P9-DMW-260

AMERICAN RADICALS:

Some Problems and Personalities

AMERICAN RADICALS:
Some Problems and Personalities

Harvey Goldberg, *Editor*

"The world will be saved, if it can be,
only by the *unsubmissive*."
André Gide, *The Journals*

MODERN READER PAPERBACKS
NEW YORK AND LONDON

Copyright 1957 by Monthly Review, Inc.

First Modern Reader Paperback Edition 1969

Modern Reader Paperbacks are published by
Monthly Review Press
116 West 14th Street, New York, N.Y. 10011
33/37 Moreland Street, London, E.C. 1

Manufactured in the United States of America

Library of Congress catalog card number 57-7984

All rights reserved.

E
663
.G6

To I. F. STONE

thirty-five years a fighter for justice

135289

WITHDRAWN
EMORY & HENRY LIBRARY

Contents

Foreword

American radicals have honored democracy by trying to make it better. With the courage and conviction to stand hard against the current, they have contributed new ideas and helped to build better institutions. For this they have won love and affection from some of their fellow Americans, while drawing the resentment and fear of others. But their record stands well in a democracy, which requires far more than lip service for success. Out of both conviction and necessity they have sought to give it what it needs—vitality, variety, choice. Their offense against timid society has been the recognition that "faith without deeds is dead."

For very compelling reasons, the study of American radicals should be essential homework for this generation: because their record can give heart and stomach to Americans who are watching democracy weaken under the weight of conformism; and because their insights and errors, their accomplishments and failures can cast light, even many years later, on the problems of the present.

There are many threads that tie the essays in this volume together, although it makes no attempt to be a systematic treatise on American radicalism. It is far from that. But it certainly suggests the richness and variety, the resources, the individuality, as well as the dilemmas, of the radical past. To the extent that it succeeds, it will be a blow against today's counsels of conservatism.

My deep appreciation goes out to the men who contributed the essays and displayed unfailing patience toward an inexperienced editor. The entire enterprise depended on the constant support of my good friends Leo Huberman and Paul Sweezy, who encouraged the idea and published the volume, and on the great editorial skill of John Rackliffe. Throughout the venture, I was sustained by the generous friendship of Russell McMasters and Kenneth Hamman.

But at bottom these essays belong to the bold men and women who built our heroic past and to uncounted others who can yet chart a great future. "For where the people are is the land that never hath an ending, that never hath an ending, that never hath an ending."

HARVEY GOLDBERG

Columbus, Ohio
September 1956

AMERICAN RADICALS:

Some Problems and Personalities

Introduction: Thoughts About American Radicalism

HARVEY GOLDBERG and
WILLIAM APPLEMAN WILLIAMS

I. The Heart of Radicalism

WHAT IS IT TO BE A RADICAL, to take a position at once denounced as corrosive and welcomed as life-giving? In its most general meaning, the one that unifies otherwise disparate programs and ideas, it is to be of a certain temperament, to have a spirit of steadfastness which sustains man's adherence to principle over any opposition, except new truth. Henry Demarest Lloyd lost friends, Heywood Broun his employment, LaFollette a political party, Veblen all academic respectability, and John Brown life itself. But at the crucial moment of pressure, recantation seemed a far greater price than loss of constancy.

In this sense, "radical" defines a nature different in quality from the temporizing "liberal" spirit, so expert in weighing principle against expediency. Broun made the point with characteristic directness: "In the final court of reckoning I believe the angels will indulge in few long cheers for any liberal. With minor exceptions he's a trimmer. 'There is much to be said on both sides' is one of his favorite sayings, or 'The truth lies somewhere between the two.' Thus split, he conciliates. It is hard enough to draw the mote from any eye, and if a man must drop that every now and then to take a yank at some beam in the opposite camp, he will accomplish little in the space allowed us." [1]

The substantive meaning of liberalism as a creed is not at stake

[1] Reference notes are placed at the end of each chapter.

1

here, for one may have a radical devotion to some of its cardinal principles. The main tenets of liberalism were recently summed up by Charles Frankel[2] as faith in reason, devotion to civil liberties, subordination of clerical influence, government economic interference for the benefit of the many, and optimism about future progress. But if the advocate of any of these puts his words to rest at the doorstep of action, if, after sifting evidence through a maze of gray, he fights shy of supporting white over black, then he has bartered radical responsibility for liberal respectability. Joseph Conrad understood the process far better than some contemporary "liberal" intellectuals, who appear to find the current retreat from protest justified by "the large measure of common ground occupied by liberals and conservatives alike."[3] In *Nostromo,* his great novel of 1904 about a South American republic in social ferment, he expressed a "feeling of pity for those men [the liberals], putting their trust in words of some sort, while murder and rapine stalked over the land. . . ."[4] If men can fall into the formalism of words in the face of frontal acts like "murder and rapine," then the plunge is far easier when the symptoms of lie and injustice are more subtle.

Morris Cohen once set up as opposites the reckless, impetuous radical and the searching, critical liberal.[5] Yet the radical proves to be sober who refuses to yield up his deeply conceived principles; and the liberal is reckless when he gambles with his beliefs. It is yet to be proved that the hairsplitter emerges from life with a much better harvest than a fistful of hair.

To be radical, then, is to be steadfast, but steadfast for what? The equation must be filled out in order to differentiate radicals from other varieties of extremists—nags and cranks espousing such assorted causes as perpetual motion and reincarnation, or rip-roaring reactionaries utterly devoted to the cause of feudalism (economic or social). Already the adjective "radical" has come into sociological literature to modify the noun "Right." In a perceptive study of right-wing political extremism in the United States, Seymour Lipset justified this use of the term. "This group is characterized as radical because it seeks to eliminate from American political life those persons and institutions which threaten either its values or its economic interests."[6] So defined, "radical" fails of precision, requiring another term, like Right or Left, to give it substance.

But radicalism points to the unattained future, not the once-attained past. If radicals stand fast and want change, they desire also a society of greater liberty and equality. Perhaps the view of Comte, who divided the world into a party of order and a party of progress, was too extreme. But the general drift seems perfectly clear; and the radicals belong to the side of progress. In all its complex parts their creed has been summed up by Russell Fraser into this organic whole: "Radicalism is here affirmed to be, neither a handy surrogate for those disgruntled persons not fed at the breast of their mother, nor pleased in their choice of a father, nor yet an ardent interlude through which young romantics must travel on their way to the 'real world' beyond, but rather a way of life humanitarian in the best sense, because it entails the most entire, the most reckless in point of self-interest, indeed the most fanatic, consecration to the common weal." [7]

The United States has had its radicals, a fair number, at times acting alone and at times in concert, men who devoted themselves exceedingly well to the common weal. The record of a handful of them, so meaningful in their successes and instructive in their defeats, constitutes the bulk of this volume. But the truth must be faced, however disillusioning, that the richest tradition of American radicalism belongs to a small minority of courageous men and women; that their achievements, while outweighing their numbers, included neither a lasting mass movement nor a profound shift of power; that a greater number of radicals than these have failed to measure up to the standards of profundity and constancy required of them.

What are the chief difficulties that have blocked the way of a genuine radical success? And what is the challenge that is now posed? The obstacles have been ideological and institutional, the difficulty of overcoming that popular American elixir of the frontier on the one hand and the problem of confronting hostile power on the other. But why bother at all to study the barriers or those who scaled them? The radical legacy is, in fact, the foundation upon which a more humane America can be built. This convolution in which the seeming dead end of yesterday becomes the highroad of tomorrow appears to be the path upon which moves the continuity of history. And it is only through understanding and accepting this irony of history that contemporary radicals can grasp the meaning of the history of American radicalism, diagnose its present condition, and plan its future.

II. The Challenge of Expansionism

America's central conception of the world, or philosophy of history, has always rested on the assumption that there was enough at hand, or within easy reach, to meet and satisfy the needs and desires of all segments of the nation. And this presumption was anchored well enough in the realities of immediate experience to circumscribe the radical analysis of society, and to limit its effectiveness in acquiring sufficient power to effect fundamental changes in the institutions and mores of America. Thus present-day radicals, if they are to understand and learn from their predecessors, must comprehend the extent to which American radicals have been prisoners of their own experience.

Perhaps the clearest way of describing this limitation on American radicals is to define them as thinkers and doers who set themselves in opposition to the dream of an ever-expanding frontier. The frontier thesis was America's *de facto* philosophy of history long years before Frederick Jackson Turner distilled it into one dramatic, seemingly iconoclastic essay in 1893. From 1700, if not earlier, Americans began dealing with their difficulties by expanding westward across the continent and outward across the high seas. Two of their deepest grievances against Great Britain stemmed from the Crown's effort to restrict this expansion by means of the Navigation Acts, which limited their overseas activities, and the Proclamation of 1763, which erected a barrier in the West.

The famous compromises over the extension of slavery further illustrate the way in which Americans circumvented or postponed their problems by expansion. Dividing land (and business openings), whether the opportunities were at hand or yet to be conquered, was the technique of resolution. Such militant rallying cries as "Texas and Oregon!" and "On to California!" serve to symbolize this outlook.

Confronted by none but weak enemies, as with the Indians and the Mexicans, or preoccupied opponents, as with the Spanish, the French, the Russians, and the British, this philosophy of history seemed foolproof. Perhaps this, among other reasons, explains why it was linked to the Almighty in the terse phrase "Manifest Destiny," which came to serve as a substitute for thoroughgoing analysis and wise policies, and as justification for almost any conduct toward the rest of the world. And the Civil War offers the final proof of this interpretation. For that conflict came only when it was no longer possible to evade the issue of slavery by further expansion.

Turner's classic statement of this expansionist philosophy of history came, revealingly enough, at the hour of that major *national* crisis, the panic and depression of the 1890s. In formulating once again the popular belief in the frontier, it had three principal effects: it rekindled the old faith in the technique of evading predicaments by resolving them into larger issues which, more often than not, were coincidentally defined as problems of foreign policy (as with Woodrow Wilson and Franklin Roosevelt, for example); it renewed the vigor of the blatant expansionists (such as Henry Cabot Lodge and Theodore Roosevelt, to name only the earliest); and it dramatized, for incorruptible thinkers like Eugene Debs, Thorstein Veblen, and Charles Beard, the necessity of dealing directly and at home with the domestic dilemmas of American society. Debs, Veblen, and Beard, however, and their sympathizers as well, faced four fundamental handicaps in coping with the quandaries of an industrial America. A brief statement and analysis of these difficulties and their consequences casts much light on the subsequent history of American radicalism.

(1) Confronted by the crises of the twentieth century, and at the same time reassured by popularization of the frontier idea of their own valid understanding of the nation's history, many Americans saw economic and ideological (and to some extent even political) expansion as the solution to their contemporary problems.

(2) America's non-imperial conservatives and radicals had first, therefore, to wrench themselves out of this tradition before they could grapple with the central crises at hand. This would have been an extremely difficult exercise in emotional and intellectual discipline under ideal circumstances, and it was in practice vastly complicated by three factors:

(A) America's industrial strength was so overpowering, and increasingly so, from 1900 to 1950, that a policy of overseas expansion could be continued and extended, by those who favored this approach, without seeming to contradict the traditional American ideology of anti-imperialism. Indeed, this overseas expansion was easily explained and justified as the task of carrying civilization and liberty to the benighted masses of the world. And as illustrated by the history of the Progressive movement, and the New and Fair Deals, this was the path of least resistance taken by most American liberals and so-called radicals. Both these movements espoused, with but brief interludes under Presidents Wilson and Franklin Roosevelt, foreign policies of expansion.

(B) Two world wars further complicated the effort of radicals to break free of the pattern of solving crises by expansion. American entry into both wars, but more especially the second, could plausibly be analyzed and righteously vindicated as an action taken to defend America's right and opportunity to work out its problems in peace.

(C) The Russian Revolution also compounded the difficulty of establishing an American radicalism. By its very existence it exercised a powerful attraction for radicals looking for inspiration and practical guidance. But the crude transportation of Russian thought and practice to America not only proved unsatisfactory in and of itself; it was also the material out of which the opponents of radicalism created a stereotype of the American radical as an unthinking, bomb-throwing, conspiring revolutionary in league with dangerous foreigners. Such an image was progressively extended to those American radicals who did not limit their horizons to the confines of Moscow's Red Square.

(3) American radicals who did free themselves of the expansionist philosophy of history were confronted, therefore, by the necessity of establishing a beachhead of freedom within their own country. Thus they had even less energy left to devote to the central problem of working out a coherent and integrated radical program for America. Even in 1956, for that matter, the radicals have yet to outline a general program that will match the sometimes fumbling but sometimes exceedingly rational corporatism of such men as Herbert Hoover, Peter Drucker, and the *Fortune* intellectuals.

(4) And finally, even assuming the existence of a core of leadership with a program, American radicalism had to win enough long-term popular support to enable it to enter the lists and compete for peacetime power, or even to be ready for revolutionary action should such circumstances ever arise.

But, over and above these handicaps of ideology and strategy, American radicals, both leaders and the courageous rank and file, faced (and do face now) a framework of powerfully sponsored hostility sufficient to bend the back of all but the hardiest.

III. The Framework of Hostility

Ultimately history has come to honor many a lonely thinker and to institutionalize the most vigorously resisted social changes. For it is possible to believe, with Diderot, that "although a lie may serve for a while, it is harmful in the long run; and contrariwise, truth necessarily is best in the long run, even though it may do harm at the moment. From which I incline to think that the man of genius who denounces a common error or who establishes a general truth always deserves our veneration. Such a man may fall a victim to prejudice or existing law; but there are two kinds of laws—those based on equity, which are universally true, and those based on whim, which owe their force to blindness or local necessity. These last cast odium on their violator for only a brief moment, an odium which time casts back upon the judges and peoples who carried the law." [8]

But the belief that a fresh theory, if true, or a new institution, if just, will finally triumph has itself failed of permanence as an idea. Each age has girded itself against innovation while throwing radical critics to its own special lions. In modern American society the radical dissenter, whether bearer of a theory or builder of an organization, has at times shared in the fate of ridicule, ostracism, or worse. If the great genius of the United States for technological change has yielded an especial receptivity to the scientific innovator, its firmly entrenched economic and social interests have organized strong opposition to critics of the culture or opponents of the power structure. Leaders of labor, who were once isolated like some poisonous bacilli, have now won their place, to be sure, within the fabric of national life; but this has been managed only after that heavy dilution of militancy with opportunism currently called "responsible leadership." The radical intellectuals, however, have come increasingly under attack for their searching analyses and criticisms of prevalent practices. The result has been, in the phrase of Alfred McClung Lee, "a pall of orthodoxy." [9]

The difficulty of holding firm and fast to a radical position has been increasingly intensified in our modern industrial age by a combination of the unprecedented power of vested interests under capitalism and the calculated manipulation of public opinion through the mass-communications media. They have produced at times a feeling of futility, at times fear. The enormous concentration of corporate wealth in the United States, a condition generally withheld from the view of a public conveniently drugged by the opiate called "free enterprise," was yet convincingly revealed in the reports of such New Deal agencies as the National Resources Committee and the Temporary National Economic Committee.[10] As for the roseate myth which has accompanied postwar American prosperity—that capitalism has approached a level of economic equality in a stage "beyond socialism"—it runs counter to the results of the few revelant penetrations into the actual nature of contemporary income distribution.[11]

The present sources of power, as C. Wright Mills has recently demonstrated,[12] derive not only from economic positions; they flow also from political and military roles. The personnel of these three institutional orders are now intertwined in a complex, almost kaleidoscopic structure, or "power elite." "The inner core of the power elite consists, first, of those who interchange commanding roles at the top of one dominant institutional order, with those in another: the admiral who is also a banker and a lawyer who heads up an important federal commission; the corporation executive whose company was one of the two or three leading war materiel producers who is now Secretary of Defense; the wartime general who dons civilian clothes to sit on the political directorate and then becomes a member of a leading corporation." [13]

In response to this tight structure radicals have felt ineffective, almost helpless. So fraternal has the play of power become that these groups no longer balance out; instead "the major vested interests compete less with one another in their effort to promote their several interests than they coincide on many points of interest and indeed come together under the umbrella of government." [14] Where and how have radicals turned to find a lever for the redistribution of power? They have more and more felt, like those Sartre characters, in a condition with "no exit."

In the most recent years, when the economy has usually been able to offer apparent rewards to those who have gone after them, the willingness to hold fast to radical integrity has been doubly sapped. For the cutting edge of criticism can be easily dulled by the soft center of personal gain. As William Newman has recently written, "it is difficult to be critical and even sarcastic about a political and economic system whose main weapon is to cloy the senses with a succulent, velvety, gummy unreality. . . . It is the atmosphere of futility and dream which creates the basic difficulty of being radical, not the lack of 'issues' or 'crises.' " [15]

But when radicals have scaled this barrier of frustration and given voice to their principles, they have usually encountered not sympathy but great public hostility toward the dissenter and rebel. "The spectacle of an efficient elite maintaining its authority and asserting its will over the mass by the rationally calculated use of irrational methods of persuasion is the most disturbing nightmare of mass democracy." [16] In so writing Edward Carr might well have been thinking of the American community where irrational opposition has too frequently been directed against agitators who disturbed the tranquillity of accepted norms. "We Americans—and I now apply the term to the people who have occupied the present United States since the first English settlements in North America—have never been slow to resort to violence, sometimes in passion, sometimes in the conviction that legal processes were either inadequate or too slow in their operations, sometimes simply because the law interfered with what we wanted to do." [17]

The unthinking dislike of radicals, that cultural xenophobia which underlies the community to the discouragement of dissent, exists as a mere preface, however, to the powerful organization of press, radio, motion pictures, and television for retaining unchanged the established order of things. The pervasive science of advertising, lending support to special interests, has made putty of a receptive public. "For a judging public is unfree if it has to judge not between competing theories of what an agreed set of facts means, but between competing distortions of what is, at the outset, unedifying and invented mythology." [18] When the tide of a fabricated public indignation has receded and the toll of damage has been calculated, the capacity and desire to dissent has almost always reckoned as the chief victim. In his survey of the "red scare" of 1919-1920, that first major experience in manipulating a national hysteria, Robert Murray found at its end that "civil liberties were left prostrate, the labor movement was badly mauled, the position of capital was greatly enhanced, and complete antipathy toward reform was enthroned." [19]

This is an age in which science, whether social or physical, has come increasingly to serve the existing institutional order, a state of affairs in which prime actors are historians who gloss robber barons into industrial statesmen,[20] physicists who contribute without fear of consequences to the greater capacity for military destruction, and sociologists who lend their finely honed methodology to a variety of callous purposes.[21] But the most startling recent challenge to the position of the radical has come through the effective linking of clinical psychology and acceptance of the status quo in search of what is called "normal adjustment."

The psychological charge against radicals has by now a familiar ring. In their intransigent and unyielding stand, in their refusal to compromise and to split truth or principle, radicals are accused of being suspiciously maladjusted, harboring dangerous hostilities. But the new concept of adjustment, as Robert Lindner warned, "enjoins men to conform, to adopt an attitude of passivity and a philosophy of resignation. . . . Implicit in the concept is a pessimistic conviction of man's helplessness before an unfriendly universe whose circumstances can be deplored but never changed." [22] In consideration, therefore, of radicals, past and present, their particular stand has seemed considerably less important than their driving resentment or disorientation. The way is thus cleared for compromisers and hairsplitters to adorn themselves with the certification of mental health for their sweet reasonableness.

Of course, the work of radicals, whether in the realm of ideas or of political action, should be weighed and evaluated in terms of its own internal validity and external result. The psychological accusation against rebels seems largely dust in the eye, blinding one to the true weight of their work. But even if the greatest wisdom rendered to this generation were a prescription for "normalcy," it would still be necessary to demonstrate conclusively that the radicals of the past have been conspicuously maladjusted while those of the present are doomed to storm and stress. Yet no body of clinical literature exists upon which to rest the charge that critics of the status quo rather than the established order itself bear the signs of disease.

Since it is perfectly demonstrable, however, that the injustice or inadequacy of institutions and ideas have often generated the discontents of dissenters,[23] the new shamans in the campaign for "normal adjustment" have posed a serious threat to the progress that springs from radical opposition. "The heresies we may suppress today," warned Laski, "may be the orthodoxies of tomorrow. New truth begins always in a minority of one; it must be someone's perception before it becomes general perception." [24] The danger of stifling radicals in the name of the demigod of adjustment has moved certain social scientists and psychiatrists to stern warning. A few, for example, have answered the charges of Harry Stack Sullivan, an influential, well-known psychiatrist.

Sullivan phrased the prevalent distrust of the extreme nonconformist very succinctly. "The person who believes that he *voluntarily* cut loose from his earlier moorings and *by choice* accepted new dogmata, in which he has diligently indoctrinated himself, is quite certain to be a person who has suffered great insecurity. He is often a person whose self-organization is derogatory and hateful. The new movement has given him group support for the expression of ancient personal hostilities that are now directed against the group from which he has come." [25] To this notion that radical views are the symptom of personal insecurity Helen Lynd at once replied sharply: "No one would deny that some radicals are neurotic. But that is a very different thing from saying that only neurotics develop radical social views, or that radical programs are necessarily evil or undesirable." [26] Very recently again, Herbert Marcuse excoriated Sullivan's position: "Deep conformity holds sway over this psychology, which suspects all those who 'cut loose from their earlier moorings' and become 'radicals' as neurotic (the description fits all of them, from Jesus to Lenin, from Socrates to Giordano Bruno), and which almost automatically identifies the 'promise of a better world' with 'Utopia,' its substance with 'revery' and mankind's sacred dream of justice for all with the personal resentment (no more injustice for them) of maladjusted types." [27]

The reaction to the cult of passivity has yielded more than a mere denial of its validity, however. Certain theorists have pleaded for rebellion as a guarantee of cultural vitality and expansiveness. Lindner has insisted again and again that "rebellion can be positive; it can be affirming; it can be rectifying." [28] While classifying as ill the rebel without cause, who merely gratifies his inner destructive urges, he points to the positive rebel as the essential engine of a progressive culture. "He is essentially a catalytic agent whose very presence within a society energizes its members and recruits them on the side of progress by calling forth their rebelliousness. Often, in worldly terms, he may be 'unsuccessful,' but the core of the matter is that he is psychologically successful *within himself* in that his rebellious instinct is constantly in expression." [29]

To assume the radical stand, subject to hostile power and publicity, is to accept a way at once vulnerable, lonely, even dangerous. Some who have embarked upon the path of dissent, oblivious to its deepest challenges, have failed along the course. This is especially true in the American tradition where a beguiling optimism and a faith in relentless progress have ensnared people into the belief that the new could be painlessly won. So to believe was to be "spared the heinous task of applying those draconian measures, that root and branch reconstruction that are the only remedy for a system diseased in its parts." [30] The American dream has been a seduction, for social and intellectual change can demand sacrifices monstrous in degree. The European radical, consistently sensitive to the difficulties of challenging a class system, could be broken and yet rise again. But those who were persuaded of Crèvecoeur's vision—that America was ever unique and near-perfect, that reform would be simple and easily accepted—they either toughened their hides or fell away when the reality replaced the dream.

Now especially, because the resources for a wonderful life have become more bountiful at the very time that radicalism has become so difficult, dissenters are confronted with the need to survive, to analyze, and to function. They may find their battleground different from that of depression days; they may extend the range of their concern to new issues, knowing "that the struggle for civil and intellectual liberties is as important as the struggle for industrial democracy; that the increasing rate of mental disorders are as significant signs of the decay of modern culture as economic injustice; and that the general alienation of men in modern society is as pervasive in the sphere of leisure as in the sphere of work." [31] But whatever the definition of the social and cultural problem, the need for constancy remains central. For with it, some radicals have moved mountains; without it, they have been snowed under.

IV. Success or Failure?

From the careers of those who are considered in the chapters that follow, two striking facts cast real light on the integrity of the best of

American radicals. One is the almost painful search for a valid and true view of life, painful because it involved movement from position to position until the focus was correct. For some it meant transcendence of personal comfort and security for a life devoted to a larger than egotistical principle. Altgeld and Dreiser, both of them driven by the vision of material success, turned dream into reality. But when the cold, hard cash revealed a cold, hard world, both turned into blazing radicals. Altgeld moved from the Haymarket pardon and sympathy with Pullman's workers to direct attack on the concentration of wealth. Dreiser, "having proved that he could force his way across the tracks," set himself to tell "the truths that the orthodox and well-born saw not and dared not tell."

For LaFollette and Broun, the presence of injustice in the fabric of American life intruded upon conscience until well-ordered careers exploded into radical instruments. Shocked by Senator Philetus Sawyer's attempt to bribe him, LaFollette began his flight beyond the boundaries of ordinary party lines until he reached an unforgettable insurgency. Broun could have chosen to cling to all the comforts of lucrative journalism; but threats to civil liberties and barriers to free development plunged him into a swift-rising spiral of radical campaigns.

The careers of John Brown and Walter Weyl offer examples of the search for method, a search that moved them far from an initial moderation. For Brown it had become imperative to do something "in a practical way for my poor fellow-men who are in bondage . . ." But the inadequacy of so small a conception as opening a school for Negroes gave way finally to Brown's formidable plan for an armed attack against the slaveholder South. Weyl's great concern from the time of the frontal class strife of the Lawrence strike in 1912 centered on the search for a substitute in some mild reform effort. But "Weyl, in 1912, was a man heavily committed to a theory that seemed to be contradicted by the evidence before his eyes." By 1919, however, "the apparent success of the Soviets completed the disintegration that the Lawrence strike, the decline of the progressive movement, the war, and the lost peace had already begun."

If integrity can be somewhat measured by this willingness to evolve and move, regardless of cost, then the deep searching of some radicals can be judged by the great variety of ends and means devised to achieve the sounder, more equitable life. Man, without fetters and free of insecurity, was in general the objective. It was the aim that sent John Brown to Harpers Ferry on July 4, 1859, to fire up by direct action the cause of abolition; for only in the freedom of the slaves would the democratic ethics commence. And it was the same aim that sent Henry Demarest Lloyd and Bob LaFollette against the new slavery imposed by monopolistic capitalism. If Lloyd with typical acuity assumed the permanence of bigness and urged community control, LaFollette, chasing the mirage of petty enterprise, sought trust-busting techniques. But, let it be noted, both were tough, implacable fighters against the giants.

Such devoted radicals have avoided, better than most, the blindness to fact that springs from desire and the smug satisfaction that accompanies arrogance of position. They have realized that "harmony and balance perhaps demand a degree of inclusiveness and completeness sufficient to nourish every kind of nature, to create the fullest variety in unity, to do justice to every occasion." [32]

But to date radicalism in the United States has failed to bring profound changes or to build a lasting movement. However comprehensible this is in the light of the American dream, the instruments of power, and the relentless demands on courage, it is tragic. But the failures themselves are meaningful instruction. Even the very best of American radicals have found difficulty in avoiding strategic pitfalls. The hope of charting a way at once more humane, just, and true has at times exacted high toll from the very logic of their position. They have been sorely tempted to close their eyes to developing realities that ran counter to original perceptions. This weakness of radicals was dissected by Milorad Drachkovitch, who laid bare the unfortunate consequences for European socialists of distorting facts to fit theory.[33] Certainly it was such a tendency which constituted the chief liability in the career of a De Leon, who dissipated his devoted energy in preparation for the imminent revolution in the United States. While understanding the desire to see hopes realized, one can ask with Bertrand Russell: "Why must people persist in falling into hopeless confusion by wishing to have things turn out in a particular way? Why won't they try, for a change, to look at things dispassionately and face the simple fact that truth has nothing whatever to do with our approval or disapproval?" [34]

In the '30s and early '40s the pitfalls were deep and the failures great for American radicals. Abandoning the independence and vigor attached to the rich tradition of the men described below, many sincere men and women were tempted into the easy solution. Either they became Russophiles, or they cast in their lot with the liberals and sought to change America by using the power of the existing national government. Now an intelligent, insightful, and Marxian American Communist might have developed an argument around the thesis that supporting the Soviet Union through famine, purge, and Stalin was actually, in spite of the illiberal features of that government, the only way to establish the necessary preconditions for a truly American radicalism. For, as he would summarize his case, no American radicalism could arise and become effective unless and until the United States found itself forced to choose between, on the one hand, a war that threatened it with devastation and, on the other, a reorganization of American society. Suffice it to say, however, that the records of the American Communist Party do not reveal any such persistent analysis of the problem. But that does not alter the fact that just such a choice may now confront the United States and may, therefore, offer American radicals their most promising opportunity of the twentieth century.

That majority of American radicals who meanwhile looked to the existing state as the answer to their dilemma made two signal errors. First, they mistook the state for the fulcrum of power, whereas it is in fact (save in moments of national disintegration) nothing but a lever for power. Only a class or an alliance of groups provides a true fulcrum. Second, they found themselves, those of them who actually reached Washington, without a program, even in the opportunity of Roosevelt's One Hundred Days. Perhaps the clue to evaluating the approach of these neo-radicals lies in the fact that it took a West Pointer and a General Motors executive to begin America's disengagement from the cold war. The foreign policy of Truman's Fair Deal was more interventionist even than that of Theodore Roosevelt's Square Deal, and both their domestic social programs disintegrated in the same experience of reaping the whirlwind of an expansionist philosophy of history.

To borrow a bit of imagery from Turner himself, we might fairly conclude that American radicalism stands at its last frontier. The expansionist philosophy of history has carried the United States to the last roundup where a nation confronts itself. So the radical's chance is still the present. And the issue is clear: who is to outline, plan, and direct America's effort to live at peace with itself and the world?

The conservatives and their compatriots of the devitalized Center are by no means as close to final decay as some liberals and most radicals labor to convince themselves. For if nothing else, they still hold power. And such conservatism, given the continuing maturation of the Russians, can quite probably muddle through for a considerable time yet. After all, the British Empire hung on for nearly two centuries after the American and French Revolutions. Such a timetable is relative, of course, but the compression of history has not proceeded at a rate sufficient to destroy the analogy. It remains, therefore, the radical's present opportunity and responsibility to demonstrate and then substantiate his claim to power.

Should American radicalism fail this challenge, the future might be shaped by the reforming Russian and Chinese Communists, or by the new breed of man which will arise as a phoenix from a nuclear holocaust. And such a social mutation will not be characterized by many traits from either contemporary American radicalism or the present American elite. Western society stands in grave need of an infusion of new humanism: it could come from a revitalized American radicalism.

NOTES

1. New York *World,* March 1, 1927.
2. Charles Frankel, *The Case for Modern Man* (New York, 1956), *passim.*
3. Arthur Schlesinger, Jr., "Conservative *vs.* Liberal—A Debate," *New York Times* Magazine, March 4, 1956, p. 58.
4. Cited in Arnold Kettle, *An Introduction to the English Novel* (London, 1953), II, 73.
5. Morris R. Cohen, *The Faith of a Liberal* (New York, 1946), p. 8.
6. Seymour M. Lipset, "The Sources of the Radical Right," in Daniel Bell, editor, *The New American Right* (New York, 1955), p. 166.
7. See below, Chapter 12, p. 220.
8. Denis Diderot, *Rameau's Nephew* (New York, 1951), pp. 12-13.
9. Alfred McClung Lee, *How to Understand Propaganda* (New York, 1952), p. 252.
10. See the interesting commentaries on some of their work in two papers by Paul Sweezy, *The Present as History* (New York, 1953), pp. 158-196.
11. See, for example, W. A. Williams, "Babbitt's New Fables," *The Nation,* January 7, 1956, pp. 3-6.

12. C. Wright Mills, *The Power Elite* (New York, 1956), *passim*.
13. *Ibid.*, p. 288.
14. *Ibid.*, pp. 266-267.
15. William Newman, "The Importance of Being Radical," *Dissent* (Spring 1956), III, 165-166.
16. Edward H. Carr, *The New Society* (London, 1951), p. 78.
17. Paul M. Angle, *Bloody Williamson* (New York, 1952), p. ix.
18. Harold Laski, *Liberty in the Modern State* (New York, 1949), pp. 131-132. For the startling figures on concentration of control in the communications industries, see Lee, *op. cit.*, pp. 240-250.
19. Robert K. Murray, *Red Scare* (Minneapolis, 1955), p. 19.
20. For some comments on historical revisionism by Harvey O'Connor, see below, Chapter 4, pp. 87-88.
21. See especially the sharp warning on this point to social scientists by Reinhard Bendix, *Social Science and the Distrust of Reason* (Berkeley, 1951), p. 42.
22. Robert Lindner, *Prescription for Rebellion* (New York, 1952), p. 11.
23. For a discussion on this point, see Carey McWilliams, *Witch Hunt* (Boston, 1950).
24. Laski, *op. cit.*, p. 75.
25. Harry S. Sullivan, *Conceptions of Modern Psychiatry* (Washington, 1947), p. 96.
26. Helen M. Lynd, "Must Psychology Aid Reaction?" *The Nation*, January 15, 1949, pp. 75-76.
27. Herbert Marcuse, *Eros and Civilization* (Boston, 1955), pp. 256-257.
28. Lindner, *op. cit.*, p. 219.
29. *Ibid.*, p. 226.
30. See below, Chapter 12, p. 231.
31. Lewis Coser, "What Shall We Do?" *Dissent* (Spring 1956), III, 161-162.
32. Lewis Mumford, *The Human Prospect* (Boston, 1955), p. 319.
33. Milorad Drachkovitch, *De Karl Marx à Léon Blum* (Geneva, 1954).
34. From a conversation between Russell and Dilip Kumar Roy, in D. K. Roy, *Among the Great* (Bombay, 1950), p. 151.

I

Declarations of Independence

"The new polarizing element is the concept of
the person: the last term in the development of
the organic world and the human community."

Lewis Mumford, *The Human Prospect*

1

John Jay Chapman and the
Insurgent Individual

MELVIN BERNSTEIN

I

To HIS CONTEMPORARIES at the turn of the century he was widely
known as "mad Jack Chapman." Fifty years later he is remembered
by only a handful of people. His obscurity is unmerited, for his radicalism is tonic to our times.

John Jay Chapman all his long life spoke out against the conservatism
of mealymouthed acquiescence in things as they are. His perfectionism
provoked him to write some twenty-five books, hundreds of speeches,
and thousands of letters on a distracting number of subjects—disarmament, literature overprotected by Germanic specialism, immigration,
education, Harvard, Prohibition, Roman Catholicism in America—but
it was in his political agitation that his radicalism was the strongest.

For less than ten years Chapman hurled himself with concentrated
energy against his times. He singled out for his attack what John
Adams had called "the Devil's own incomprehensibles"—New York
politics. Out of this experience came a strange name-calling periodical,
two books on the urgency for reform of conduct in political life, and,

ultimately, a disillusionment of achieving a victory over the evils he defined. Out of this disenchantment came also a modified form of radicalism which achieved a monumental simplicity and naked communication that in its individuality compels the attention he sought to direct to the matter. The flow and ebb stages of Chapman's radicalism can symbolize but not exhaust the man and his contribution to American ideas and society.

Chapman did not stumble accidentally into political agitation and reform. He came to intellectual maturity when the corrupt concomitants of the Gilded Age in America had become so noisome as to ask for relief from them. Besides, Chapman was well-born to a family whose sense of public responsibility and activity in its behalf was matched by an equally strong sense of private integrity. The opportunity and the tradition coalesced in the 1890s when Chapman, fresh from Harvard Law School, cast about for an outlet for his energies and found New York politics, manipulated by Tammany's Richard Croker and Republican "easy boss" Thomas C. Platt, in need of a moralist's admonitions and adjurations. But first a look at Chapman's early career and the ideal of public service that he carried in his memory.

II

The hub of John Jay Chapman's world was New York City where he was born in 1862. His father, Henry Grafton Chapman, was a broker, his mother, Eleanor Jay Chapman, was an ambitious and talented woman, and his older brother Henry was one of his formative intellectual antagonists, helping him to crystallize his opinions. Private tutoring, St. Paul's School in Concord, New Hampshire, Harvard (Class of '84), travel in Europe, Harvard Law School, and the New York bar brought him to a profession he did not especially like, the difficulties of making a living, and marriage to Minna Timmins (1889). After the birth of their third son, Mrs. Chapman died. In 1898, he married Elizabeth Chanler, holding himself and his family heroically together while he fought domestic calamity and what was to be his losing battle against politics. Active in a dozen civic organizations, working beyond his nervous strength, in 1901, just before his son Chanler was born, he suffered a nervous breakdown and retired temporarily from political agitation. It was in this period that the first stage of Chapman's radicalism was worked out. These years saw the publication of the gadfly journal, *The Political Nursery* (1897-1901), and two books devoted primarily to the political situation as it qualified American society, *Causes and Consequences* (1898) and *Practical Agitation* (1900).

In 1912 he returned publicly to immediate political issues in a personal protest against lynching. In 1913 in a biography of William Lloyd Garrison he held up to the times the example of the man of action, the doer, the agitator for principle and his indelible influence upon a critical period of American history. This was the ebb stage in his radicalism. It must be understood that these stages are artificial, that they sketchily report the man who steadily, until his death in 1933, spoke out against what he thought was wrong with life in America.

The Ariadne's thread that leads us through the maze of Chapman's many activities is his attested awareness of the values of his Jay-Chapman ancestry. His inheritance positively shaped his energies.

The Jay family were French Huguenots who, uprooted by the revocation of the Edict of Nantes, emigrated to England and America. The public services and offices of John Jay as chief justice and governor of New York need no review. He was an indefatigable writer and propagator of "causes": international arbitration, the manumission of slaves, education, and Protestant Christianity. One of his sons, William Jay, followed him in the law and continued to promote anti-slavery agitation, international arbitration, and disarmament. His son, John Jay (Chapman's grandfather), defended runaway slaves in court, agitated for Negro enlistments in the Union army and the admission of Negro churches and students to Episcopal conventions and seminaries, and against the spread of Catholic parochial education in America.

The Chapman inheritance was no less rich in storied incidents of virtuous private conduct and public agitation. Grandfather Henry Grafton Chapman had been a church-outed minister of the Unitarian church because of its lethargy in speaking against slavery. Grandmother Maria Weston Chapman had been an international personality, friend and biographer of Harriet Martineau, polemicist of anti-slavery agitation, right-hand helper of William Lloyd Garrison, poet, moralist, and political journalist of hortatory prose studded with complimentary references to great dissidents like Wat Tyler, Wycliffe, Knox, and Luther.

This, then, was the family image—good bourgeois leading American society to the fulfillment of the American Enlightenment promise—which was an insistent goad to Chapman's public service. We can accept literally Chapman's words written when he was thirty-four and in the middle of learning the political game in New York City; thinking of his grandfather Jay, he wrote: "The fact is that his name and the family tradition have been controlling ideas with me ever since I can remember—perhaps too much so, and while I do not speak of them very often they are in my mind about all the time." [1] Both the Jays and the Chapmans had set the example. Chapman reveled in anecdotes of his forebears and soaked up their enthusiasms for causes from their pamphlets and books in the overflowing family libraries. He was religious by upbringing and by education at St. Paul's; his family ideals had the confirmation of religion, and religion had the confirmation of the practical and happy example of his ancestors. His family had been public leaders acting according to principle not expediency. They had acted out of an educated opinion that expressed their citizens' responsibility to lead benevolently. Significantly, they had agitated by any good means at hand to arouse the conscience of their times to that perfectibility of man potential in a militant Christianity and in the instrumentalism of ethical American government. These lessons his ancestors taught; Chapman practiced them—with equivocal results.

III

One intellectual force in the maturation of the mind of Chapman must be added to this awareness of the civic responsibility of the educated man in America. This was his reading in and enthusiasm for Ralph Waldo Emerson. Emerson convinced Chapman of the rightness of protest and the primary value of the individual:

> While the radicals of Europe were revolting in 1848 against the abuses of a tyranny whose roots were in feudalism, Emerson, the great radical of America, the arch radical of the world, was revolting against the evils whose roots were in . . . tyranny, and by bringing back the attention of political thinkers to its starting point, the value of human character, he had advanced the political thought of the world by one step. He has pointed out for us in this country to what end our efforts must be bent. [2]

This was Chapman's starting point and his lifelong concern: renovated and rededicated individuals. The individual must perceive first the threats to himself, then resist them, and finally encourage others by example and personal influence to help still others, creating, as it were, widening concentric circles of right doing and practical reform ultimately touching and enclosing all of society. The grievances that Emerson had had against America—moral cowardice, the tyranny of democracy, political conservatism, commercial self-interest, unimaginative religious or moral perceptiveness—were the very grievances that Chapman nurtured against his own times. What was there to do about them? Speak out against them.

He spoke out in this early stage of his radicalism backed by his youthful Emersonian idealism, his reservoir of nervous strength, his ready wit, and his hope that his class might reassert its natural aristocracy and recapture its defaulted leadership. In the early flush of his protest, Chapman joined groups of political independents. He was an active member in many civic organizations, among them the Good Government Clubs, the City Reform Club, and the Citizens' Union. He made cart-tail speeches before elections and watched the polls during elections. He lectured around the state, organized dinners where political talk could be open, wrote newspaper appeals enlisting public support for protest groups against grab legislation, and arranged delegations to Albany. He was a prolific letter writer, unburdening his energy and stirring controversy wherever he could. (The quantity of his unpublished writing, housed in Harvard's Houghton Library, is gigantic.)

One goad to his class was what amounted to his personal magazine. *The Political Nursery* was on the average a four-page journal issued thirty-six times between March 1897 and January 1901, and sold for ten cents. The title was satirical and didactic: the truths of morality and conduct were simple nursery truths. The masthead of the buckshot journal declared war on the New York *Times, Herald, Sun, Post,* and *The Nation,* and on evildoers everywhere:

> The object of THE NURSERY is to tell the truth. There is no publication at present which seems to cover this exact field. Truth is the best seen by the light of example, hence THE NURSERY does not shun personalities, when they are in point.

At first Chapman, who was practically the sole editor with occasional help from a fellow idealist, Isaac H. Klein, believed that humor (with which he was generously, cleverly, delightfully supplied) was better than denunciation. Eventually he tried both. He meant to confront his subscribers—his clubmen friends and relatives, the respectables, the "phylacteried individuals," the better element of both Republican and Democratic parties—with the facts of their hypocritical life. He enjoyed the news that *The Nursery* was removed from the files of the Chamber of Commerce.

His central theme—if so miscellaneous a periodical as *The Nursery* can be said to have a theme—was: "We endow politics with mystery. . . . But, really, politics is as simple as money can make them." [3] Money-dominated politics proliferated an endemic disease. "The canker of the times is moral cowardice." [4] It corrupted men and institutions. "Boss Platt is not an originator of evil; he is a political servant of corrupt banks, syndicates, and politicians." [5] As for the unnamed president of a gas company who contributed $20,000 to a political campaign, why that was "a business investment without any damned nonsense about it." [6] Governor Theodore Roosevelt's refusal to help civil service reform showed "the most conspicuous Mark of the Beast which he has yet displayed. . . . He worships neither God nor Mammon, but the Deity known as The Boys." [7] When Seth Low's campaign behavior didn't please Chapman's principles he parodied:

> Sweet and Low, sweet and low
> Wind of the western seas
> Blow, blow—blow high, blow low,
> Anything to please. [8]

In the manner of Carlyle's Teufelsdröckh, Chapman berated his fellow citizen, "the American-at-home . . . the whipped animal" [9] :

Do you not think, you, Mr. Church Deacon Bank-President, you, Mr. Senior Warden Gas-President, you, Mr. Franchise Grabber Charity-Patron, you, the Rev. Politic Polyglot, you, Dr. Millionairist Physic, you, Lawyer Corporation-Fee-Taker, you, Architect Smug-Face, you, Merchant Food Adulterator, you, Manufacturer Short Roll, you, Gentleman Do Nothing, and all you other innumerables who go to make up the upper ten, the Heavy Respectables, the persons who have influence in the community because of their money, or their clothes, or their social position, or their God-Knows-What, possibly ancestors' swindling, certainly not because of righteous thinking or righteous dealing, do you not think that you had better stop this prating about your own desire to vote according to the dictates of what you are pleased to call your conscience,

and about your fear that other persons will not vote according to theirs?
Do you not think that you had better begin to ask whether you are not
a humbug? [10]

These excerpts from *The Nursery* show Chapman as an agitator;
Causes and Consequences and *Practical Agitation* show him as a
reformer and a critic of American values. In the two books he not
only gave a more coherent picture than he had in *The Nursery* of the
consequent evils of commercialism as it infiltrated American society
but he also elaborated on why and how a man might by personal influence effect personal revolutions in his community.

In *Causes and Consequences* he located the abuse of government in
the historical experience of America subsequent to the Civil War.
"Misgovernment in the United States is an incident in the history of
commerce." [11] The Gilded Age had drawn the best men from government into business expansion. Business then used these men to get
control of the machinery of government. "Party" after the Civil War
became sacred; the "machine" became the profane engine of "boss"
and party. Rascal politicians bought out lawyers who had to choose
between lucrative malpractice and thankless honesty. Although their
choice was the first, no one apparently minded, for "bribery, in one
form or another, is part of the unwritten law. It is atmospheric; it is
felt by no one." [12] The hookup of the professional classes with the
corrupt politicians was most shocking to Chapman who was then an
ardent idealist, a lawyer whose family motto, *Crescit sub pondere
virtus*—"Virtue increases under a burden"—was threatened by vulgar
marketplace discount:

> Since the days of David, the great luxury of the powerful has been to be
> free from the annoyance of other persons' opinions. The professional
> classes in any community are parasites on the moneyed classes; they at-
> tend the distribution.[13]

Clearly, he would have no part in this liaison with dishonesty. The
truth of this oppressive conjunction of dishonesty and power must be
published, especially since free speech, the very agency that could
clamor against this perversion, was being bought off and silenced. The
powerful would not be unmindful of Chapman's accusation. He would
speak out, to them, against them. "Free speech is a habit. . . . As free
speech goes out the rascals come in." [14]

So pernicious, indeed, was the evil of the times that the very catchwords of democracy, he charged, were used to intensify the tyranny of conformity. A dissenter from current malpractice became downright unpatriotic:

> A distrust of the individual running into something like hatred may be seen reflected in the press of the United States. The main point is that Americans have by business training been growing more alike every day, and have seized upon any and every authority to aid them in disciplining a recusant.[15]

The omens of the very degradation of democratic dogma and the reduction of the individual to a cipher were in these patterns of business, government, law, journalism, and social conduct. Civil liberty itself was submerged in the boss system. History was forgotten. The example of the American Revolution—a revolution of sense and virtue—was lost. The future was compromised. American life—an experiment in living that ought to provide a pattern for Europe—was a sad spectacle unworthy of imitation:

> . . . a civilization based upon a commerce which is in all its parts corruptly managed will present a social life which is unintelligent and mediocre, made up of people afraid of each other, whose ideas are shopworn, whose manners are self-conscious.[16]

Yet there were portents of hope. (There were always bright sides to Chapman's strictures.) The guerrilla warfare of reformers, philanthropists, and settlement workers who resented the treason to the American practice of self-government was one such portent. "If commerce has been our ruin, our form of government is our salvation. . . . In spite of this corruption and debauchery, the American people, the masses of them, are the most promising people extant." [17] At this point in his career his appeal was to Everyman to educate himself to the responsibilities of principled self-government. "No religious revival will help us. We are religious enough already." [18] The instructions for Everyman's education were in *Practical Agitation*.

IV

It was at first Chapman's modest intention to create a ferment in the the drawing room, a commotion in the civic consciousness of those "children of captivity, the upper bourgeoisie." [19] But by the time he

had thought out *Practical Agitation* he broke through the class barrier
and hoped to fire the man-in-the-street with the right feeling that
follows right doing. He now desired to stir the age. He dismissed the
socialists and trade unionists as being too materialistic. Besides, they
suffered from the same faults as the sporadic political reform organizations like the Good Government Clubs and Citizens' Union. First,
precisely because they were organizations they were wasteful of men's
time and energy. Second, like Walpole's men, they could be bought.
"A political organization is a transferable commodity." [20] Nevertheless,
all of the political action groups, including a third party, did serve one
good purpose: they were "the very elixir of reform. People are forced
to think. It hurts them." [21]

By 1900, disenchanted with his group political experience, Chapman
addressed himself to the individual, to "the conscience of the unknown
man," [22] and to the reformer or independent who didn't get elected to
office where he might advance the new day. Agitate, he wrote, for the
good idea and the good deed in private conversation, in your own business ventures, at your club, in your community organization. Accept
your aloneness. "Do not think you are wasting your time, even if no
one joins you. The prejudice against the individual is part of the evil
you are fighting." [23] Between elections maintain your honesty. At
elections vote honestly. Understand that you do not throw your vote
away when you vote independently. Speak out against dishonesty,
prejudice, mistaken party loyalty, indifference, expediency wherever
you see it. This is reform. "Reform consists in taking a bone from a
dog. Philosophy will not do it." [24] Wherever you speak out against
wrongdoing you are using your personal influence as an individual in
a democratic manner for an unselfish purpose. Who can estimate ac-
curately where and whom the last ripple of the wave of the widening
concentric circles of rectitude will touch? Rejoice when you see an
indignant man, deny that "the system is at fault," disregard the masses
("There are no masses in America . . . only individuals" [25]) and,
above all, urge young men to enter politics to crack "the gloomy ice-
field, the American civic consciousness." [26] This practical and individual agitation was the alternative to revolution in America. Do not
despair. Take inspiration from John Stuart Mill, Kant, Tolstoy, Garrison, Moses, and Jesus—individuals all of heroic influence.

The end of *The Political Nursery* came a few months after the publication of *Practical Agitation*. *The Nursery* puts the period to Chapman's agitation in a way that *Practical Agitation* does not. It will be recalled that in 1898 Chapman had denied the necessity for a religious revival to clear away the muck of corruption and that for almost a decade he had given himself to organization work for good government. Exhausted now by care and work and defeated by the lack of success, he found solace in the Bible. He retired to a position he called non-resistance, and announced in verse in the May 1900 *Nursery:*

> Must you be propping others with your crutch?
> Just stand alone and show us how it's done.
> Your plan of walking doesn't matter much
> So long as you apparently get on.
> Just walk alone.

Chapman disappeared from public life, slowly healed his wounds, wrote plays and essays, gradually took on the world again as an antagonist, and in 1912 he walked alone, a tenderhearted protestor, for the world to see. Meanwhile the comfort of specific Christian hope and grace did its work in him.

V

In Coatesville, Pennsylvania, on August 12, 1911, a Negro, "Zach" Walker, was burned to death by white lynchers. Under conditions unverifiable because his victim was dead, Walker had killed a man, attempted to run away, and had shot himself to elude his pursuers. Dragged from his hospital-jail, he got a hasty death—because he was not white. The case was brought to national attention, dragging on for several years. The prosecution failed to secure a conviction and the state and local agents withdrew. The National Association for the Advancement of Colored People continued to investigate quietly. It retained two Burns detectives who by opening a restaurant and by collecting information found out who the chief instigator was. The matter never came even to indictment, Governor Tenner of Pennsylvania cryptically admitting that the lack of convictions in this case was one of "the failures of my administration." [27]

The case did not escape Chapman's earnest attention. On the anniversary of the sordid murder, he went to Coatesville, hired a store for a memorial prayer meeting, and spoke. The meeting was attended by two people. Fortunately, the speech, reprinted and widely distributed then, is preserved in Chapman's *Memories and Milestones* (1915):

> We are met to commemorate the anniversary of one of the most dreadful crimes in history—not for the purpose of condemning it, but to repent our share in it. We do not start any agitation with regard to that particular crime. . . . The failure of the prosecution in this case, in all such cases, is only a proof of the magnitude of the guilt, and of the awful fact that everyone shares in it. . . . As I read the newspaper accounts of the scene enacted here in Coatesville a year ago, I seemed to get a glimpse into the unconscious soul of this country. . . . I seemed to be looking into the heart of a criminal—a cold thing, an awful thing. . . . The subject we are dealing with is not local. . . . The trouble has come down to us out of the past. The only reason that slavery is wrong is that it is cruel and makes men cruel and leaves them cruel. . . . A nation cannot practice a course of inhuman crime for three hundred years and then suddenly throw off the effects of it. . . . Whatever life itself is, that thing must be replenished in us. The opposite of hate is love, the opposite of cold is heat; what we need is the love of God and reverence for human nature. . . . The occasion is not small; the occasion looks back on three centuries and embraces a hemisphere. Yet the occasion is small compared with the truth it leads us to. For this truth touches all ages and affects every soul in the world.[28]

The Negro in America had been on Chapman's conscience, as on the conscience of his family for generations before. Perhaps that is why Owen Wister, a lifelong friend, characterized Chapman too simply as "a belated abolitionist." [29] The difference between his ancestors and him was that they had been collective agitators against injustice to the Negro; Chapman played the lone reformer. To those who would legislate fair practice and outlaw lynching, Chapman's argument and example, simple and noble, are not very compelling; but there must be men like Chapman to remind public opinion and legislators of the moral sanction that causes the law to be formulated and promulgated. The penitential pilgrimage to Coatesville must have made the life and times of Garrison terribly real to Chapman who was then at work on his biography, published the next year.

William Lloyd Garrison was a partisan, passionate book about a hero. The Bible-led editor, orator, agitator, and radical of international significance had purged slavery from America. He had redeemed belief in America's Declaration of Independence and the world's Bible. He had been a moral shock to America like Lovejoy's murder, like John Brown's raid. He had unmistakably branded slavery as sin and had named the evil in America: "It was Garrison who saved this nation. In his youth he gave us the issue through which alone salvation could come; and by his life he created the spirit through which that issue triumphed." [30] If Garrison could end Negro slavery, and if Emerson's voice were heeded and the moral slavery of corruption ended in America, were there not new horizons of greatness visible for America and the world?

It was a natural step from Garrison to *Notes on Religion* (1915) and *Letters and Religion* (1924), in which Chapman celebrated the moral heroes of the Bible and the world-embracing insights of their ethical affirmations. The political arena was no longer a serious attraction to Chapman. He had the comforts of poetry, plays, Greek, German, Italian, and the Bible. On each of them he left his calling card marked distinctively with the Chapman crest.

VI

John Jay Chapman held no public office and there seems to be no evidence that he sought it. For a while in the very middle of New York City politics he tried to lead his contemporaries to forswear the Machiavellianism that served a brutish hunger for economic gain. During the last half of his life he intermittently coached from the sidelines. He set himself against the grain of American society. He desired for America a Greek philosopher's intelligent democracy and invoked it with the passionateness of a Hebrew prophet. America to Chapman stood for an idea qualitatively different from its boast that it improves the world by keeping stock quotations above par.

Granted the economic gigantism in the history and development of the United States, Chapman protested against identifying uncritically the fat prosperity of corporations with the character of life in the United States. The American economic promise of a padded and pillowed existence had in small print a price tag of tyranny over politics, law, journalism, religion, education, the arts, social life—a tyranny affecting every individual who made up these abstractions. The ideals, institutions, and daily private life of Americans were being vulgarized, prostituted, and depersonalized. Chapman stood at the vestibule to the period of the muckrakers pointing the direction social protest in America was going to go, capitalizing the tendency of sentient Americans to repudiate the excesses of America's expansionism. Commercialism was the barometer of his times; democracy he called a man-ometer.[31] In so far as the individual was bought at election time, silenced in the interim between elections, fed deceit by the kept press, hypnotized by technologists, entranced by pallid productions of the arts, and taught by timid teachers, to this extent was the degradation of American life an accomplished fact. Individual regeneration, more education, and conscious altruism were the cures to the American condition.

In speaking out against and for so many things in which he saw organic disease (and sometimes health), it is understandable that Chapman is at times open to criticism for his occasional hasty scholarship, his reformer's heat where there should be light, his agitator's slashing tactics, his moralist's confidence in absolute values, his religious man's insistence upon the authenticity of his witness, and his gentleman's conviction of the rightness of his taste.

He was the conscience of his class, but his class did not listen to him except to mark him as an eccentric, a crank, a Quixote. He is today more significant than having been the Oliver Goldsmith of the depopulated drawing room. He expressed noisily, arrogantly, polemically, radically his perception of the captivity of the potential of man for goodness, private and public, domestic and international. He was not unaware of the plight of the underdog, the poor, the immigrant, the anonymous underpaid worker in the great industries, the efforts of the union organizer, and the victims of racial lynchings. His self-appointed task was not to delineate the shame of monopolies and slums. Burdened gracefully with a family history of being and doing, John Jay Chapman practiced and by example taught the self-respecting therapy of speaking out. He belongs to the time in America when radicalism spoke out and took pride in agitating against injustice, against infidelity to ideals, and against treason to the hearts of men everywhere. No "revisionist" history written in the age of creeping conservatism can deny this achievement to John Jay Chapman.

NOTES

1. Letter to his mother, quoted in M. A. DeWolfe Howe, *John Jay Chapman and His Letters* (Boston, 1937), p. 11.
2. *Emerson and Other Essays* (New York, 1898), pp. 107-108.
3. *The Political Nursery,* September-October 1900. (The present notes, for purposes of convenience, disregard the change in title from *The Nursery* to *The Political Nursery* in October 1898.)
4. *Ibid.,* March 1897.
5. *Ibid.,* April 1897.
6. *Ibid.*
7. *Ibid.*
8. *Ibid.,* Midsummer 1897.
9. *Ibid.,* April 1897.
10. *Ibid.,* Midsummer 1897.
11. *Causes and Consequences* (New York, 1898), p. 3.
12. *Ibid.,* p. 25.
13. *Ibid.,* p. 56.
14. *Ibid.,* p. 65.
15. *Ibid.,* p. 61.
16. *Ibid.,* p. 64.
17. *Ibid.,* p. 131.
18. *Ibid.,* pp. 131-132.
19. *Ibid.,* p. 132.
20. *Practical Agitation* (New York, 1900), p. 23.
21. *Ibid.,* p. 16.
22. *Ibid.,* p. 28.
23. *Ibid.,* pp. 24-25.
24. *Ibid.,* p. 140.
25. *Ibid.,* p. 76.
26. *Ibid.,* p. 143.
27. Quoted in the NAACP magazine *The Crisis* (February 1913), p. 192.
28. *Memories and Milestones* (New York, 1915), pp. 225-232.
29. Owen Wister, *Two Appreciations of John Jay Chapman* (privately printed, 1934), quoted in Howe, *op. cit.,* p. 10.
30. *William Lloyd Garrison* (New York, 1913), p. 252.
31. *Causes and Consequences* (New York, 1898), p. 126.

NOTE. The writer wishes to acknowledge the help of the Alfred University Research Foundation, Mr. Chanler Chapman (executor of the Chapman papers), Mr. Harvey Goldberg, the staff of the Houghton Library of Harvard University, Mr. Carey McWilliams, and Mr. H. H. Wilson.

BIBLIOGRAPHICAL NOTE

Works by Chapman

Emerson and Other Essays (New York, 1898).
Causes and Consequences (New York, 1898).
Practical Agitation (New York, 1900).
Learning and Other Essays (New York, 1910).
William Lloyd Garrison (New York, 1913).
Memories and Milestones (New York, 1915).
Dante (Boston, 1927).
Lucian, Plato and Greek Morals (Boston, 1931).
New Horizons in American Life (New York, 1932).

NOTE. A complete file of *The Nursery* and *The Political Nursery*, Chapman's magazine effort to stir up New York City to political reform, is in the Princeton Library; less complete files are available at the New York State Library at Albany, at the Cornell University Library, and in the Duyckinck Collection at the New York Public Library.

Works on Chapman

Howe, M. A. DeWolfe, *John Jay Chapman and His Letters* (Boston, 1937).
Wilson, Edmund, *The Triple Thinkers* (New York, 1948).

2

Theodore Dreiser: Ishmael
in the Jungle

JOHN LYDENBERG

I

"I WAS AN ISHMAEL, a wanderer."[1] So Dreiser spoke of himself during his homeless newspaper days in the 1890s. Did he think of himself as an outcast, too? As the son of Hagar, the slave girl, instead of Sarah, the proper wife? Whether he did or no, his birth on the wrong side of the Terre Haute tracks marked him as drastically as did Ishmael's birth in the wrong tent. America does not cast out the sons of its servant girls to wander in the desert, but in the 1870s it did not readily accept them as priests in its Back Bay or Fifth Avenue temples. If not an outcast, Dreiser was at least an outsider.

At one time the outsider seemed about to push his way in. Only a few years after he had stood on the banks of the East River so lonely and disheartened that he planned to jump in, he was a $10,000-a-year editor of the Butterick publications. Flashily dressed, confident behind his shiny desk, he fashioned articles that would please the new-rich ladies who sought culture and chic in the slick pages of the *Delineator*.

37

Dreiser had the force, the ability, and the drive to make his way in, and he could have stayed in and huckstered his way ever onward and upward like a good American.

But stronger than the allure of success was something in this out-sider which made him reject respectability, or even sheer unrespectable power. Dreiser was by instinct a loner, an *"isolato,"* to use Melville's term, like so many of our great writers. As an outsider he wanted to get in, to glitter among the strong, the rich, the admired. But he could never *be* one of them; he could never wholemindedly accept their ways or their views. So having proved that he could force his way across the tracks, he withdrew, not to his natal place on the wrong side, but to the tracks themselves, where he could stand alone, exposed, and observe both the sides that he knew so well from experience and sympathy.

The term "rugged individualist" is peculiarly appropriate for Dreiser not merely because of the ironic implications of applying it to him, but because it is literally so apt. His pictures show him rough, solid, and hard despite sagging flesh, big-boned and forbidding. Anecdotes reveal him alone and aloof at parties, shy and a trifle wistful, but withdrawn chiefly because he chose to remain outside, wondering and watching. Society could not soften him; nor could either hostile critics or friendly guides polish him. He was immobile and unmalleable. He was what he was—not pretty or pleasing, not a good writer by most standards, not even very intelligent, but integral, a whole man.

In *My Life with Dreiser,* Helen Richardson shows how little even the love of one he loved could tame or mold him. She lived with him most of the time from about 1920 until he died, marrying him in 1942 after the death of his long-estranged wife. She had to learn to take him as he was and to endure his desertions, his moods, and his tempers, for he could not be changed, only escaped, and she would not escape at the price of losing him. His friend, admirer, and defender, H. L. Mencken, tells of the "gigantic steadfastness" with which Dreiser ignored all his attempts "to entice him in this direction or that, fatuously presum-ing to instruct him in what would improve him and profit him." [2] Mencken's flinty barbs could not even scratch Dreiser's adamant. Muckrakers, reformers, radicals of all sorts tried to draw him into their camps where each was so sure that Dreiser belonged. But they were no more successful than Mencken: Dreiser would write as he pleased. Of course the genteel critics and all the respectable defenders of the purity of the American Girl and the happiness of the American Way flung taunts, arrows, and stink bombs at him continuously from *Sister Carrie* in 1900 until his death. He was impervious to the Methodists as to Mencken.

The latter described Dreiser as the Hindenburg of the American novel. Today a bulldozer might provide a more appropriate image. Caring nothing for shouts or shots, unable to see or to save the flowers of the tender saplings, he drove his bulldozer over the whole terrain, shattering the old buildings and pushing aside the rubble until the ground was cleared and the foundations laid bare. He demolished not out of hatred but out of a feeling that the structures, with their conventional fronts or painted with familiar slogans, served to hide the realities of life, and these he had to uncover at any cost.

Instead of steel or ice in his heart, there was bewilderment and wonder and pity. This was the quality that Sherwood Anderson chose to emphasize in the foreword of *Horses and Men,* which he dedicated to Dreiser:

> Long ago when he was editor of the *Delineator,* Dreiser went one day, with a woman friend, to visit an orphan asylum. The woman once told me the story of that afternoon in the big, ugly grey building with Dreiser, looking heavy and lumpy and old, sitting on a platform, folding and refolding his pocket-handkerchief and watching the children all in their little uniforms, trooping in.
>
> "The tears ran down his cheeks and he shook his head," the woman said, and that is a real picture of Theodore Dreiser. He is old in spirit and he does not know what to do with life, so he tells about it as he sees it, simply and honestly. The tears run down his cheeks and he folds and refolds the pocket-handkerchief and shakes his head.

II

Dreiser's position in American literature is very special. He was the first important writer to come from a non-Anglo-Saxon, lower-class background. It was not simply a matter of coming from relatively poor or humble folk—that was indeed more usual than unusual among American writers: witness, for example, Thoreau, Whitman, Twain, Howells, and Crane. Nor was it a matter merely of feeling isolated; we have only to think of others like Poe, Hawthorne, Melville. The difference was that all of these "belonged" in a most essential respect.

They came from the old settlers; they were of the great white Protestant middle class that dominated nineteenth-century America and its literature, and that determined what was orthodox and genteel. Whatever their personal or psychological problems, however they might intellectually or emotionally reject the standards of their society, they were insiders. They scarcely knew of the existence of that strange new society that was growing unrecognized beneath the crust of the old America.

Both Dreiser's parents were German immigrants, his father a fiercely puritanical Catholic and his mother a Mennonite whose original piety had become overlaid with a pagan mysticism. Dreiser was one of eleven children. His family's attempt to rise in the American way had ended with an accident to his father shortly before Theodore's birth. Thereafter, the father's work was intermittent and never such as to support the family. The younger children stole coal from the Terre Haute railroad yards in the winters, and the older sisters took up with men who could offer them temporary financial security if not matrimony. When Theodore was eight, the mother took him and the three younger children off—not to seek anyone's fortune, but as Dreiser would say, in a vagrom search for a less uncomfortable life, somewhere.

In Vincennes, Indiana, they lived with a friend over the fire station until they discovered that the rest of the quarters were being used as a bawdy house. In Sullivan, Indiana, they moved into a barren box of a house adjacent to the railroad yards; there the mother took in washing and rented out a scarcely-spare room. Then one day the glamorous older brother Paul—already famous as songwriter Paul Dresser—turned up and suggested they move to Evansville where he had a pleasant cottage for them. This he rented from his mistress—a local madam and the original of "My Gal Sal"—until the affair broke up and the Dreisers had to move on again. After a year in Chicago they went to Warsaw, in northern Indiana, where for the first time, at thirteen, Theodore was permitted to go with Protestants to a public school instead of to a Catholic school, and where also he heard the local sports crack wise about the difference between his sisters and the nice middle-class girls they would later marry.

Dreiser was brought up properly to believe in the standard American moralities. Good and evil could be distinguished readily according to the rules taught in schools, Sunday and weekday; the rewards for following the good and scorning the evil were clear, and the punishments for doing otherwise were certain.

In glaring contrast to the morality he was taught was the life he observed and lived. His kind, patient, beloved mother said nothing and held the family together as best she could: when a virginal daughter handed her ten dollars proffered by a local lawyer, she took it and bought food without a word to condemn the coming loss of "virtue." "Proper" morals came from those young Dreiser had no love for. They came through his broken father, who would turn up at their latest home, sick, hungry, jobless, but not too cowed to shout imprecations at his daughters for their immoral ways and to warn them of the vast punishments they were heaping up for themselves. They came through his respectable acquaintances in Warsaw who looked up to their own protected sisters and down upon the sisters they casually ruined across the tracks. Paul rose in the artistic demimonde, brother Rome dropped down through gambling and drink. Rome may have been "bad" but Paul certainly was not "good." What mattered, so far as Theodore could see, was not their morality or immorality; the significant difference was that Paul, like his mother, was always kind and generous, Rome boastful, unfeeling, and selfish. On the porch of the Sullivan rooming house old men rocked away their lonely last years; did their fate have any relation to their virtues?

The world he was taught about had a nice clear-cut meaning; his experience showed him a world which denied that meaning and seemed to have no other. What, possibly, could the defeat of these helpless old men be said to mean? Where did one see the working out of the principle that virtue was rewarded and only vice punished? People did what they had to do, what they could do. They survived. What grounds could there be for praise or blame? Certainly none were to be found in any of the official moralities. In the last analysis all that remained was "goodness of heart," the quality Dreiser attributed to Jennie Gerhardt and knew in his mother.

He did not formulate his thoughts this way at the time. He was simply bewildered, dreamy, unhappy, but thrilled and excited by the life of the big city to which he returned, on his own, in 1887. He drifted through odd frustrating jobs for a few years and then into reporting in 1892. Newspaper work was the training ground for many authors from the '90s on, and the breeding ground par excellence of cynicism. At no time was life in America more raw; never did the disparities between precepts and practices gape more widely and openly; and no experience was as effective as the journalist's in preventing a man from comfortably ignoring the raw disparities. It was only too easy to conclude with one of Dreiser's first editors that "Life is a god-damned stinking, treacherous game, and nine hundred and ninety-nine men out of every thousand are bastards." [3]

The adoption of that attitude would have provided one solution for Dreiser—and had he accepted it, we would never have heard of him. Happily he couldn't, for he was too much a child of his time, the young man from the country, fascinated at the shiny fruit dangled before him, bright-eyed at the wonders of the city, enthralled by the men and women in their fine clothes and handsome carriages, the grand gay hotels, the wonderful insolence of the powerful. For all he was an outsider, he was also the typical American with the conventional goals: "My eyes were constantly fixed on people in positions far above my own. Those who interested me most were bankers, millionaires, artists, executive leaders, the real rulers of the world." "No common man am I," he said then of himself as he dreamed of a Horatio Alger rise from rags to riches. [4]

But he had neither the cynicism nor the blindness needed for one who would successfully follow that dream. The ultimate effect of his newspaper experience, superimposed upon that of his youth, was to make him not a cynic but a skeptic, a questioner, a seeker. Like Lincoln Steffens, he saw a world made up of the strong and the weak instead of the good and the bad. The strong were successful, and success brought its rewards, but these were scarcely the rewards of virtue, however much the conventionally pious would like to think it so. Nor were the rewards the Devil's brand, as some reformers would have it; the sentimentalist's equation of strong with bad and weak with good was simply the converse of the orthodox view and no less inapplicable to the real American jungle. One could only say that people were what they were, that victory in the battles was sweet but impermanent, that defeat was more common, and that it was a pity the world had to be so:

For myself, I accept now no creeds. I do not know what truth is, what beauty is, what love is, what hope is. I do not believe any one absolutely and I do not doubt any one absolutely. I think people are both evil and well-intentioned.[5]

III

This, then, was the Dreiser who at the age of twenty-eight sat down to write his first novel. The life he had experienced was neither gracious nor moral. He had succeeded as a free-lance writer in the great New York city that had so frightened and appalled him at first. He had learned that the fight was as ruthlessly ungloved in the publishing world as in that of the new industrialists whose life stories he had been writing. And he had made his way up in that world so that in 1899 he was sufficiently well known for the first edition of *Who's Who in America* to include his name, listing him as "Journalist-Author."

"Author" was, as a matter of fact, a misnomer. Though in his early newspaper days the example of some of his colleagues had led him to attempt a few plays and short stories, he had done so only halfheartedly and he quickly gave up. He was as exceptional among American authors in his lack of literary training and ambitions as in his family background. The other novelists who had started out as newspapermen had, with few exceptions, seen their journalism as preparation for "serious" writing. They recognized a literary tradition and sought to be "writers" within that tradition.

Dreiser had a call, as do all great artists, but it was not a call to "write." What he had to do was simply *describe* the America he had experienced, tell how he felt about the life he had known, point out the bewildering, contradictory, unadmitted truths. No other important American author showed such a lack of concern for the craft of writing. Paradoxically, this was for him a source of strength as well as a weakness. Scorning the tricks of fine writing, he never succeeded in developing grace or beauty or even facility, but by the same token he never succumbed to the temptation to follow one or more of the roads to popularity. When *Sister Carrie* failed, instead of trying to find a manner that would satisfy readers, critics, and publishers, he simply abandoned fiction and responded again to the siren call of success. But at the *Delineator* desk his own personal call soon came back again, louder, irresistible; and he gave up editing to be an author, cost what it might. Like Thoreau, whom he later came to admire greatly, he

marched to a drummer that no one else heard; like Emerson and
Thoreau, he found that he must follow his own genius, wherever it led,
that to be a man and a writer he must be a nonconformist however
much the world might whip him with its displeasure.

In *A Book About Myself,* Dreiser tells how his budding desires to
write short stories had been nipped by his reading of the magazines.

> I set to examining the current magazines. . . . I was never more con-
> founded than by the discrepancy existing between my own observations
> and those displayed here, the beauty and peace and charm to be found in
> everything, the almost complete absence of any reference to the coarse
> and the vulgar and the cruel and the terrible. . . . But as I viewed the
> strenuous world about me, all that I read seemed not to have so very
> much to do with it. Perhaps, as I now thought, life as I saw it, the darker
> phases, was never to be written about. Maybe such things were not the
> true province of fiction anyhow. I read and read, but all I could gather
> was that I had no such tales to tell, and, however much I tried, I could
> not think of any. The kind of thing I was witnessing no one would want
> as fiction.[6]

Yet he had tried a few short stories while vacationing with Arthur
Henry, an old newspaper friend from Toledo. Then in the fall of
1899, only half in earnest, he responded to Henry's insistence that he
should try a novel. According to his account, he put the words "Sister
Carrie" atop a blank page of paper, with no idea of what he was
going to say, and then went on to write the first half of the novel with
no planning and little difficulty.

He was able to do that because he was simply recording his own
experiences and emotions instead of trying to tell a tale that would
belong to the "true province of fiction." Indeed, one could say that in
Sister Carrie Dreiser was not writing a novel at all; he was simply
transcribing a part of his version of the American experience. Although
taken scene by scene or character by character almost everything in it
could have been found in preceding novels, taken as a whole it was
unique as a social novel. Its uniqueness lay in the fact that Drouet,
Carrie, and Hurstwood were facets of their author; whereas in other
novels the drummer, the poor girl from the country who fell to the
wiles of the city slicker, the flashy front-man who absconded with the
cash and paid with his soul or his life, these were either stock figures
or at their best characters observed from above with varying degrees of

condescension or sentimentality. If Dreiser could not write popular magazine fiction because he was outside the official American culture and the conventional literary circles, he could write something different and true and lasting because he was inside the jungle of the new urban, industrial society.

Henry James and Edith Wharton wrote about their American aristocrats from intimate acquaintance. Howells and a multitude of now-unread minor novelists described with authority the life of the old middle class. Train, and after him Howe, Frederic, Garland, gave authentic accounts of the rural societies they had grown up in. All of them sensed the changes in postbellum America, and most of them tried in one way or another to show these changes in their books. But none of them could deal directly, from firsthand experience, with what was most distinctive about the new society. Novelists had, of course, already written about the ignorant, destitute immigrants from southern and eastern Europe, about tenements and saloons and sweatshops, about jobless workers, radicals, labor organizers, prostitutes, industrialists, political bosses; and between *Sister Carrie* and *Jennie Gerhardt* a spate of muckraking novels exposed in ever more odorous detail the great American Augean stables. Most of these were righteous, indignant novels describing the evils in lurid detail, and implicitly or explicitly urging the good people to do something, to throw out rascals or rescue the perishing or care for the falling. And most—possibly all—were written by the old insiders who could only see from the outside this world across the tracks.

Howells's streetcar strike is viewed from an easy chair, not from the carbarns and the strikers' saloons as is Dreiser's. Crane, the rebel against his respectable Protestant background, observes Maggie the girl of the slums and the streets sardonically, ironically, and so unsentimentally as to shock his friends; but Carrie is Dreiser's sister. It is significant that Howells liked *Maggie,* ignored *Sister Carrie.* McTeague's disintegration is depicted with a fine use of symbolic actions selected by Norris with care (and remembrance of Zola); Hurstwood's decline is that of the old men Dreiser had known, and it is given added poignancy by the fear never far from the surface of Dreiser's heart that he might one day join the Hurstwoods in breadlines and flophouses. One might claim a similarity between Dreiser and Robert Herrick, in the fact that Cowperwood—the subject of a trilogy, *The Financier*

(1912), *The Titan* (1914), *The Stoic* (1917)—was modeled closely after a real tycoon, Yerkes, as Herrick's American citizen, Van Harrington, the hero of *The Memoirs of an American Citizen* (1905), was based on the careers of the great meat packers. But the difference is more significant: Professor Herrick could never have been his Van Harrington, whereas, in at least a part of him, Dreiser was Cowperwood, sharing his drive for power and his love of ostentation and luxury, his inability to accept official views of right and wrong, and his disdain for the *unco guid* who hid their weaknesses behind a cloak of reformist morality. Clyde Griffiths in *An American Tragedy* (1925) was but another part of Dreiser—his background and his longings; and as Clyde stole money to buy his teasing Hortense a coat, so Dreiser himself had once "borrowed" twenty-five dollars from his employer that he might be more nattily attired. Of all his novels we can say, paraphrasing Whitman, Dreiser was the man, he was there, he suffered.

Dreiser was as alone and as integral in his art, if such we can call it, as in his life. Where other novelists adopted a literary theory and tried to make their fiction fit it, or introduced a particular subject matter because they thought it should be dealt with, Dreiser wrote only about what he knew, as he knew it. Traditionless himself, he was unable or unwilling to adopt the traditions, literary or social, of the genteel arbiters of the thought of his day. And so, all unwittingly, simply because he looked at the world about him with untrained, uncultured eyes and insisted on being himself, he brought a revolution to American literature.

As he accepted no literary formulas, so he adopted no political or social formulas—at least as far as his fiction was concerned. T. S. Eliot's observation about Henry James that "he had a mind so fine that no idea could violate it" is possibly even more applicable to Dreiser, at least if for "fine" we substitute "honest" or "stubborn." At first glance this assertion may seem absurd, for Dreiser was continually being seduced by plausible theories. Indeed he fancied himself a Thinker and went around arguing the Big Questions with anyone he thought had a new idea. He even published several volumes in which he essayed to formulate the philosophical or social theories that currently attracted him, dreary writings that merely express in pseudo-intellectual terms his inability to "understand."

Understanding of this sort was not his forte. Lionel Trilling in a righteous Columbiad has cited Dreiser's intellectual failings as symbolic of the degeneration of the liberal imagination. Such an attitude is almost as perverse as the simple moralism of Stuart Sherman, literary critic of the 1920s, which supporters of Dreiser regularly use to show the myopia of his contemporaries. For one thing, Dreiser was no more of a "liberal" than Thoreau. More important, the power of his novels lies precisely in the fact that they were not illustrations of any political ideas or social theories. When he introduces his jejune philosophizing into his novels, we hurry ashamedly over the turgid, pretentious passages, ignoring them as intrusions. His strength lies not in his thought but in his observation of the social milieu, his feeling for the way people lived and dreamed and despaired. His account of the American experience of his time, of the lure of wealth and power and the fear of poverty and defeat, of tawdry dwellings and gaudy hotels, of the weak and the strong, the seeker and the sought, is unsurpassed because in his novels his mind did remain inviolate and he saw his American scene not as revealing any dialectical process, or endorsing any moral or political theory, but simply as being Life, wonderful, terrible, very mysterious.

IV

Until he had finished all his major novels, Dreiser resisted the appeals of the Left as firmly as he did the admonitions of Comstockery. In 1916, Floyd Dell exhorted him in the old *Masses:* "Life at its best and most heroic is rebellion. All artists, big and little, are in their degree rebels. You yourself are a rebel. . . . Why do you not write the American novel of rebellion?" [7] But Dreiser stubbornly insisted that he was an observer and an artist. Alongside his sympathy for the downtrodden lay his empathy for those who strove greatly and successfully for power. Much as he would have liked to see a better world, he did not see how it could be brought into being, nor could he imagine what it would be like—except, vaguely, that it should contain less suffering and more goodheartedness. When tempted to explain his views he would sometimes castigate American ideals and institutions and hypocrisies as the source of social injustices, implying that changes should be made.

More often he would assert that the world's ills were ineradicable because some men were born strong and some weak, and suffering lay in the nature of things. In *A Traveller at Forty* (1913), he wrote:

> There are those who still think that life is something which can be put into a mold and adjusted to a theory, but I am not one of them. I cannot view life or human nature save as an expression of contraries—in fact, I think that is what life is. . . . I cannot see how there can be great men without little ones; wealth without poverty. . . .
>
> I did not make my mind. I did not make my art. I cannot choose my taste except by predestined instinct. . . . I indict nature here and now, as I always do and always shall do, as being aimless, pointless, unfair, unjust. I see in the whole thing no scheme but an accidental one—no justice save accidental justice.[8]

He insisted that he cared more for the spectacle of contending forces than for any permanent good that might come out of them. "I like labor leaders," he wrote in the same book. "I like big, raw, crude, hungry men who are eager for gain—for self-glorification."[9] Over a decade later, when he was working in Los Angeles on the tragedy of Clyde Griffiths's America, he gave a reporter an interview which showed him little changed:

> I want to be back where there is struggle. . . . I like to wander around the quarters of New York where the toilers are. . . . That's health. I don't care about idlers or tourists, or the humdrum, or artistic pretenders that flock out here, or the rich who tell you—and that is all they have to tell—how they did it. They would have interested me when they were struggling. . . .
>
> It is wrong and can't be righted. When you know that, the unalterableness isn't going to cause you any tears. I don't worry about it. One could lose his mind if he took it to heart.
>
> I don't care a damn about the masses. It is the individual that concerns me.

Despite the element of pose in that public statement, it suggests the essential character of Dreiser's social views as they informed his fiction. He was concerned above all with the individual. He enjoyed struggle and admired the victors. But he did not think for a minute that the mighty were right. If he pretends sometimes to amorality, he here shows his real feelings by characterizing the outcome of the struggle as "wrong." Only when he denies that it causes him any tears is he really disingenuous. No tears in the *American Tragedy?*

The popular success of *An American Tragedy* (no other novel of Dreiser's came close to being a best seller) brought him increased attention from reformers of all sorts. The Soviet Union invited him to visit the country as a guest, promising, on his insistence, that he would be free to see what he wanted and say what he thought. He was interested in Russia because of "its change, its ideals, its dreams," skeptical about it because he was an individualist. On leaving, he publicly criticized many aspects of the new society, concluding that "more individualism and less communism would be to the great advantage of this mighty country." [10] But at home he defended the Soviets against what he considered complacent or dogmatic American criticisms. Communists were outsiders as he had been, and he would stand up for them against the smug insiders. There were also important things to say in favor of Russia: for all her poverty, she had no unemployed and no breadlines as did the rich United States even during the boom of the 1920s.

With the coming of the depression, Dreiser found himself drawn more and more into political controversies, until finally they came to occupy almost his entire attention. The reasons for the shift were many: his passive sympathy for the poor turned into an active insistence that something had to be done to stop the rapidly increasing misery; the social consciousness and political involvement of writers of the '30s was so pervasive and so pressing that few could remain aloof; after *An American Tragedy* Dreiser was for the first time relatively free from financial worries and the pressure to publish; and apparently he felt a growing need to escape from his loneliness.

It would be easy to say that the Communists got their ring through his nose and led him along their twisting line from 1930 until his death in 1945. Nor would it be entirely inaccurate. For he did follow along their line. Yet, like the led bull, he was not the tame creature of his leaders; he conceded to them none of his integrity or spirit of independence. By the early '30s, Dreiser had become a signer and a joiner. He would give his name to any good cause; he soon learned to speak in public, something he had always dreaded and avoided; and reporters could now get from him impassioned, partisan, newsworthy statements where formerly they had simply been told that life was unknowable and social forces uncontrollable. If it was Communist guidance that he most often seemed to take, that was partly because the Communists, typically, were most assiduous in wooing him, and partly because he saw them both as maligned victims of all the American reactionaries, and as clear-sighted, open-minded (so it really seemed to Dreiser and to many others then) analysts of the middle-class hypocrisies and illusions. But he was not a party man; he was still his old self, and on occasion he resigned from an organization that he decided was really Communist-dominated and following paths he did not wish to take.

But while he was fighting alongside the Communists for the Scotts-boro boys, the Spanish Loyalists, nonintervention during the days of the Nazi-Soviet Pact, and a second front almost immediately there-after, he was at the same time pursuing another, apparently divergent, course. The mysticism that had always lurked behind his materialism came increasingly to the fore. Having rejected the conventional abso-lutes of American orthodoxy, he sought restlessly for an absolute of his own. The outcome of this search appears in his posthumous books, on which he had worked intermittently between *An American Tragedy* in 1925 and his death. *The Stoic,* last volume of the Cowper-wood trilogy, ends with the heroine's rather soggy conversion to Yoga. *The Bulwark* much more convincingly depicts a Quaker's doubts and his ultimate reconciliation to religion as he comes to recognize the beneficence of the life force working through all things.

On Good Friday of 1945, Dreiser took Communion in a Congre-gational church. In the fall he joined the Communist Party, issuing a statement written for him by his Communist friends, but insisting that he still remained his own master and would continue to speak his own mind.

Failure of nerve? Betrayal of radicalism? Possibly both, in a sense. But neither action was entirely inconsistent with his earlier attitudes, and neither was a denial of his integrity. Despite his constant excoria-tion of religionists and moralists, he had always had a strong religious, mystical strain. He had always wanted to discover final answers to the whys of existence. He had always longed to find some all-embrac-ing meaning to his life of wandering and the struggles and heart-breaks of his fellows. If, toward the end, he found some peace in the mysticisms of Eastern religion, or the mystery of the sharing of Christ's body and blood, or the symbolism of world brotherhood in

Communism, this did not mean that he had fallen into acceptance of his father's puritan moralism or Russia's totalitarianism.

And in the last analysis these two acts did not matter, just as his writings since 1925 do not matter much now. This Ishmael had, in his old age, tried on the mantle of Isaac, but what we will remember and cherish is the bitter fruit of his days as Ishmael the outcast, wandering alone in the desert, telling the truths that the orthodox and well-born saw not or dared not tell.

V

Dreiser's books seem to have been hewed out of stone. Uncouth and often ugly, so bold that they were hard to read, they were ignored or derided when Dreiser was erecting them on the foundations he had laid bare. But they last. The paint flakes off the fashionable wooden structures built on sand, and the boards rot and fall off. Who now reads David Graham Phillips or Robert Herrick or our American Winston Churchill? Garland, Frank Norris, even Howells as social realist, have faded. And it is not at all unlikely that Dos Passos and Steinbeck will shortly recede as Sinclair Lewis is already doing.

Dreiser was a radical in the great, and much dishonored, American tradition because he insisted on being himself. He resisted the admonitions and cajoleries of the critics; he saw through all the creeds of the orthodox and accepted none from the reformers. Because he had the courage, the stubbornness, the lack of literary sensitivity to write as he did, Dreiser built far better than he or his contemporaries knew. No novelist today would think of using his fiction as a model. But none will write social novels with such lasting power unless he has Dreiser's essential qualities of integrity and independence, wonder and pity.

NOTES

1. Quoted in F. O. Matthiessen, *Theodore Dreiser* (New York, 1951), p. 34.
2. Edmund Wilson, editor, *The Shock of Recognition* (Garden City, N. Y., 1947), p. 1160.
3. Dreiser, *A Book About Myself* (New York, 1922), p. 59.

4. *Ibid.*, pp. 33, 34.
5. Dreiser, *A Traveller at Forty* (New York, 1913), p. 4.
6. *A Book About Myself,* pp. 490-491.
7. Quoted in Bernard Smith, *Forces in American Criticism* (New York, 1939), p. 298, from *The Masses,* Vol. VIII, No. 10 (August 1916), p. 30.
8. *A Traveller at Forty,* p. 34.
9. *Ibid.*, p. 178.
10. Quoted in Robert Elias, *Theodore Dreiser: Apostle of Nature* (New York, 1949), p. 298.

BIBLIOGRAPHICAL NOTE

Works by Dreiser

Sister Carrie (New York, 1900).
Jennie Gerhardt (New York, 1911).
The Financier (New York, 1912).
A Traveller at Forty (New York, 1913).
The Titan (New York, 1914).
The "Genius" (New York, 1915).
Twelve Men (New York, 1919).
A Book About Myself (New York, 1922); reissued as *Newspaper Days* (New York, 1931).
An American Tragedy (New York, 1925).
Dawn (New York, 1931).
The Bulwark (New York, 1946).
The Stoic (New York, 1947).

Works on Dreiser

Dreiser, Helen, *My Life with Dreiser* (Cleveland, 1951).
Dudley, Dorothy, *Forgotten Frontiers: Dreiser and the Land of the Free* (New York, 1932); republished under the title *Dreiser and the Land of the Free* (New York, 1946).
Elias, Robert, *Theodore Dreiser: Apostle of Nature* (New York, 1949).
Kazin, Alfred, and Charles Shapiro, editors, *The Stature of Theodore Dreiser* (Bloomington, Indiana, 1955). This collection of biographical and critical essays on Dreiser contains an extensive bibliography of Dreiser criticism.
Matthiessen, F. O., *Theodore Dreiser* (New York, 1951).

3

Heywood Broun: A Free Man's Faith

HARVEY GOLDBERG

In the annals of modern journalism, no newspaperman sur-passes Heywood Broun in devotion and dedication to his craft. And in the record of creative radicalism, no journalist since Steffens even approaches Broun in his inspired use of the great commercial press to criticize, to propose, and to prepare a better life. However gentle his nature or precarious his security, he would not jibe and run. To attack first and equivocate later has been the unfortunate hallmark of the liberal. But to stand ground firmly for unvarnished truth against organized power, to translate words into action and action into deeds, this was the way of Broun. And it is the way of the radi-cal. "In the final court of reckoning I believe the angels will indulge in few long cheers for any liberal. With minor exceptions he's a trimmer. 'There is much to be said on both sides' is one of his favorite sayings, or 'The truth lies somewhere between the two.' Thus split, he conciliates. It is hard enough to draw the mote from any eye, and if a man must drop that every now and then to take a yank at some

53

beam in the opposite camp, he will accomplish little in the space allowed us." [1]

I

In the decades before 1940, when journalism was considerably more personal and creative than today, less synthetic and drained of blood, Broun honored his profession by setting high the minimum standards for a newspaper and its staff. Always against the subordination of news to dogma which served the special interest of owner or advertiser, he had a code for the honest newspaperman that rested on a foundation of skepticism, idealism, and talent. "The very function of a newspaper," he wrote, "should make it skeptic. The business of reporting is to ask questions and check them up." [2] When conservatives like the clerical columnist Dr. Frank Crane, self-appointed guardians of public morality, suggested that news ought to be suppressed by papers if its consequences might be disquieting to the public, Broun thundered back: "The public has a right to resent being coddled into salvation. We don't want to look at the world through the eyes of some kindly mentor intent upon offering us recommended lists of facts. If certain truths are troublesome and dangerous we demand them just the same. Truth is worth many tons of complacency." [3] Yet Broun was never a destructive cynic. With the courage to stand against authority, the great journalist required the imagination to stand for principle. "All revolutionists have been like that. They have refused to accept some prevailing concept. After pounding it to dust with doubt, they have built something better out of faith and imagination." [4] But whether critical or creative, Broun insisted upon talent in journalism, upon the ability to think clearly and to communicate effectively, free in the writing from all that is turgid, pompous, or equivocal. Once he had said: "Much that is written for the moment has at least a year or two of vitality. Perhaps there is a little which deserves even longer life." [5] But this high praise for journalists is far better applied to Broun than to the craft as a whole.

However great and radical his talent, Broun might easily have been suffocated by repression or devitalized by use in the small, sectarian papers if he had not found possible a long alliance with the *New York World*. The *World* was a commercial operation, to be sure, and Broun came to eventual clash with its ownership. But under editors like Swope and Cobb in the 1920s, the paper stood strongly for talent (gathering to its pages as columnists in the '20s men like Broun, Woollcott, F. P. A., Deems Taylor, Allan Nevins, Frank Sullivan, Ring Lardner, Samuel Chotzinoff, and Mencken). And it stood for a time on the principle of courage enunciated by Joseph Pulitzer upon establishment of the *World* on May 10, 1883:

> An institution that should always fight for progress and reform, never tolerate injustice or corruption, always fight demagogues of all parties, always oppose privileged classes and public plunderers, never lack sympathy with the poor, always remain devoted to the public welfare, never be satisfied with merely printing news, always be drastically independent, never be afraid to attack wrong, whether by predatory plutocracy or predatory poverty.

A startling principle for a great daily organ? But it came from a period when American capitalism seemed sound in its present and secure in its future. Broun wrote in the twilight of that age, when lengthening shadows came to be cast upon intellectual freedom, but the twilight was still light enough for his wide-ranging efforts.

II

It would be inaccurate in the extreme to etch a portrait of Broun steeped in Marx and mired in poverty. Family background, education, social life, personal comportment would all give the lie to such a picture. Born in Brooklyn, New York, on December 7, 1888, he was the son of an English immigrant father who prospered in the printing business and cultivated a love of wines, sports, and bridge. Young Heywood grew up, in fact, in a congenial household, adorned for a time with a French butler and an Irish nurse. From private school (Horace Mann at 120th Street and Broadway) to Harvard College in 1906 seemed a normal progression, and he entered the class of 1910 along with Walter Lippmann, John Reed, Stuart Chase, Alan Seeger, and Bronson Cutting. Others may have foreshadowed their future development, but not Broun. Failing three times to make the staff of the *Harvard Crimson,* failing ultimately to attain a degree because of a deficiency in elementary French, displaying only desultory interest in socialism, he left college in 1910 with few marks on his record to presage a future as a noted journalist and a humanitarian socialist.

Broun's career in journalism, uninterrupted until his death at fifty-one on December 18, 1939, began in 1910 on *The Morning Telegraph,* a post to which the oversized, affable, yet intensely sensitive young man came through the influence of his father.[6] On the *Telegraph,* and from 1912 on Whitelaw Reid's *New York Tribune,* Broun performed a tremendous variety of journalistic tasks, but emerged finally as a reporter of sporting and cultural events. Except for a brief period as a war correspondent in France, he wrote mainly about pennant races, plays, and new books, and became a central figure in the fabled Broadway life, symbolized by the famous Round Table at the Algonquin Hotel. But if other members of that group, like Benchley, George Kaufman, Woollcott, and F. P. A., were likewise great wits and fine writers, only Broun emerged from the sparkling surface of this intellectual night life to undertake a highly serious appraisal of the world about him.

But this Broadway reputation seemed to haunt Broun. For some, especially in the radical camp, he remained always a whiskey-drinking, poker-playing, stage-acting comedian, who preferred the locker room of the Giants to the picket line of a strike. In the pages of the *Daily Worker* he was generally caricatured as a bourgeois clown who merely toyed with left-wing causes. Broun, of course, could not or would not change his epicurean habits. If he rose late in the day, loved the company of pitchers and actors, burst the puritanical bounds that humorless radicals sought to impose, it may have weakened his reputation but never his integrity. Like many others before him, he suffered from the debilitating tendency in the history of radicalism whereby some militants seem always to suspect the purity of others. In deep earnestness, therefore, he turned on such detractors during his campaign for Congress on the Socialist ticket in 1930 with a blunt statement: "There has been considerable comment on the fact that there are a number of actors actively supporting my candidacy. People seem to think there is something funny about actors in public affairs, just as they seem to think it's funny for a newspaperman to get into politics. The truth is that unemployment has hit the actors harder than almost any other group of workers."[7] But a word can actually be said for the detractors.

When Broun expressed serious thoughts in brilliant phrases, he assuredly reached a huge audience. Yet there lurks the danger that the lesson is lost while the phrase remains. Commenting on his defeat in the 1930 Congressional campaign, for example, Broun stressed the need for elaborate organization, but added: "I shall begin tomorrow to build up that organization. I won't get up at 9 o'clock to do it, that's too early, but at about 3 o'clock." [8] But what a small defect in a man who never defected! For a massive audience, Heywood Broun, however he lived (or perhaps because of that vast joy of living), was both radical and consistent. Bruce Bliven said that quite pointedly soon after Broun's death: "He had a million friends he did not know, in addition to ten thousand he had heard about. He gained this million by being himself, by using his great gifts on their side in a battle where the shiniest armor and the brassiest hats go to those who cross over to the enemy." [9]

III

On the morning of September 7, 1921, the eighteen-year run of Heywood Broun's "It Seems to Me" began in the *New York World* of Herbert Bayard Swope. One can search out the essential keys in the transition of this famous column from informed, witty commentaries on the arts to vigorous fighting for personal freedom and social justice without achieving conclusive results. But certain components of Broun's radicalism can be isolated. At bottom, Broun was a profound humanist, whose love of life, whose poet's sensitivity to the sounds and smells of nature, to the verve and thrill of cities, yielded a radical resentment of all those institutional barriers that blocked man from fulfillment. [10] American industrial society seemed full of such barriers. Thus, when Henry Ford declared grimly that "history is bunk," he seemed to sum up for Broun America's crushing subordination of human learning and enthronement of mechanical success. "Like all practical men and a good many impractical ones as well, Mr. Ford is in a terrible hurry about things. He would organize the world as tightly and as quickly as a factory." [11] Like certain other writers of this time, Broun saw the dangers in a culture whose standards of material success and physical strength were sapping the sensitivity of man and turning his community into a Darwinian jungle.

What, asked Broun, has business enterprise to do with genuine learning? "Business saves its warmest welcome for youngsters who look well about the place and play creditable golf over week-ends. Banking and bond-selling and all the rest of it are largely an extension of the college club and fraternity system." [12] And as for the American cult of strength, Broun spoke bluntly: "Muscularity has no necessary relation to force, either temporal or spiritual." [13] If conformity to prevalent values and obedience to contemporary institutions served to paralyze man, Broun urged nonconformism and disobedience. Therein lay his admiration for lonely pioneers. Therein lies a clue to his radicalism.

The particular stimuli to Broun's growth in the 1920s emerge, however, from the history of the day. There is a neat legend about the postwar decade, 1920 to 1929, propagated by an assorted company of golden-age worshippers, that those were years of universal prosperity and perpetual gaiety. But historians have demonstrated otherwise when describing the misery of the farmer or the coal miner in the '20s. And novelists like Sinclair Lewis, Dos Passos, and Upton Sinclair struck deeply at the culture of American capitalism in their attacks upon vulgar materialism, rampant nationalism, the corruption of political and educational institutions. For in fact, the USA of the '20s, in its thought as well as its resources, seemed to become ever more cartelized, more controlled. It was in vigorous defense of the open society against the closed, of the unfettered mind against the conformist, that Broun moved closer to political radicalism. On censorship, on racial discrimination, on academic freedom—on these three aspects of the question he wrote repeatedly.

The wave of censorship against books, movies, and ideas rested upon a nervous postwar fear of social change and a strange hangover of repressive puritanism. Broun attacked the movement systematically. It was his belief at the outset that censorship actions, almost without exception, covered private interests in the cloak of public welfare, exactly the kind of hypocrisy that sickened him: "I wish that when America decides to do something from sheer self-interest it would label it as that and not insist on calling the action altruism and even adding highfalutin adjectives." [14] But for Broun censorship was not only hypocritical; it was often useless, destined at most to retard, not to efface, a movement or a thought. Reflecting wisely on the attacks against the teaching of evolution theory, he wrote: "Censorship is centuries too late. Biology, for instance, cannot be amended with blue pencils and shears." [15]

Yet even assuming the validity of suppression and its ultimate effectiveness, what standards, challenged Broun, were available to the censor, enabling him infallibly to distinguish truth from error, the moral from the immoral, the American from the un-American? Mayor Hylan of New York, "not quite the average citizen, but not much below that mark," [16] seemed hardly suited to urge the removal of MacMonnies's statue "Civic Virtue" as immoral. The standards set by the National Motion Picture League were, of course, absurd in demanding the elimination from films of "all scenes depicting hatred, intrigue, unfaithfulness, indecency, envy, superstition, deceit, irreverence and lawlessness." Broun commented with sharp sarcasm: "The scenario writer who can follow all the instructions of the League and write any story at all must be hailed as a genius. The only possible clash in his story must be built up around the terrific conflict between perfect virtue and absolute goodness." [17] No, the censor was decidedly not moved by a divine infallibility but rather by a human lust for power. "In some respects the life of a censor is more exhilarating than that of an emperor. The best the emperor can do is to snip off the heads of men and women, who are mere mortals. The censor can decapitate ideas which but for him might have lived forever." [18]

Presaging his monumental fight on behalf of Sacco and Vanzetti, Broun did continuous battle with the censors. To those, for example, who sought to prevent lectures by Margaret Sanger out of their hostility to birth control, he insisted upon the indivisibility of freedom: "We must bring ourselves to realize that it is necessary to support free speech for the things we hate in order to ensure it for the things in which we believe with all our heart." [19] And having defended such serious works of art as Lawrence's *Women in Love* and Anderson and Stallings's *What Price Glory?* against charges of obscenity and actions of suppression, Broun reminded the public that the artist's contribution lay in revealing the totality of human experience: "You cannot discard grossness until you have laid hand upon it and named it and numbered it. We think of the ostrich as a great fool because he hides his head and fancies that he has stepped out of time and space. Our own practice is just as silly." [20]

It was a constant with Broun—this struggle against suppression—and not always easy. "Disagreement disturbs me. Argument gives me indigestion and palpitation." It would have been easier to let the democracy founder and to join the crowd. But no, the growing threat to American mobility prodded Broun to militancy. "I shall keep on, for by practice I may learn to hold like a freeman this fine, fizzy wine of challenge." [21]

Discrimination against the nation's racial and religious minorities accompanied the suppression of unpopular causes. Negroes, Jews, Catholics, Orientals—in fact, any foreigners as defined by that strange "Anglo-Saxon" standard—were increasingly victimized in this period of irrational ultra-patriotism. Broun would make no compromise with intolerance, acting as he did out of deep Christian love and democratic faith. He talked of the Negro problem as the dilemma of democracy long before Professor Myrdal did: "As long as the Negro problem persists, we shall be confronted with the task of conducting a democracy in the face of the fact that from one vast bloc of States we can seldom expect representation except through Bourbons and demagogues."

An intellectual who drew deeply from wide culture and sober reason, Broun saw in discrimination and prejudice more than a force corrupting political and economic democracy. It was a disease, paralyzing the reasoning faculties of man, and putting blind emotion in their place. "Anti-Semitism," he wrote one morning, some five years before he finished a full-length book on the subject, "is a state of mind which may not be pacified by any offering of reason. The man from Russia who upholds his own customs and culture, even for a single generation, is assailed as a foreigner who is incapable of assimilation in American habits of mind and action. The intellectual young Jew of the schools and colleges meets reproaches, and he is called a grind and pedant." [22] In the same vein of irony he tossed solid fact against poisonous fiction in fighting against the Nordic theories of such notorious bigots as Madison Grant. But ultimately he understood the bigot as well as the argument, penetrating to that gnawing personal insecurity which leads a man to divide society into superiors and inferiors: "Being a member of a superior race is trying business. Conviction must ring ever in the ears and so they move about, these beleaguered Nordics, tolling the bell, straining at the rope,

panting, sweating, aching in back and shoulders. Nothing much comes
to the world from these people along the rain-swept fringe. They have
no time for other tasks, for their job is to carry the white man's burden
and be dominant." [23]

But, characteristically, Broun did not view this problem, or any,
with despair. He urged and practiced exposure of the practices of
discrimination and the ideas of intolerance. He urged especially the
courage of experience, the growth of contacts with minority groups—
the kind of action, in fact, recently taken to desegregate school children. Commenting on a three-year experience of dining with a Negro
in Memorial Hall at Harvard, during which all tensions disappeared,
Broun remarked pointedly: "The tragedy of race discrimination does
not lie in the fact that nothing can be done about it but that something can." [24]

While the public attention of the '20s remained riveted on stock
exchange, hip flask, and sports page, Broun became increasingly anxious
about the nation's schools and colleges. Education is a crucial key
to the functioning of a democracy, but the schools at all levels, reflecting control of the educator by the businessman, seemed geared
for training mediocre conformists and discouraging independent
thinkers. Regretting the lack of vigorous radicalism, and understanding precisely that the cry of self-appointed censors against "sub-
version" represented an attack against a small but independent minority
among teachers and students, Broun called lie to charges being aired
in those days: "The college radical finds himself a lone and rather
unpopular innovator entirely surrounded by Babbitts. The codes of
the colleges are far more rigorous than those which most of the students are likely to encounter in later life. Not radicalism but priggish-
ness rides rampant in American colleges." [25]

When John T. Scopes, a biology teacher in Dayton, Tennessee,
was brought to trial on July 10, 1925, for explaining to students the
theory of evolution despite the legal injunction imposed by that fun-
damentalist commonwealth, the contrast between the search for truth
and the imposition of dogma was glaring enough to enlist as the legal
representatives of science and myth respectively the great Clarence
Darrow and the senile William Jennings Bryan. For Broun, the issue
yielded one of his endless newspaper campaigns in favor of academic
freedom. At the very outset of the case, he underscored two lessons. If

special interests were to dictate the teachings of the classroom, the capacity of students to see clearly and to think critically would be lost. But despite obnoxious pressures and dangerous consequences, there were fortunately teachers like Scopes, making their sacrifices for truth. In a final evaluation of the case, Broun found a great moral victory (despite the legal defeat) in the performance of Darrow, who "showed the pitiful inadequacy of reasonable mental processes at the back of Bryan's Fundamentalism." Casting light for a future in which academic freedom would become far more viciously assaulted, he defined the high task of its defenders: "The processes of education and enlightenment move too slowly. The salvation of man will not come until skepticism sends out its circuit riders." [26]

IV

Writing frequently and rapidly, Broun was no conscious system-maker. Yet behind every line, his eye seems consistently alerted to the regimentation and suppression that choke off social change. The greatest regimentation of all was war, so often clothed in the ugly garb of imperialism. The enforced conformity masking blatant selfishness, the brutal carnage of the innocent made him a lifelong pacifist: "The man who says, 'I will not fight at all, no matter what the issue may seem to be,' may run the risk of missing one or two righteous crusades, but he's almost sure to escape an even greater number of bloody and useless shambles. This reasoning makes me pacifist." [27] Upon all the many "just causes" in the record of imperialism he heaped his scorn. When Secretary of State Kellogg explained American intervention in Nicaragua in 1927 as an effort to suppress incipient Communism, Broun suggested an alternative expedition: "Instead of sending armed forces down to Nicaragua, might it not be an excellent idea to ship Mr. Kellogg to Jung or Freud? Our Secretary of State seems overladen with what psychiatrists call free-floating fear." [28]

But as Broun attacked, so he proposed. Even in that age of nervous frivolity and pseudo-prosperity, he searched again and again for the roots of a radical position. Unlike those Nietzschean intellectuals who may relish their isolation as prophets, Broun hoped for and wrote for the organization of the masses. In a democracy, the mass of men have numbers on their side, to be used for the reconstruction of society. But without organization they are controlled and beaten. As early as 1921, in a remarkable essay, "How to Be a Lion Tamer," Broun, having discussed the easy domination of lions, went on to speak of men:

> Perhaps it is not quite fair to go on as if lions were the only living creatures in all the world who are swayed and cowed by firmness and authority. The same weakness may be found now and then among men. All too many of us, if hit on the nose with iron bars, either real ones or symbols, do little more than lions in similar circumstances. We may growl and roar a little, but we do not show resentment in any efficient way. And like lions, we are singularly stupid in not making working alliances with our fellows against the man with the iron bar.[29]

With this lesson in mind, Broun, who became in the most literal sense a leader of labor during the decade of depression, urged now the union of workers during the decade of injunction and lockout.

But Broun was no simple utilitarian, preaching organization simply to satisfy the self-interest of the majority. Social movements must spring from a sense of mutual love and brotherhood; they must produce a more beautiful morality. His radicalism was rooted in ethics, and the ethics were tied to religion. When he entered the Catholic Church a few scant months before his death in 1939, Broun had merely reached another phase of a lifelong search for a valid religious force behind social behavior. He had waged always-relentless war against that substitution of form for spirit which marked so conspicuously the American churches of the twentieth century. "It seems to me that the fundamental features of primitive Christianity might well promote the creation of a better and more kindly world, but I do not find these fundamental features highly regarded in the Churches of America." [30]

He found instead a sterile fundamentalism, a doctrinal imperative, an empty social teaching. Fundamentalism he challenged in his many encounters with the flamboyant Baptist preacher John Roach Straton. In Straton's raucous railing against individual immorality, Broun found never an encouragement of man's love in life but a warped consciousness of his sins. Giving insight into true and false religion, Broun once compared a Straton sermon to a Chaplin movie:

"And while Dr. Straton has been thus engaged in debasing the ideals of mankind, Charlie Chaplin has brought to great masses of people some glint of things which are eternal. He has managed to show us beauty." [31]

Quite clearly, Broun was religious, but his faith meant neither Biblical passages nor perverse asceticism. Religion was an emotion, a power of love, just beyond reason or logic, the basis for a communal fraternity. "My own faith," he once wrote, "is an early, fundamental Christian mysticism. There is no church for it, which is very convenient for me." [32] Eventually, he accepted the confines of the Catholic Church. T˙e two brief public references [33] which he made to a seemingly surprising move were gentle pleas for privacy. What is clearly ascertained in his record, however, is Broun's radical constancy until death. What may therefore be inferred is his belief, whether valid or not, that Catholicism could deepen and further that radicalism.

The insistence upon democratic organization and the ethics of brotherhood fill out only one side of the equation. Of course Broun was a socialist. At a precise moment in 1930 he joined the Socialist Party, which he left not long afterwards. But he was a socialist outside of and beyond that concrete commitment, socialist in the very marrow of his thought and action. Yet because his belief was strong and not blind, well-founded and not dogmatic, he ran afoul of some of the narrow sectarians who had settled on the Left. As an acute critic of high literary taste, Broun fought against the habit among some Communists of evaluating a work of art solely on its social message. Several years after Broun had engaged in a bit of fascinating dialectic with the Communist writer Mike Gold on the function of the artist, he answered quite crisply a question on the subject posed by the *New Masses:* "In a certain sense every creative person is a reformer, but this does not mean that he must be in his work a propagandist for good roads, shorter hours, and a low tariff. All these are excellent things, but they need not be the concern of the artist." [34] The artist's eye must penetrate to the truth of a matter, but when he "puts his thumb to his nose and keeps it there, his vision is curtailed." [35] Broun's love was deep for Whitman, Shaw, Twain, and Ibsen, all of them social writers. But ideological sympathy never blinded him to artistic failure.

Such independence of mind strengthened the fiber of Broun's socialism and made it strong. Without a profound knowledge of economic theory, he viewed carefully the problems of his time, and came to consider capitalism as neither sacred nor permanent: "If it is sound to say that capitalism ought to be preserved at such times as it serves the best interests of labor and employer, then it is just as reasonable to agree that something else ought to be tried when private enterprise makes a mess of things." [36] Yes, the faith was there, deep and ready; two events expanded it into a formidable socialism—the case of Sacco and Vanzetti, and the crisis of the depression.

V

The case of two poor Italians—one a fishpeddler, the other a shoemaker—battered the conscience of a decade. Accused because of their anarchism (frequently called Bolshevism in the irrational atmosphere of 1920), Sacco and Vanzetti were tried in Dedham, Massachusetts, between May 31 and July 14, 1921, for a double holdup murder in South Braintree, Massachusetts. On the slightest evidence, they were found guilty. Judge Webster Thayer, shorn of every shred of judicial impartiality in his hostility toward the accused, imposed the sentence of death. Despite the emergence of new evidence, despite learned denunciations of the original trial, all applications for appeal were refused.

For years the case dragged on as a growing minority of shocked men and women pleaded for some action to prevent the death of two men for their political ideas. By 1927, only Governor Fuller could save the steadfast pair. Speaking with completely unequivocal bluntness, Broun entered the affair. He urged the governor to grant commutation of the death sentence: "The case against the men is one of the flimsiest on which conviction was ever obtained. That they are wholly innocent of wrongdoing seems much the likeliest contingency. Obviously the wholly extraneous issue of radicalism and opposition to the war entered into the deliberation of the jury." [37] The case symbolized the struggle against all those who were hell-bent on closing the open society. Broun would have none of the refined calm being urged by certain liberals: "Why should any of us consent now to be polite about Judge Webster Thayer and the dirty work in Dedham?

The reproaches ought to ring in the ears of the old man from Worcester." [38]

Fuller appointed a committee of three respectables, President Stratton of MIT, a retired probate court judge, and President Lowell of Harvard as chairman. They declared the original trial fair, and in effect blocked any further action by the governor. From the moment of their report on August 3, Broun began a continuous stream of articles to rouse an apathetic public and to save two innocent lives. He wrote in a blazing white heat: "Scratch through the varnish of any judgment seat and what will you strike but hate thick-clotted from centuries of angry verdicts? Did any man ever find power within his hand except to use it as a whip?" [39] The lesson of the case was clear—that democracy is defeated when it is class-controlled: "And popular government, as far as the eye can see, is always going to be administered by the Thayers and Fullers." [40]

Heywood Broun had wide fame and earned a large salary. But neither acted as a brake on his conscience. On August 6, 1927, he ended a frontal attack on the Lowell Committee with words that tore completely the mask of respectable society: "From now on I want to know, will the institution of learning in Cambridge which once we called Harvard be known as Hangman's House?" [41] In tone and content these words were in utter contrast to those of the equivocating editor of the *World,* Walter Lippmann, whose liberalism was slipping badly. From August 7 until the 17th, not a word from Broun appeared in print. By August 17, he explained his absence publicly. The *World* had refused to print his Sacco-Vanzetti material; and he had refused to write about noncontroversial matters. The crisis underscored the growing difficulty of expounding an independent radicalism in the great commercial press: "By now I am willing to admit that I am too violent, too ill-disciplined, too indiscreet to fit pleasantly into the *World's* philosophy." [42] Several months later, on January 2, 1928, when Sacco and Vanzetti were safely in their graves, Broun returned to his old column. But he made no recantation—far from it: "My opinion in the matter remains unchanged." [43]

The case of Sacco and Vanzetti, like the case of Captain Dreyfus in France, virtually divided the United States into two camps, one of light and the other of darkness. Broun could make no accommodation to ironfisted reactionaries or timid liberals. Obviously his days with the *World* were numbered. When the final break came, Broun had precipitated it with a blunt accusation of cowardice against his paper. Writing in *The Nation* on May 4, 1928, he cited the absence of a courageous liberal daily in New York City. The *World?* No, it was much too inconsistent: "So constant were the shifts during the Sacco-Vanzetti case that the paper seemed like an old car going up a hill." [44] The next day Broun was fired because "his disloyalty to this paper makes any further association impossible." He moved over to the Scripps-Howard *Telegram* (which by 1931 in fact became the *World-Telegram*) and held on there until fired again, a few weeks before his death in December 1939. Near the end, he returned with undiminished wit to the circumstances of the earlier dismissal: "I did object to the word ['disloyalty'] because the casual reader would hardly know whether I had robbed the till or sat on the editor's hat." [45] Broun was unmasking duplicity again; for at issue, of course, was not his loyalty but his radicalism.

Years later, Broun wrote a final line to the tragedy of Sacco and Vanzetti. It was the eleventh anniversary of their death, and Broun was now witnessing in the Dies Committee the resurgence of the witch hunt, and in the politics of the late '30s the death of a reform movement. He had thought the case was dead: "Now I know that I was wrong, for in Washington, I saw the shadow of the dead hand dance upon the wall. . . . Fingers of bone clutch at the bridle of progress. It is death condemning life." [46]

VI

The depression of the '30s took the hide off a nation, battered its faith, destroyed its hope. If ever the time was right for a significant redistribution of power, it was now. And no one eclipsed Broun in writing and working for that genuine reconstruction. The Broun of the '30s was dead serious, even more acute, somewhat less genial: "This is no time for jokes. And I was never very good at them anyhow. I don't pretend to be a profound economist or commentator. But good or bad, the very best that I can do is to urge upon readers that cooperation which is necessary to salvation. And if this proves to be boresome, all I can say is that I know nothing more tiresome to a man or woman than to want a job and have none." [47] It was the time when he did what few writers have ever done; he erased all lines between thought and action. What he wrote about, he tried to do; what he tried to do, he wrote about. The journalist as radical and the man as radical were merged.

Readers of the *New York Times* learned on the morning of August 4, 1930, that "Heywood Broun, newspaper columnist, will be the Socialist candidate for Representative in the 17th Congressional District against Representative Ruth Pratt, Republican, and City Magistrate Louis Brodsky." Officially, Broun had joined the Socialist Party in May of that year, although he himself indicated a far greater antiquity for his socialist sympathies in a rare bit of humor he penned some years later. At Harvard, he explained, he had taken a course in economic theories from the arch-conservative Thomas Nixon Carver. The professor had outlined the theories of the radicals in the fall term, and proposed to demolish them in the spring. But the Boston Red Sox commanded Broun's attention in the spring, and he never heard the answers to the radicals: "Tris Speaker was batting .348 and Carver wasn't hitting the size of his hat. . . . I went out into the world the fervent follower of all things red, including the Boston Red Sox." [48]

In his campaign for Congress, he made an earnest plea for socialism to solve the horrible catastrophe of the depression. "I am appealing for votes," he proclaimed, "to all people who feel that drastic remedies must be adopted to relieve the unemployment situation. This is a silk stocking district, I am told, but there is plenty of rayon still in it. After all, it is only one block from the big crowds milling around the unemployment agencies on Sixth Avenue to the big houses and hotels of Fifth." [49] The election went finally to the Republican incumbent, but only after a remarkable campaign by Broun, during which he was arrested for picketing in a dressmakers' strike and was banned from speaking at Hunter College. From the experience, he only strengthened his urge to participate.

Among his own kind of men, Broun left his tallest monument of radical action. It was the American Newspaper Guild, a trade union for the working press, which Broun headed and guided in the crucial years of its history. The need for an organization of newspapermen was drastic. Veteran reporters with twenty years of experience were averaging $38 a week in 1933. Child labor and long hours were likewise characteristic of the atrocious working conditions.[50] The anti-labor policies of reactionary publishers had gone long unchallenged, aided in large measure by the unfortunate myth that newspapermen, as professionals, were above the workers. By 1933, however, three years of depression had erased this prejudice, and the organizational spur produced by NRA yielded spontaneous unionization among journalists in several major cities. The New York Guild was founded in September 1933, and the following December, in Washington, the American Newspaper Guild was launched—with Heywood Broun as president.

Unions are not formed by decree alone. The organization of the Guild, momentous in itself, prefaced a grim struggle by the newspapermen against their employers, organized since 1887 in the American Newspaper Publishers Association "to protect newspaper publishers against labor." Employers declared war on men who dared to join the Guild, and a series of crucial strikes resulted. Broun was omnipresent among his men, exhorting them to courage, stating their case in public, joining their picket lines, and formulating their demands. In the *Newark Ledger* strike, which raged for four months in 1934, the right of unionization was at last recognized. In the *Wisconsin News* strike in Milwaukee in 1936, the empire of Hearst was successfully invaded for the first time. Broun was on that picket line and arrested for it. Late in the same year, a great strike against Hearst's *Post Intelligencer* in Seattle cracked the West Coast for the Guild, and brought agreements with the major San Francisco papers. "By the middle of 1937 membership had risen to 11,000. Seventy-eight newspapers had signed contracts recognizing the Guild, including the New York *Daily News* with the largest circulation of any newspaper in America."[51]

Broun's vision as a labor leader, however, extended far beyond the newspaper industry alone or labor questions in the strictest sense. Fighting without exception for the cause of beleaguered workers, he exposed the wild power of the "haves" and the endless misery of the "have-nots." With all his energy, for example, he supported the great West Coast waterfront strike, led by Harry Bridges in 1934. When the strikers were brutally assaulted, in defense of "life and property," Broun, viewing a naked class society, asked bluntly: "Just which lives and whose property are the police and the soldiers supposed to protect?" [52] But as important as unions are, they were for him the start, not the end, of a better society, the instrument for replanting the roots of society. As head of the Guild, Broun hurled its weight behind the broadest possible program of progressive legislation and against the terrible growth of fascism. Finally, in June 1937, at the fourth annual convention of the Guild, he led his men enthusiastically into the CIO, then the most militant and creative American labor organization of the century.

VII

In the last six years of Broun's career, editors trimmed the length of his column, while he expanded the breadth of his vision. Untutored in the buoyant economic effects of great military expenditures, Broun simply saw the end of capitalism in the massive depression. But however wrong in that prediction, he was unerring in his view that "no sane person can possibly believe that industry in America will ever be carried on in precisely the same forms which obtained in 1929." [53]

In the crucial years of depression, Broun was convinced that the time was ripe for a broad socialist movement. He called repeatedly for an economic order planned to achieve distributive justice: "Common sense in any clime would seem to suggest some possible connection between the labor of making goods and the capacity of the current market to absorb them." [54] In his search for this better economic order, he rejected sharply the romantic snare of those who preached small-scale, competitive capitalism: "The worker has nothing to gain from the small entrepreneur. A higher standard of living and shorter hours and a shorter working week can never come out of the cut-throat competition of little fellows struggling one against the other." [55] The answer for the better life assuredly lay with the great productive capacity of modern industry.

Just as Broun had found an economic organization to solve labor problems, so he sought a political organization to effect social change. It is perhaps the essential tragedy of the history of modern American radicalism that no organization emerged to absorb the great leadership of men like Broun. The Socialist Party, marked by "a slothfulness, almost a timidity," he rejected as an instrument of change. In fact, about to be expelled in April 1933 for sharing the lecture

platform with Communists on behalf of Tom Mooney and the
Scottsboro boys, Broun blasted the inaction of the Socialist Party imposed by its anti-Communist intransigence. And he added, in the
simplest terms, the philosophy of the popular front: "I don't expect
the Communists to love me, and I'm not going to love them. I hope
from time to time to say many things about them, and I expect the
same in return. . . . But I think it would be a fine idea not to fight
until Mooney is free and the Scottsboro boys are acquitted." [56]

Despite the many accusations by witch hunters, Broun was far from
joining forces with the Communists. They were active, to be sure,
and often sincere. He would work with them for a just cause. But
he could find no home inside a movement which had "deserted sound
radical principles on many occasions for the sake of opportunism." [57]
What he sought was what has always been needed and perhaps naively
hoped for—a major third party, a labor party, uniting in tolerance the
forces of the Left. Disillusioned with Democratic patchwork, he urged
such a movement for 1936: "A Presidential field consisting of Roosevelt, Huey Long, and Hoover, or his equivalent, ought to constitute
a very pressing invitation for the formation of a labor party." [58] For
a passing moment his hopes were high for New York's American
Labor Party, at whose 1936 convention in the Hotel Astor he made the
most stirring and radical speech. But hope vanished again and again
for the broad front he envisioned: "As yet," he said wearily, "these
gentlemen have shown very little ability in getting together." [59] He was
left with the New Deal and with his assaults on the Right.

Broun wavered in his attitude toward the New Deal, like a man
who wanted to believe but found it hard. At the start, when everything was plastic, there seemed hope for radical progress. But when
hope deferred became hope unfulfilled, Broun wrote bitterly: "The
plain truth of the matter is that the movement which was once known
as the Roosevelt revolution turns out to be a carrousel for kiddies.
And in the big tent of NRA the patrons ride the horses and the
zebras about the circuit. . . . Nobody need worry any more that
Washington is going left. Indeed, nobody need worry that the Washington of today is going anywhere." [60] But clear-eyed though he was
about a movement which barely touched the concentration of wealth,
Broun felt, nonetheless, a sympathy for Roosevelt. He praised him for
the enemies he had made. And after hearing him at the 1936 Democratic convention, Broun even raised aloud the hope that FDR's

liberalism might serve to reshape the old party system: "In the days to come it may be used against me that I was deeply moved by Franklin Roosevelt speaking to the many in Philadelphia. His limitations as a leader of labor are too obvious to need recapitulation. But here in a rough yet exact way was the nucleus of the great party of the people's front." [61]

That nucleus never became a party, and Broun was really on firmer ground when he blasted away the pretensions of reactionaries, and laid bare a class society. For Herbert Hoover (whose weird present status as an elder statesman would have rocked him with indignation) he reserved his greatest scorn. Summing up in a line a social philosophy in the service of the rich, Broun wrote: "Mr. Hoover undertook to put a guinea hen in every chafing dish." [62] He exposed in devastating thrusts the position of such varied pundits as Will Rogers, Henry Mencken, and Walter Lippmann, who were overcome with anxiety over Big Government while cherishing so warmly Big Business. With more than a little relish he punctured the "liberal" posture of Lippmann: "If I may mix a metaphor a little, he is the sort of advocate who is quite apt to score a field goal for Harvard and a touchdown for Yale in one and the same play. But of course, he specializes in safeties. I have been watching the mind of Walter Lippmann for more than a quarter of a century, and my eyelids are a little weary." [63]

Broun never gave up. The managers of the forty-two newspapers which carried "It Seems to Me" may have complained, but he attacked without quarter and proposed anew. His tempo increased on two themes—the evils of the red hunt and the terrible dangers of fascism. Against the increasingly active witch-hunters Broun defended the essential Americanism of the radical tradition, made by a Bellamy or a Debs. When he addressed the public, he urged more, not less, radicalism to improve the democracy. Long wise to the fact that the "red scare" was a convenient pretext to snuff out social change, he fought it with might and main. And that fight was climaxed one day in August 1939, when, dragged before the Dies Committee himself, he denounced its purposes and called its notorious investigator, J. B. Matthews, a "skunk." [64]

From the very first, Broun isolated the Nazi movement as one that substituted wild hatred for social renovation. He assaulted its anti-Semitism, pleaded with America to welcome its victims, and gave the lie especially to those who insisted upon Hitler's sincerity. It was growing late, very late, and still there were men who praised fascism as the bulwark against Communism. In the midst of the Spanish War, Broun called to Franco to open his ears. In reality, he called to a public to open its eyes: "It has been said that you are a liberator who took the sword only because Spain was Red. It is redder now. Barcelona is drenched in the blood of men, women, and subversive babies. Francisco Franco, Generalissimo, how do you sleep of nights?" [65]

VIII

Broun probably anticipated great difficulties in days to come. When he reached his fifty-first birthday, however, a scant week before his death, he was closer to a radical faith, further from defeat and resignation than ever before: "At 51 I'm a better fighter than at 21. . . . Brotherhood is not just a Bible word. Out of comradeship can come and will come the happy life for all. The underdog can and will lick his weight in the wildcats of the world." [66]

Broun suffered from lack of a powerful political movement. He was victimized by the power of property on one side and narrow sectarianism on the other. But the roots of his position were too varied to die at once. His radicalism was very American in its belief in progress and passion for freedom; religious in its burning sense of brotherhood; socialist in its clear view of class injustice. Heywood Broun gave his cause thirty years of great journalism. And in the end he gave it the creed of the fighter: "In order to amount to anything a man must learn how to shiver and shake and still keep coming in." [67]

NOTES

1. *New York World,* March 1, 1927.
2. *Ibid.,* July 20, 1927.
3. *Ibid.,* September 26, 1922.
4. *Ibid.,* January 6, 1925.
5. *Ibid.,* September 30, 1922.
6. Dale Kramer, *Heywood Broun* (New York, 1949), p. 45.
7. Quoted in *New York Times,* August 24, 1930.
8. *Ibid.,* November 5, 1930.
9. Bruce Bliven in *Heywood Broun: A Symposium* (Washington, 1940), p. 4.
10. *New York World,* March 9, 1927.

11. *Ibid.*, December 3, 1921.
12. *Ibid.*, January 11, 1924.
13. *Ibid.*, January 6, 1927.
14. *Ibid.*, May 28, 1924.
15. *Ibid.*, February 2, 1922.
16. *Ibid.*, March 24, 1922.
17. *Ibid.*, September 16, 1922.
18. *Collier's*, May 14, 1921.
19. *New York World*, January 26, 1923.
20. *Ibid.*, February 14, 1925.
21. *Ibid.*, March 12, 1925.
22. *Ibid.*, May 31, 1926.
23. *Ibid.*, January 14, 1925.
24. *Ibid.*, January 18, 1923.
25. *Ibid.*, November 3, 1925.
26. *Ibid.*, June 5, 1925.
27. *Ibid.*, May 13, 1927.
28. *Ibid.*, January 14, 1927.
29. *Seeing Things at Night* (New York, 1921), pp. 21-22.
30. *New York World*, March 20, 1924.
31. *Ibid.*, February 15, 1922.
32. *Ibid.*, February 12, 1926.
33. *Broun's Nutmeg*, June 10, 1939, and *New Republic*, July 26, 1939.
34. *New York World*, August 26, 1926.
35. *Ibid.*, April 25, 1922.
36. *Ibid.*, May 10, 1926.
37. *Ibid.*, April 18, 1927.
38. *Ibid.*, April 19, 1927.
39. *Ibid.*, August 5, 1927.
40. *Ibid.*, August 6, 1927.
41. *Ibid.*, August 7, 1927.
42. *Ibid.*, August 17, 1927.
43. *Ibid.*, January 2, 1928.
44. *The Nation*, May 4, 1928.
45. *Broun's Nutmeg*, December 9, 1939.
46. *New York World-Telegram*, August 24, 1938.
47. *Ibid.*, May 22, 1933.
48. *New Republic*, November 17, 1937.
49. *New York Times*, August 4, 1930.
50. Bruce Minton and John Stuart, *Men Who Lead Labor* (New York, 1937), p. 135.
51. *Ibid.*, pp. 138-139.
52. *New York World-Telegram*, July 19, 1934.

53. *Ibid.*, January 3, 1933.
54. *Ibid.*, June 19, 1934.
55. *Ibid.*, June 9, 1933.
56. *Ibid.*, April 29, 1933.
57. *Ibid.*, April 28, 1933.
58. *Ibid.*, February 25, 1935.
59. *Ibid.*
60. *Ibid.*, January 29, 1935.
61. *Ibid.*, June 29, 1936.
62. *Ibid.*, September 6, 1934.
63. *Ibid.*, November 21, 1933.
64. Roger Baldwin, in Bruce Bliven and others, *Heywood Broun: A Symposium* (Washington, 1940), p. 5.
65. *New York World-Telegram*, March 21, 1938.
66. *Broun's Nutmeg*, December 9, 1939.
67. *New York World-Telegram*, September 22, 1939.

BIBLIOGRAPHICAL NOTE

Works by Broun

Seeing Things at Night (New York, 1921).
Pieces of Hate: And Other Enthusiasms (New York, 1922).
It Seems to Me: 1925-1935 (New York, 1935).
Collected Edition of Heywood Broun, compiled by H. H. Broun (New York, 1941).
In collaboration with George Britt, *Christians Only: A Study in Prejudice* (New York, 1931).

Works on Broun

Bliven, Bruce, and others, *Heywood Broun: A Symposium* (Washington, 1940).
Kramer, Dale, *Heywood Broun, A Biographical Portrait* (New York, 1949).

Newspapers and magazines in which Broun appeared regularly:

New York Tribune, 1911-1921
New York World, 1921-1928
New York Telegram, 1929-1931
New York World-Telegram, 1931-1939
Connecticut Nutmeg, later *Broun's Nutmeg,* 1938-1939
The Nation
The New Republic

II

Attacks on Privilege

"Maybe we'll fix it so life won't be printed on dollar bills."

Clifford Odets, *Awake and Sing!*

4

Henry Demarest Lloyd: The Prophetic Tradition

HARVEY O'CONNOR

I

"I AM," SAID HENRY DEMAREST LLOYD, "a socialist-anarchist-communist-individualist-collectivist-cooperative-aristocratic-democrat." [1] In less exuberant moments, the great American social reformer referred to himself as a socialist and a democrat. The two words, he insisted, were synonymous. As he thundered in book, speech, and letter against the iniquities of monopolistic capitalism and painted the glories of a social system animated by love and mutual aid, he was more the Hebrew prophet than the devotee of any "ism."

Lloyd's growing stature among the pioneers of social reform derives from his *Wealth Against Commonwealth,* the first book to describe the rise of Standard Oil. That was in 1894, but in 1881, while the Standard was still a brawling infant, he had sounded the alarm in his famous article, "The Story of a Great Monopoly," in William Dean Howells's *Atlantic Monthly.* That issue of the *Atlantic* went through seven printings (an unprecedented affair for such a staid magazine), so enormous was the interest aroused by Lloyd's article. Charles Edward Russell hailed it as "a turning point in our social history"; and it was Lloyd's article on "The Lords of Industry" in the *North American Review* of June 1884 that initiated the discussion of the general monopoly question that has continued to this day.

In later years, Lloyd was dubbed the first of the muckrakers. He wouldn't have cared for that. While working on *Wealth Against Commonwealth* he wrote his mother that it "keeps me poking about and scavengering in piles of filthy human greed and cruelty almost too nauseous to handle." [2] When the book was published, he was finished with Standard Oil and never wrote about it again. He was, he said, a reporter, and in future he would report the hope of humanity rather than its despair. From that resolve came, in his lifetime, books on co-operation and labor arbitration in Europe and Australasia that gained him international renown. More in the vein of social protest and prophetic vision were the five books published after his death, from manuscripts and addresses, bearing such titles as *Man: The Social Creator* and *Men: The Workers*.

Although a self-proclaimed socialist and an intimate friend of Eugene Debs, Victor Berger, and other leading socialists, Lloyd never joined the Socialist Party. That he intended to is attested by a manuscript, "Why I Join the Socialists," written June 4, 1903, a few months before his untimely death at the age of fifty-six. Summoned to lead the campaign for municipal ownership of the street railways, he caught cold on a drafty platform at a meeting called by the Chicago Federation of Labor, and developed pneumonia. His manuscript lay unfinished on his desk, his application for membership unsigned.

Lloyd was no Marxist. His zeal streamed down from the Hebrew prophets, from the undiluted precepts of Jesus, from the Enlightenment and its American apostles, Jefferson and Emerson, and from an infinite faith in the innate power and possibilities of human beings. Son of a minister, he had rebelled against formalized Christianity and had found divinity among his fellow men.

II

All his life, Henry Demarest Lloyd had been in the main current of reform movements, beginning in 1869 with espousal of free trade. As

a lawyer just out of Columbia, he campaigned against Tammany in
1871 and fought Greeley from the Left in 1872. He had rejected the
practice of law as "too technical and traditional"; money-making, he
said in a youthful letter, "I despise as pursuits in themselves for themselves." [3] He had no taste for the physical sciences and mere literary
culture was not sufficiently practical. Already he had broken with the
church for "I am too unconventionally and unaffectedly pious." [4] He
chose journalism and went West to accept an offer on the *Chicago
Tribune,* then a liberal paper. As financial and literary editor and
editorial writer, he gained an intimate knowledge of finance and
economics. Having married the daughter of a part owner of the
Tribune, he became financially independent and after quitting the
paper in 1885 devoted himself to pursuits of his own choice.

Lloyd boasted that he was a "reporter," although he was really far
more than that. The facts about monopoly needed to be told, but first
they must be dug out. For that task he had several advantages. His
training as financial editor of the *Tribune* helped him solve many of
the mysteries of Standard Oil financing. As an in-law of one of Chicago's wealthiest families, he himself was a member of the upper crust.
He had the leisure to study, something denied those in the everyday
ruck of existence. He understood the Rockefellers, for he had associated
with their ilk as an equal; as a result, his contempt was bottomless.
"The real truth about the Standard Oil people," he summed up, "is that
they are thieves." [5] He warned that "if merely because they are rich
and powerful, a certain number of gentlemen can take possession of
the property of their neighbors by criminal means, without punishment, the American Republic is a failure, and the dissolution of American society has begun, although the fact may not be chronicled by our
Gibbon until sometime long after this." [6]

His style, rich in allusion and somewhat Ruskinesque, could be
crisp and sparkling as he tossed off epigrams:

> Only the rich can get justice, only the poor cannot escape it.[7]
> The bird of freedom has always been a jail bird.[8]
> When monopolists succeed, the people fail.[9]
> The Standard [Oil trust] has done everything with the Pennsylvania
> legislature except to refine it.[10]

Jibing patly at the McCarrans of his time, he suggested that they turn the ancient maxim, "Nothing human is foreign to me," into "Nothing foreign is human to me." [11] Asked by a Congressional committee if he would admit anarchists as immigrants, he replied: "I wouldn't consider myself fit to be an American citizen if I wanted any man debarred on account of his opinions." [12] In regard to millionaires: "We want nothing they have that belongs to them. We want only what they have that belongs to us." [13] The people, he counseled, must be led along the path of political action "or else face the alternative of revolution, which I do not expect, or of a rotting down which I think is already well under way." [14]

Lloyd was no trust buster, yearning for simpler days. He distrusted the competition that led to monopoly as well as monopoly itself. That he pressed forward to a radical analysis can be attributed to two dominant factors: his moral revulsion from the anti-social effects of the private appropriation of the public property, and his soul-searing contacts with the effects of industrial feudalism in his home city, Chicago. The bomb that shook the Haymarket shattered Lloyd's faith in his fellow capitalists and their brand of justice. With that tottered whatever confidence he ever had in their system.

Perhaps Lloyd was just another interested citizen as he entered Judge Gary's court to scrutinize the trial of the anarchists. He quickly ceased being an onlooker. Then, as now in the Smith Act trials, the prosecution made no effort to connect the defendants with actual violence. It was a "conspiracy," and Judge Gary ignored his black robe to act as prosecutor. The trial revolted Lloyd, and he sought interviews with Lingg, Spies, Parsons, and the other anarchists. As in the Communist trials of the 1950s, the anarchists of 1886 marched to their inevitable doom of "guilty." Passionately Lloyd threw himself into the fight for commutation of the death sentence, the most to be hoped for then. Trained both as a lawyer and a reporter, he analyzed the evidence and spread his conclusions by pen and tongue. At the last, he was in Governor Altgeld's mansion in Springfield pleading for the lives of the anarchists; he succeeded in the cases of Fielden and Schwab and carried the commutation papers to them in their prison cells.

Joseph Medill, publisher of the *Chicago Tribune* (which Lloyd had quit the year before), warned Mrs. Lloyd: "Do you realize what you are doing, have you and Mr. Lloyd considered how this will influence your future?" "Do you suppose," she answered, "that any such consideration will stop Henry Lloyd from doing what he believes to be right?" [15]

Medill's warning was not exaggerated. Lloyd was ostracized by the social and financial elite of Chicago, denounced in the press along with the other "rattlesnakes" who supported "anarchy, murder and riot"; his wife's fortune was entailed, and the Lloyds were even denied guardianship and care of the property of their children. It was a foretaste of the obloquy that descended upon Governor Altgeld when in 1893 he pardoned the two men Lloyd had helped to save.

III

As a reformer, Lloyd had wept on the doorstep of a slum building after seeing for the first time how the other half lived. He might have continued through life, running from one current reform to another, had it not been for the glare that Haymarket shed upon the "lords of industry" and their social system. Now he turned to examine for himself what was going on, not in the upper reaches where the Standard Oil magnates reigned, but in the nether depths where their victims suffered.

A Strike of Millionaires Against Miners was his first book, published in 1890. In Spring Valley, Illinois, the corporations had shut down their mines to break the back of the young United Mine Workers union. The story was to be oft retold thereafter—the Rockefeller mines in Colorado in 1914, West Virginia in the 1920s, Harlan County in the 1930s. But for the first time, Lloyd lifted the black curtain that hung over the coal fields and revealed to the public the price the miners paid in starvation for their right to be union men. Spring Valley became a *cause célèbre,* its tragedies known in Europe as well as at home.

Thereafter Lloyd was in many a strike, most notably that at Pullman where he got to know Eugene V. Debs, the man of labor who most resembled him. Of such different origin and circumstance, they were bound in a common glow, an ecstatic faith in humanity that somehow, in the world of the cobalt bomb, now seems quaint and old-fashioned. In both was the fire that kindled men and bound them in high enterprise, both were inspired prophets of a new order.

Lloyd was with Altgeld the night the governor was withstanding the demands of the railroad interests to send in the militia; President Cleveland that night nullified Altgeld's stubborness. The federal troops poured in, and Debs was on his way to jail. By then Lloyd was widely known as a man who had union in his heart; the AFL already had had him address its Chicago convention in 1893. His speech, "The Safety of the Future Lies in Organized Labor," was reprinted by the AFL and found wide currency in the labor and farm press.

Lloyd's proudest moment came during the anthracite strike of 1902. He hurried to Scranton to offer his services again to the United Mine Workers and to their president, John Mitchell, who had been a youngster in the Spring Valley strike. The anthracite moguls would neither negotiate nor arbitrate. To Lloyd's enterprise we are indebted for publication of the classic statement of industrial feudalism. President George F. Baer of the Philadelphia & Reading had thus responded to a minister's letter of protest: "I beg of you not to be discouraged. The rights and interests of the laboring man will be protected and cared for—not by the labor agitators, but by the Christian men to whom God in His infinite wisdom has given the control of the property interests of the country, and upon the successful management of which so much depends." [16] Lloyd had the letter photographed and broadcast; from as far away as South Wales money poured in to sustain the strikers' families.

For the man who had never practiced law, this, boasted Lloyd, was "my first case." He got his friend Clarence Darrow to come on from Chicago. The three—Mitchell, Darrow, and Lloyd—finally induced President Roosevelt to intervene and set up the arbitration machinery the coal owners for months had spurned. Lloyd had but recently returned from New Zealand, and his book, *A Country Without Strikes,* his articles on arbitration in the leading magazines, and his speeches had familiarized the country with the technique, yet new here. The miners won. The three men returned to Chicago where six thousand workers greeted them in a great victory meeting in the Auditorium. Lloyd was humble. Speaking of the miners and their families, he said: "With their starving bodies they made a wall around all of us." [17]

To Lloyd, working people were "the only real people." [18] With them, he found not only social salvation but personal, as well. It saved him, on the one hand from a frenetic succession of reform cause enthusiasms, on the other from sectarian sterilities. The German ideologues in New York who ran the Socialist Labor Party seemed to him out of the mainstream of the democratic process (although he voted their ticket in 1896 and 1900); not until refugees from the Populist, Granger, and Greenback movements in the Middle West joined the Easterners in creating the Socialist Party around 1900 did he begin to look upon the organized socialist movement with interest. He himself had run for Congress on the Union Labor ticket in 1888 and the Populist ticket in 1894. Bitterly was he disappointed when the Populist convention of 1896 threw in its fate with Bryan and with Free Silver, "the cow-bird of the Reform movement." [19] He had fought, along with the socialists, for a collective ownership plank and had been defeated.

Lloyd had the ability to work fruitfully with the labor movement while refusing to budge from first principles, almost a unique achievement. He felt that socialism was deep in people's hearts but had never been able to find expression in this country because wealth had already entrenched itself in the avenues of communication. The people, he said, stand "paralyzed and fascinated, as if helpless under the charm of an evil eye." [20] At another time, he observed that "the most uncertain element in American political arithmetic today is in what form this unrepresented socialism of the United States will precipitate itself, and what channels it will make for itself when it begins to move." [21] In despair after the Populist debacle, he prophesied that "only adversity will teach the American people,—and *they are going to have plenty of it; . . .* they will stir when they begin to suffer." [22]

At times Lloyd entertained grave misgivings on the future of democratic action. After the Pullman strike, he felt that "in no event will the working men and farmers be allowed, no matter what their majority, to take control of the government." [23] By his nature he hated violence, war, and revolution, and called them an abdication of reason. But he could also see that "there is only one evil greater than reform by force—the perpetuation, the permanence of injustice." [24]

Parliamentary democracy he held incompatible with socialism. "Some day," he wrote, "we will supersede politics by education. . . . One of the greatest disasters the world has ever seen awaits the people who attempt to administer enterprise on socialistic principles, through present parliamentary methods." [25] Already, he observed, "the ordinary political means of voting and campaigning make it impossible for the real will and the real interests of the people to come forth as the result." [26] Lloyd never outlined definitely his ideas on non-parliamentary democracy; apparently he hoped that through the development of cooperatives and people's business enterprises, an administration of things might succeed the government of men. But he was not a bit sanguine about such hopes for this country. Lloyd was too much the realist to imagine, as he pointed out, that the United States Steel Corporation would permit steelworkers thrown out of work in McKeesport to develop their own tinplate mill. His soaring faith in the rapid growth of the socialist and cooperative movements in Europe and Australasia also ran headlong, on his return to his native land, into the realization that monopoly had dug in far too deeply here to be dislodged by methods that might be appropriate in other lands.

On monopoly, he was no reformist. The leading authority of his day on trusts in America, he disdained to offer any trust-busting proposals. "I cannot think of any remedial measure," he wrote, "to which I would attach the slightest importance except agitation to awaken the public to the necessity of themselves becoming the owners of every monopoly." [27] That expressed exactly his idea—the people owning industry. He never confused the people with the state. There was plenty of state ownership of railroads and other utilities in Europe, he said, but that did not bring socialism. Nor did he consider government ownership achieved by buying out stockholders as much of an improvement on barefaced monopoly itself. Then the people merely exchanged corporate slavery for bond slavery; the fact was that the monopolies had stolen the public's property and deserved to be shorn of their loot. If it would help any, he would maintain the owners in the luxury they were accustomed to for the duration of their lives; that, he said, was not justice, but mercy, and mercy he cherished.

As he watched with dread the growth of monopoly, concerned not so much with the pillaging of the public's purse as with the poisoning and paralyzing of the people's will, Lloyd predicted: "Our time by all its signs manifestly approaches one of the great crises which have marked off history into eras." [28] The American business kings were about to build a world empire beside which the British would be "a mere fly-speck," a process he called "the Americanization of the world." [29] On another occasion, in 1900, he foresaw that "the great political word of the twentieth century will be empires—Russian and American." [30]

IV

Despite the gloomy outlook, Lloyd held firm to his faith in man. "I believe," he wrote, "that when the people of America begin to move, they will move with great rapidity, huge energy, and with corresponding success. . . . The word the world waits for today will come from those who can disclose to humanity that the perfections it has been attributing to its gods are sparks struck out of the goodnesses it feels stirring within itself." [31] The Freudian-Niebuhrian bleakness was yet to come.

Death cut short the contribution Lloyd might have made to the development of a popular radical movement in the United States. His passion for justice, his skill in digging out the facts, his uncanny ability to strip the main issue bare from a mass of irrelevancies, his extraordinary facility as a writer, a persuader, a bringer-together, made him unique. Only Debs matched him in striking the divine spark which kindled hope and confidence among the dispossessed and gave them courage to fight on. Since then, the radical movement has tended to reflect the values created by the monopolies, becoming as hard-boiled as the system it fights, concerning itself with the quick gains to be achieved through maneuver, aiming at positions of power that prove all too illusory, neglecting to stoke the fires that Debs and Lloyd knew so well how to ignite in men's hearts.

So Lloyd is remembered mainly for his *Wealth Against Commonwealth*. Amazingly, in recent years, the book has returned to the fore as a burning issue among the professional historians. Public attention will always be attracted to John D. Rockefeller, the most ruthless and efficient monopolist of all time. For that reason, what Henry Demarest Lloyd wrote about Standard Oil in the first book on the subject will be read as long as there is monopoly; by an ironic twist of fate, Lloyd will be read only because people want to know about Rockefeller, and his own magnificent contribution to radicalism will lie barely noticed by the wayside. Nevertheless, Lloyd's book is embarrassing. There is a school among historians who insist now that monopoly was inevitable, that it fitted the times, that it was a natural evolution. Let us not denounce it; let us understand it, perhaps then it can be justified. Perhaps, too, the glittering chrome façade of American capitalism can be made as appealing morally as it is satisfying financially. It is "the American way."

For forty years, Lloyd's account of the rise of Standard Oil enjoyed the approval of historians. Charles and Mary Beard, John Chamberlain, John T. Flynn, and Allan Nevins all acclaimed *Wealth Against Commonwealth*. Nevins wrote that "it was a searching exposure, amply buttressed by detail," of "the iniquities of the trusts" and "the sordid record of business piracy" achieved by Standard Oil.[32]

By 1940 Nevins had changed his mind. The Rockefeller papers had been opened for him as he prepared a two-volume biography. In rewriting history he found himself face to face with Lloyd. Lloyd's book must be demolished if Rockefeller were to be accepted as a true patron of the American way. So *Wealth Against Commonwealth* became "almost utterly worthless" as history, not to be trusted, even dishonest.

The controversy is for the historians. For the layman, it should be noted that Nevins condemns Lloyd for failing to realize that the excesses of competition were as terrible as the ravages of monopoly; the fact is that Lloyd insisted upon exactly that and proceeded to demand public ownership of the trust, rather than the fatuous "dissolution" which was decreed by the Supreme Court in 1911. "Moral strictures," says Nevins, are beside the point.[33] But to Lloyd it was essentially a moral issue, and not one of dollars and cents: from monopoly came the corruption of public opinion and of the Republic, of which Lloyd held such fear. Lloyd could not see the "beneficial side" of Standard Oil; but then neither can many another who has had the advantage of fifty years' more acquaintance with the corporation than Lloyd had. Finally, Nevins condemns him for terming government regulation of monopoly "a dream" and "a compromise with evil." But isn't the record of the regulators being regulated by the corporations exactly what Lloyd foresaw a half century ago?

The author of *Wealth Against Commonwealth* was no "historian," Nevins concludes. Perhaps so. Nor was Isaiah when he thundered against the evils of the rich and the powerful in his day. To Lloyd, Standard was not only a corporation to be scrutinized and explained; it was a cancerous growth upon the body politic, to be excised. Far more than a historian, he was a prophet in his time, a man sensitive to injustice, to hunger, to the failure of civilization to draw out the full potentialities of humankind. His pages flame with indignation, pity, hope, and faith in his fellow men. "Nature is rich," he cried in the opening words of his great book, "but everywhere man, the heir of nature, is poor." [34] With Debs, he could bring together the dreams of men and women for a better world and clothe them with grandeur.

"The reformer," he wrote, "is a poet, a creator. He sees visions and fills the people with their beauty; and by the contagion of his virtue his creative impulse spreads among the mass, and it begins to climb and build." [35]

NOTES

1. Quoted in Caro Lloyd, *Henry Demarest Lloyd* (New York, 1912), I, 301.
2. *Ibid.*, I, 189.
3. *Ibid.*, I, 39.
4. *Ibid.*, I, 40.
5. *Ibid.*, I, 184.
6. *Ibid.*, I, 281.
7. *Ibid.*, I, 61.
8. Lloyd, *Law, Labor, and Liberty* (Tennessee City, N. D.), p. 97.
9. Caro Lloyd, *op. cit.*, I, 58.
10. *Ibid.*, I, 61.
11. *Ibid.*, I, 155.
12. *Ibid.*, I, 156.
13. *Ibid.*, II, 154.
14. *Ibid.*, I, 258.
15. *Ibid.*, I, 93.
16. *Ibid.*, II, 190.
17. *Ibid.*, II, 236.
18. *Ibid.*, II, 207.
19. *Ibid.*, I, 264.
20. *Ibid.*, I, 183.
21. *Ibid.*, I, 304.
22. *Ibid.*, II, 126.
23. *Ibid.*, I, 152.
24. *Ibid.*, I, 112.
25. *Ibid.*, I, 296.
26. *Ibid.*
27. *Ibid.*, I, 292.
28. *Ibid.*, II, 11.
29. *Ibid.*, II, 127, 181.
30. *Ibid.*, II, 161.

31. *Ibid.,* II, 163.
32. Quoted in Earl Latham, editor, *John D. Rockefeller: Robber Baron or Industrial Statesman?* (Boston, 1949), p. 91.
33. *Ibid.,* p. 112.
34. Lloyd, *Wealth Against Commonwealth* (New York, 1894), p. 1.
35. Caro Lloyd, *op. cit.,* II, iii.

BIBLIOGRAPHICAL NOTE

Works by Lloyd Published During His Life

A Strike of Millionaires Against Miners, or The Story of Spring Valley (Chicago, 1890).

Wealth Against Commonwealth (New York, 1894) (condensed edition, National Home Library, Washington, 1936).

Labor Copartnership: Notes of a Visit to Cooperative Workshops, Factories, and Farms in Great Britain and Ireland, in Which Employer, Employee, and Consumer Share in Ownership, Management, and Results (New York, 1898).

A Country Without Strikes: A Visit to the Compulsory Arbitration Court of New Zealand (New York, 1900).

Newest England: Notes of a Democratic Traveller in New Zealand, With Some Australian Comparisons (New York, 1900).

Posthumous Works

Man: The Social Creator (New York, 1906).

A Sovereign People: A Study of Swiss Democracy, by John A. Hobson, from Lloyd's notes (New York, 1907).

Men: The Workers (New York, 1909).

Mazzini and Other Essays (New York, 1910).

Lords of Industry (New York, 1910).

Works on Lloyd

Aaron, Daniel, *Men of Good Hope* (New York, 1951) (chapter on Lloyd: "The Middle Class Conscience").

Latham, Earl, editor, *John D. Rockefeller: Robber Baron or Industrial Statesman?* (Boston, 1949) (articles touching on Lloyd and *Wealth Against Commonwealth* by Allan Nevins, Chester McA. Destler, reprinted from *The American Historical Review;* Destler has been working on a life of Lloyd, as yet unfinished).

Lloyd, Caro, *Henry Demarest Lloyd,* 2 vols. (New York, 1912).

5

Robert M. LaFollette: The Radical in Politics

CHARLES A. MADISON

IN AN EVALUATION of the 1924 candidates for the Presidency, William Allen White wrote about "Fighting Bob" LaFollette: "He is a man of the highest personal character. Personally he is incorruptible. Politically he is immovable in his determination to battle in his finish fight for what he deems a just and righteous cause."[1] Indeed, for more than thirty years LaFollette had distinguished himself from most other liberals not only by his persistent radicalism but by his steadfast fight for principles in the face of, at times, almost universal condemnation. So firm was his belief in democracy that political success whetted rather than warped his humanitarian goal.

I

Robert Marion LaFollette, son of Huguenot and Scotch-Irish pioneers, was born in Primrose, Wisconsin, on June 14, 1855. Eight months later his father died, and his widowed mother worked hard to provide the bare essentials for her four children. Robert managed to enroll in the state university in 1875 and supported himself by teaching school and editing a student periodical. His first ambition was to go on the stage, and to that end he concentrated on public speaking. In his senior year he won the interstate oratorical contest with an interpretation of Iago's character. Having about that time been persuaded by a visiting actor that a thespian career was not for him, he decided to study law. Early in 1880, after less than a year of effort, he was admitted to the bar.

With legal work scarce for the neophyte, LaFollette was attracted to the office of district attorney, which paid a salary of $800 a year plus $50 for expenses. The local Republican leader had endorsed another candidate, but young LaFollette campaigned hard among his farmer neighbors on an economy platform, and surprised the politicians by emerging as victor at the polls. This experience taught him the importance of appealing directly to the voters—a lesson he never forgot.

Twenty-five years old and earning a regular salary, LaFollette was able to marry Belle Case, a classmate with whom he had long been in love. From the first his wife became his closest counselor. In possession of a keen mind, imbued with like ideals, and equipped with a legal training, she provided him with the advice and encouragement that sustained him in defeat and steadied him in victory.

In 1882, having demonstrated his concern that justice be done despite the obstacles put in his way by entrenched politicians, he was the only Republican to win locally. Two years later, he decided to run for Congress. Again he was opposed by the Republican machine, and once more he followed the formula of going directly to the people—trudging along from farm to farm and from house to house to remind voters of his readiness to represent their interests in Washington. And the people trusted him and enabled him to win both the nomination and the election. At twenty-nine he was the youngest member of the House of Representatives.

In Washington he was befriended by Senator Philetus Sawyer, a rich lumberman and Wisconsin's leading Republican. This powerful politician soon found LaFollette too honest and conscientious to take advice on matters affecting the public good. When Sawyer sponsored a bill that would have given the railroads millions of acres of Indian land in the Dakotas, LaFollette fought it stubbornly. Both Sawyer and Henry C. Payne, Wisconsin's influential lobbyist, threatened angrily to put an end to his political career, but LaFollette remained firm in his opposition and helped to limit the grant to the normal right of way.

If he was in the 1880s uncompromising and incorruptible, he was as yet no radical. In Congress he followed the leadership of his party except where the weal of the public was concerned. His interest in populist reforms seemed academic. In 1889 he worked and voted for Thomas Reed as Speaker. His appointment to the powerful Ways and Means Committee was gained in part because of an effective speech in favor of a tariff bill. He was therefore thoroughly disappointed when he failed of re-election in 1890; he was partisan enough to resent the idea of having been defeated by a Democrat. Once out of office, however, he concentrated on his legal practice and prospered.

II

Not long after his return to Madison, LaFollette underwent a traumatic experience. The Democratic victors in office were suing the state treasurers of the previous twenty years—all of them Republicans who had banked public money to their own considerable benefit—for the interest that rightly belonged to the state. Senator Sawyer, having been bondsman for some of them, approached LaFollette privately in an effort to have him influence his brother-in-law, Judge Robert G. Siebecker, who was to preside at the trial. The offer of the "retainer" deeply shocked the honest lawyer-politician. Years later he wrote: "Nothing else ever came into my life that exerted such powerful influence upon me as that affair. It was the turning point, in a way, of my career. . . . It shocked me into a complete realization of the extremes to which this power that Sawyer represents would go to secure the results it was after." [2]

He saw no alternative but to tell Judge Siebecker of the interview. The latter at once excused himself from the case. When Sawyer issued a denial, LaFollette made the story public. He was at once attacked as a notoriety seeker, and politicians sought to destroy his reputation and his practice. The acid of ostracism corroded his spirit. He knew he had done right and resented the unwarranted punishment. For months he was in a state of acute depression. Long evenings of brooding over the wrong done to him convinced him that the power of the corrupt political machine had to be broken.

From that time to the end of his life he was a dedicated man. It was he and the people against the iniquitous rich and venal politicians. Endowed with exceptional oratorical ability and armed with hard facts, he took every opportunity to preach his message. He ignored the snubs of political leaders and was active in the 1892 campaign. Two years later he challenged them at the polls—having persuaded the liberal Nils P. Haugen to oppose the party nominee for governor. With the aid of many college students, LaFollette carried the fight against the machine leaders to most of the voters of the state, and Haugen lost the nomination only because Sawyer and his men used every weapon to block this insurgence.

Defeat did not daunt LaFollette. Believing that time was on his side, he continued to address the farmers and tradesmen of the state and to circularize his speeches to the extent of his financial ability. In 1896 he himself challenged the machine. Independent Republicans came to his aid. By the time of the convention he had a majority of the delegates pledged to vote for him for governor. The party bosses, however, by means of cash payments or promised preferment, obtained enough of these votes to rob LaFollette of the nomination.

He now realized that the caucus and convention system, always subject to manipulation by unscrupulous politicians, would never truly express the will of the people. Having meantime heard of the direct primary reform, he began to study it with the enthusiasm of a convert. In an address on the subject at the University of Chicago he said with persuasive solemnity:

This is the modern political machine. It is impersonal, irresponsible, extra-legal. The courts offer no redress for rights it violates, the wrongs it inflicts. It is without conscience and without remorse. . . . Go back to the principle of democracy; go back to the people. Substitute for both the caucus and the convention a primary election—held under the sanctions of law which prevail at the general elections—where the citizen may cast his vote directly to nominate the candidate of the party with which he affiliates and have it canvassed and returned just as he cast it. . . . The nominations of the party will not be the result of "compromise" or impulse or evil design . . . but the candidates of the majority, honestly and fairly nominated.[3]

This speech he delivered at county fairs, at various meetings, and on the Chautauqua circuit. Numerous weeklies distributed a total of 400,000 copies plus a primary bill to their subscribers. LaFollette and some friends also issued a weekly entitled *The State* and made it the vehicle of their reform program.

In 1898 he again came before the party convention as the favored gubernatorial candidate, but Sawyer was still in control and once more defeated the choice of the people. Two years later, however, Sawyer was dead and all opposition to LaFollette collapsed. His election by a large majority followed despite the implacable opposition of the conservatives.

LaFollette assumed office determined to destroy the party machine and to carry out the chief planks of his reform program—the primary law and the corporate tax act. His opponents fought him doggedly— and they still controlled the legislature. Their leader, Charles Pfister, bought the Milwaukee *Sentinel*, then the only liberal newspaper in the state, and turned it into a violently anti-reform vehicle. The railroad lobbyists also campaigned against the reform bills with extreme lavishness. When the measures came to a vote, their defeat was inevitable.

LaFollette would neither compromise nor retreat. To a group of farmers he declared: "Selfish interests may resist every inch of ground; may threaten, malign, and corrupt; they cannot escape the final issue. That which is so plain, so simple, and so just will surely triumph." [4] He therefore took every opportunity to attack his political opponents and to castigate the recreant legislators. In 1901 a serious stomach ailment kept him relatively inactive for nearly a year and his enemies would have surely defeated him for re-election if he had not been aided by liberal Democrats.

During his second term as governor, again in good health, he renewed the fight for his reform measures. In addressing a joint session of the legislature on the desired railroad laws, he analyzed the rates in nearby states and showed that in Wisconsin "151 towns were paying on an average 39.9 percent more for their transportation charges than towns located at similar distances from markets in Illinois and Iowa." [5] When railroad representatives questioned the accuracy of his data, he sent the legislature a special message, prepared by a staff of state accountants, offering detailed and irrefutable evidence. The railroads thereupon brought prominent shippers to testify against the measure.

But public pressure in favor of the bill was equally strong and the legislators compromised by enacting the equalization tax bill and defeating the measure to regulate railroad rates. The direct primary bill was fought with like ferocity, and when its passage became unavoidable its opponents managed to put it to a referendum vote at the next election. Another reform that passed at the same session was a graduated inheritance tax ranging from 1.5 to 15 percent.

With his reform program still incomplete, LaFollette decided to break with tradition and seek a third term. He felt absolutely sure that another two years in office, with a more sympathetic legislature, would establish self-government in Wisconsin. His political enemies were equally determined to balk him. When they failed to control the nominating convention, they bolted and put up a separate slate of candidates. The state supreme court, however, validated the liberal faction as the legitimate Republican Party. Confident of his own victory, LaFollette campaigned hard for a progressive legislature. "I determined," he wrote, "to get a legislature of the right kind. It was nothing to me to be governor of Wisconsin without being able to accomplish anything." [6] When the votes were counted, his slate and the primary law won handsomely.

LaFollette was now in complete control of the state's political machinery. To him this was merely a means of carrying out his reform program. First he furthered a strong railroad regulation law. As finally passed, it provided for a commission with power not only to fix rates but to control service and to make complete physical evaluation of all railroad property in the state. It was more sweeping than any legislation enacted by any state up to that time. During the same year he had the satisfaction of signing the following acts of legislation: a strong anti-lobby law, a corrupt practices act, a state civil service law, a forest conservation measure, workmen's compensation and various other social service provisions, and insurance regulation. Although he had been elected to the Senate the previous January, he continued to serve as governor until his reform program was enacted into law and made Wisconsin the most progressive and best-governed state in the Union.

"The Wisconsin Idea"—government by experts for the benefit of all the people—was his legacy to the state. It was his energetic initiative that greatly enlarged the facilities of the University of Wisconsin and established close cooperation between its scholarly faculty and state officials. And his loyal followers and successors in office proceeded to turn the state into a progressive political laboratory, with expert commissions attending to its tax, railroad, banking, conservation, insurance, public service, and industrial problems. The legislative reference service headed by Professor Charles McCarthy became a model for similar services in other states. LaFollette was satisfied with his work as governor and with the functioning of his own "machine," but he knew that much remained to be done. "While much has been accomplished, there is still a world of problems yet to be solved; we have just begun; there is hard fighting, and a chance for the highest patriotism, still ahead of us. The fundamental problem as to which shall rule, men or property, is still unsettled." [7]

And this problem he hoped to bring up for settlement in the Senate.

III

LaFollette was treated scornfully by the dominant group of Senators. He was not given the committee posts he wanted and he was generally cold-shouldered. "I was again alone," he later reminisced. "When I entered the cloakroom, men turned their backs on me and conversation ceased. Members left their seats when I began to speak. My amendments to bills were treated with derision. . . . They did not know the iron that had been driven into me years before." [8]

Shortly after entering the Senate, he disregarded accepted custom and made a three-day speech on the Hepburn railroad bill, then under consideration. He had studied the measure thoroughly, and although he favored its general purpose he found it quite inadequate. Alone of all Senators he contended that the federal government could and should regulate railroad rates. The leaders were not interested. They resented his impertinence and determined to snub him. He had no sooner begun to speak when they rose one after the other and left the chamber. Stung by this insult he declared prophetically:

> Mr. President, I pause in my remarks to say this: I cannot be wholly indifferent to the fact that Senators, by their absence at this time, indicate their want of interest in what I may have to say upon the subject. The public is interested. Unless this important question is rightly settled, seats now temporarily vacant may be permanently vacated by those who have the right to occupy them at this time. [9]

President Theodore Roosevelt sympathized with some of LaFollette's proposals but refused to support him in the face of strong opposition. If Roosevelt's liberalism was more verbal than veritable, most Senators were practical politicians and devoted to their financial backers. The idea of legislation that would keep the public domain from private exploitation or curb corporate profits for the benefit of the public seemed to them socialistic and therefore subversive. Because LaFollette persisted in introducing bills for just such purposes, they considered him a radical and troublemaker. Again and again they quashed his proposals and voted down his amendments. On his part he acted the watchdog against bills favoring corporations at the expense of the public. And so cogent were his factual arguments and so broadly humane was his social outlook that in time he began to win the friendship of Senator after Senator. By 1909 he had with him a compact little group of insurgents—all excellent speakers—fighting the Payne-Aldrich tariff bill. In the same year he established *LaFollette's Weekly Magazine,* later changed to a monthly, which became a forthright advocate of political and social reform.

Around 1910, liberalism spread like a rising tide. Influenced by the writings of the muckraking journalists and the provocative speeches of LaFollette and his fellow insurgents, and alarmed by the gigantic growth of monopolistic corporations, voters everywhere expressed their sympathy with the Congress radicals and their disappointment in President Taft's conservatism. In the elections that fall the Democrats won a majority in the House, and progressives in both houses gained considerable strength.

Stimulated by the hope of electing a liberal President in 1912, the leading progressives of the nation met in LaFollette's home in January 1911 and organized the National Progressive Republican League. When Theodore Roosevelt, back from Africa and coyly perched on his political fence, declined to join the League, LaFollette became its obvious choice for the Presidency. Louis Post wrote in *The Public:* "The logical candidate of the Republican Progressives is Senator LaFollette who led the advancing column when others feared or faltered, who has proved his constructive skill, and who does not compromise." [10]

LaFollette was willing to lead, but he was too skilled a politician to disregard the possibility of his being used as a stalking horse for Roosevelt—whom he never trusted and whose recent behavior he considered enigmatic and equivocal. To Gifford Pinchot, one of his financial backers and a close friend of Roosevelt, he pointed out that it would be unfair to himself and harmful to the Progressive movement if a switch of candidates were made in the middle of the campaign. But Pinchot assured him that Roosevelt was not a candidate and would support him. Thereupon LaFollette announced his candidacy.

The response was gratifying, especially west of the Alleghenies. In October key Progressives met in Chicago and their endorsement of LaFollette was enthusiastic. Yet the stronger the movement became the more inclined were certain of the leaders to insure success at the polls by giving it the fillip of Roosevelt's name. These admirers of the former President believed that LaFollette was too radical and too uncompromising to win a national election. The situation became confused when George W. Perkins, wealthy banker, began to finance Roosevelt's candidacy and when other rich men, fearing that President Taft had no chance of re-election, likewise made known their preference for Roosevelt over LaFollette. When the Colonel intimated that he might be drafted, he quickly attracted a number of LaFollette's backers. LaFollette protested in vain that his withdrawal would be a betrayal of progressivism and make the campaign a contest to nominate Roosevelt rather than to advance a cause.

Invited to speak in Philadelphia before the country's influential newspapermen, LaFollette accepted despite the fact that he was suffering from extreme fatigue and was deeply distressed by fear for his younger daughter who had to undergo serious surgery the following day. Weak and tense, and irritated by the obvious conservatism of his audience, he failed to speak with his usual effectiveness; in his anxiety to stress the thesis of his address—the control of business by men who considered themselves above the law—he continued speaking long after his audience had dwindled.

Gifford Pinchot and others of his sponsors seized upon this incident to abandon him as a candidate. Still others followed suit when Roosevelt openly announced his readiness to run. LaFollette, recuperating from his physical exhaustion, felt tricked and troubled. What he feared had come to pass. The very men who had backed him most enthusiasti-

135289

EMORY & HENRY LIBRARY

cally were deserting him for a popular opportunist. He at least would
not yield to expediency. That week he announced on the front page of
his magazine:

> I shall continue in the contest as a candidate for well-defined principles
> and for a definite program of legislation which, once enacted into law,
> will break the hold of privilege on the industrial life of the people and
> free them from the burden imposed by thousands of millions of ficti-
> tious capitalization.[11]

If Roosevelt, aided by a large campaign fund, showed remarkable
strength in the primaries, he failed to attract a number of prominent
liberals. They did not trust his progressivism and resented his shabby
treatment of LaFollette. Senator Joseph L. Bristow of Kansas spoke
for many when he pointed out that "LaFollette's superiority over
Roosevelt . . . is in the fact that he has definite and specific notions as
to what ought to be done to correct the evils which exist." [12] Louis D.
Brandeis, similarly cool to Roosevelt, declared: "No man in public
life today expresses the ideals of American democracy so fully as does
LaFollette in his thought, his acts, his living. No man in public life
today has done so much toward the attainment of those ideals. He is
far-seeing, of deep convictions and indomitable will; straightforward,
able, hardworking, persistent and courageous." [13]

At the Republican convention LaFollette refused to join the Roosevelt forces and thus made it easier for the conservative bosses to re-
nominate President Taft. When the thwarted liberals organized the
Progressive Party with Roosevelt as their standard bearer, LaFollette
refused to bolt with them. He did not believe in founding a new party
to satisfy the ambition of a single individual. During the campaign he
praised Woodrow Wilson as a real progressive, and in November Wisconsin went Democratic.

IV

Wilson and LaFollette respected each other's liberalism. The latter
was naturally sympathetic to the New Freedom program of legislation
and was the only Republican Senator to vote for the Underwood-Sim-
mons tariff bill. On his part he was grateful to Wilson for signing the
Seamen's Act, a measure which he had long sponsored and which in

his view "blots out the last vestige of slavery under the American flag." [14]

LaFollette also approved of Wilson's initial patience toward Mexican developments. When the clamor for war with the agitated nation to the south of us was at its height, he called for understanding and peace:

> It is well to remember that war is always cruel; that its iron tread means destruction and devastation, whether the march is across Europe or from Atlanta to the Sea; that war arouses all the fiercest human passions; that there are always cases of brutality and outrage—and usually there is quite as much of it on one side as upon the other.[15]

This position he maintained when war broke out in Europe, and he strongly defended Wilson's observance of strict neutrality.

When the agitation for war against Germany became intense and nationwide, putting Wilson on the defensive, LaFollette increased his opposition to military appropriations. He asserted that the preparedness propaganda was largely instigated by munition makers, and he advocated the nationalization of the arms industry. During the 1916 campaign he concentrated on his own re-election and presented his constituents with a platform that emphasized peace and social welfare. Victorious by a large majority, he felt confirmed in his assumption that most voters favored peace.

Early in 1917, when Germany resumed its unrestricted submarine warfare, Wilson broke off diplomatic relations. His request of Congress for power to arm American merchant ships was opposed by LaFollette as a prelude to war. In a forceful editorial in his own magazine he argued that war solved nothing, that both England and Germany were guilty of violating our neutral rights, and that peaceful solutions were more permanent.

> Shall we, to maintain the technical rights of travel and the pursuit of commercial profits, hurl this country into the bottomless pit of the European horror? Shall we bind up our future with foreign powers and hazard the peace of this nation for all time by linking the destiny of the American democracy with the ever-menacing antagonisms of foreign monarchies? [16]

He insisted that he was fully aware of the "supreme principle for which men must fight to death as a last resort," [17] but the United States was not yet at the point of last resort. He reminded his fellow Senators that the people had voted for peace the previous November and that if again given the opportunity "they would with even greater voice pray God that this country be kept out of war." [18]

A month later the country was at war. LaFollette and his few colleagues—Wilson's "little group of willful men"—had fought to the last moment against an overwhelming majority. Defeat brought them condemnation and ostracism. Nevertheless they continued to perform their duties as Senators with the utmost conscientiousness, concentrating their efforts on the honest and democratic execution of our war activity. Of the sixty Administration measures voted on during the first eight months of war, LaFollette supported no less than fifty-five. He did oppose the draft, espionage, and other restrictive acts, and fought hard but in vain to amend the War Revenue Act so as to meet war costs out of current profits and large incomes.

On September 20, 1917, in St. Paul, while addressing a meeting of the Nonpartisan League (founded in 1915 in North Dakota as an organ for insurgent farmers) he remarked in reply to a question that although he had opposed the war against Germany, "I would not be understood as saying that we didn't have any grievances. We had." The Associated Press garbled the report and quoted the reply to read, "We had no grievances [against Germany]." The country's leading newspapers at once headlined the misleading story and accused LaFollette of disloyalty. The charge was taken up by his enemies in the Senate, several members denounced him as a traitor, and a committee was appointed to consider his expulsion.

The fury generated by this incident beat about the victim's head. Everywhere he was execrated and condemned. In his home city of Madison, students burned his effigy, a club voted to oust him, and a round robin signed by 92 percent of the university faculty denounced him as pro-German. Alarmed by this outburst of hysterical intolerance, he obtained the floor of the Senate on October 6 and made a forthright defense of free speech in wartime.

> I maintain that Congress has the right and the duty to declare the objects of the war and the people have the right and the obligation to discuss it. American citizens may hold all shades of opinion as to the war; one citizen may glory in it, another may deplore it, each has the same right to voice his judgment. . . . If the American people are to carry on this great war, if public opinion is to be enlightened and intelligent, there must be free discussion.[19]

Many months later the Associated Press admitted its blunder and apologized. The Senate committee delayed its report for sixteen months and finally cleared him. Four years after the incident, the Senate voted to pay him $5000 for expenses incurred in his defense.

When the fighting in Europe ended, everyone talked about the terms of peace and the projected League of Nations as if the world had really been made safe for democracy. LaFollette was skeptical. Although he approved of the Fourteen Points, upon which the armistice terms were based, he trusted neither Wilson nor the Allied leaders. As eager as anyone to destroy the seed of future wars, he knew that the European peacemakers were too involved in their own schemes of power to agree upon a genuine league for peace. In his magazine he maintained that such a league must be based on two conditions: abolition of enforced military service and a referendum of qualified voters before war is declared.

An examination of the peace treaty brought back from Paris by Wilson convinced him that no real peace was achieved and that the League was in effect an alliance of the victorious powers for the exploitation of their imperialistic designs. He criticized it for not including all nations and for not insuring peace by effective disarmament. And though disdainful of aligning himself with the reactionary Senators, he could not but vote against the unamended treaty.

V

On domestic issues LaFollette resumed his forthright advocacy of political and social reforms. Early in 1919 he filibustered against the sale of valuable coal and phosphate lands to private interests, and thereby saved the nation about a billion dollars. He fought with fierce zeal against the return to private management of the railroads, which had been taken over by the government during the war. Fully familiar with railway finance and administration not only in the United States but the world over, he was convinced that only government ownership and control would give the nation adequate service at reasonable cost. But his arguments and proposals had no effect on Senators immersed in party politics and straining to capitalize on the postwar disillusionment in order to launch the spirit of "normalcy" of the 1920s. For the time being his was indeed a voice crying in the wilderness.

In the fall of 1922 he campaigned for his fourth term in the Senate.

Four years earlier he had been denounced throughout Wisconsin as pro-German and a traitor. In the postwar reaction, as the patriotic fervor of his constituents subsided, they began to evaluate the causes and consequences of war more realistically. A majority again felt fresh faith in the principles which LaFollette had championed right along. These voters now hailed him as their first citizen and great progressive leader. Nor did he slur over his wartime position. He boasted of his anti-war views and of his fight against war profiteers. "I would not trade my war record with any man in the world," [20] he asserted. By the time he completed his speaking tour his popularity reached new heights, and at the polls his majority was the largest in his entire career.

As the warmth of resurgent popularity began to melt the glower that had darkened his mien during the war period, he once more turned his mind to the Presidency—keenly aware that advancing age was affording him his last chance. Tending to identify a cause with his own part in it, he came to believe that a well-organized progressive movement, with himself at its head, might dislodge the old-guard oligarchy from the seat of government. In 1921 he helped to establish the People's Legislative Service for the purpose of spreading broader participation in governmental affairs. A year later the Railroad Brother-hoods—among his most grateful adherents—discussed with other unionists and prominent liberals ways and means of promoting La-Follette's candidacy for President. This preliminary meeting was followed by another in December. A month prior to the conference, leading progressives met with LaFollette to formulate campaign plans. The problem of a third party troubled all present. Knowing that his chances of election would be infinitely greater on the Republican ticket, the group agreed to do nothing definite, except to work hard for his nomination, until after the convention. Their views and decisions became the agenda of the meeting in Cleveland, later known as the Conference for Progressive Political Action.

The conference reassembled in St. Louis on February 11, 1924. Delegates from liberal, labor, farmer, and socialist organizations expressed themselves in favor of political candidates pledged to the interests of the producing classes and to the principles of genuine democracy in agriculture, industry, and government. Although no formal action was taken, the delegates indicated their determination to back LaFollette for President even if they had to form a new party to do it.

Meantime, fearful of the effect of Communist adherence on many potential voters and apprised of the Communist control of the Farmer-Labor Party, which announced its readiness to name him as its candidate, LaFollette bluntly rejected its support:

> To pretend that the Communists can work with the progressives who believe in democracy is deliberately to deceive the public. The Communists are antagonistic to the progressive cause and their only purpose in joining such a movement is to disrupt it. . . . I most emphatically protest against their being admitted into the council of any body of progressive voters.[21]

On July 4 the convention of the united liberal and labor groups was called to order in Cleveland. The Republicans had ignored LaFollette and his reform planks in their stampede to nominate President Coolidge, leaving the liberals no alternative but to form a political organization of their own. The delegates generated much enthusiasm. So unified were these dissidents in their fight for a candidate who truly sympathized with their grievances that even the Socialists, who had always insisted on a ticket of their own, and the leaders of the American Federation of Labor, who had never before deviated from their position of political neutrality, joined the other delegates in pledging full support to "Fighting Bob" LaFollette. His letter of acceptance, read to the convention by his son Robert, reaffirmed the principles and beliefs which had guided his political activity for the past thirty years.

> To break the combined power of the private monopoly system over the political and economic life of the American people is one of the paramount issues of the 1924 campaign. . . . The private monopoly system has grown up only through long-continued violation of the law of the land and could not have attained its present proportions had either of the Democratic or Republican parties faithfully and honestly enforced the law. . . . We are unalterably opposed to any class government, whether it be the existing dictatorship of plutocracy or the dictatorship of proletariat. Both are essentially undemocratic and un-American. . . . The supreme issue, involving all others, is the encroachment of the powerful few upon the rights of the many.[22]

The delegates eagerly bent their will to his. They agreed to campaign as independents, rather than as a third party, in order to avoid the stigma of radicalism. Likewise they accepted his Wisconsin platform, essentially a populist document adapted to 1924 conditions. Among its planks were government ownership and control of public utilities, conservation of national resources, tariff reductions, improved banking and financial facilities, adjustment of income and inheritance taxation, abolition of labor injunctions, outlawry of war, and reduction of armaments.

For all its intrinsic merits, this platform did not arouse the expected enthusiasm among the mass of voters. Economic conditions were generally prosperous. Urbanized Americans were becoming reconciled to the industrial dominance of large corporations. Employed and adequately fed, most workers were loath to vote for a man who was fiercely attacked as the "Wisconsin Bolshevik." Even the farmers of the Middle West, economically pressed and aware that LaFollette was their tried friend, did not vote for him in large numbers—partly because of a surprisingly fine crop that fall. Moreover, the LaFollette adherents had neither an adequate organization nor sufficient funds. Their total expenditure of $221,977 was a mere pittance when measured against the Republican outlay of $4,270,469—which was exclusive of contributions spent locally or never formally reported. When the ballots were counted, LaFollette received 4,826,471 votes, or 17 percent of the total. Wisconsin alone give him a plurality and its electoral votes, but in ten other states he led the Democratic candidate.

LaFollette was disappointed but not discouraged. "The progressives," he declared, "will not be dismayed by this result. We have just begun to fight. There is no compromise on the fundamental issues for which we stand. The loss of this one battle in the age-long struggle of the masses against the privileged few is but an incident." [23] These were brave words for a man nearing his seventieth birthday and in poor health, yet he meant exactly what he said. This was not true of the men who had urged him to run and who had worked for his election. Failure to win a larger vote caused them to backslide into their former political positions. One group after another broke away, and the last meeting of the Conference for Progressive Political Action in February 1925 was a ghostly affair.

Meantime, LaFollette's health continued to deteriorate. Pneumonia, bronchial asthma, and a coronary condition took their heavy toll, and he died on June 18, 1925.

VI

"LaFollette," wrote Professor Frederick A. Ogg of the University of Wisconsin, "was for thirty years the most spirited, resourceful and relentless fighter in the American political arena." [24] He was also the most aggressive liberal of his generation. A product of Midwestern democracy, driven by a combination of chance and dynamic ambition into political insurgency, he devoted his great oratorical talents and intense vigor to the advancement of democratic government. Nurtured on Jeffersonian precepts and therefore refusing to acquiesce in the political exigencies of an expanding industrialism, he fought resolutely against the monopolistic drives of corporate enterprise. If in the end he failed to retard the aggression of big business, his fight helped to prepare the way for the active controls of New Deal legislation.

He was ambitious. His extraordinary energy impelled him to leadership, to achieve and to enjoy the exercise of political power. He was egotistical. His strong sense of righteousness made him impatient of opposition, domineering, and tolerant of obsequiousness in his followers. Yet he was no political boss; he was primarily a crusader bent on achieving his goal. His aim in Wisconsin was not to gain the personal perquisites of political power but to turn the state into a model of good government. Professor Richard T. Ely, long a leading member of the University of Wisconsin faculty, well described his achievements as governor:

> His chief work was to transform Wisconsin into a political laboratory for advanced measures. . . . LaFollette had the zeal of a reformer. He wanted an office to fulfill his mission in life and he wished to make a name for himself. He recognized what so many reformers overlook— that to secure office he must make himself a master of political methods. He knew he must outmaneuver the old politicians—beat them at their own game. This he did—and it's an amazing story.[25]

As United States Senator, LaFollette was forced to play a largely negative role. Unable to vanquish the conservative leaders of his own party, he could only act as political goad and public conscience. It is important to note that of thirteen reform planks he submitted to the Republican convention in 1908, no less than eleven were eventually enacted; and of the eighteen proposals he made four years later, fifteen were later written into law.

As a leading anti-interventionist in World War I, LaFollette drew upon himself the hysterical abuse of patriots bent on conformity as a means of victory. Manifesting the parochial limitations of many Middle Westerners, he in fact served the democratic ideal more valiantly than those who supported the war to make the world safe for democracy. Twenty years later, Professor Ely, in 1918 one of his harsh critics, intimated as much: "In looking back from 1938 to the time of the World War, I do not feel so sure as I did then that LaFollette was wrong and Woodrow Wilson right. If LaFollette had been nominated and elected in 1912, it is quite possible that the country might be far better off than it is now." [26]

His ambition for the Presidency notwithstanding, he was too uncompromising a liberal to gain the confidence of the majority of voters. And he was too shrewd a politician not to know this. His persistence as a candidate came therefore not from blind egotism but from a desire to promote his progressive views on as broad a scale as possible. He had the insight to realize that what his opponents at first condemned as radical and subversive they would later accept as moderate and beneficial. The late Justice Robert H. Jackson, speaking of LaFollette in 1940, clearly evoked his quality:

> In his policy there was enlightenment, in his hope there was a glow that caught and held young men. I did not mind then and do not mind now that he was called a "radical." That name, always hurled at those who would right wrongs, has become a certificate of character.[27]

NOTES

1. W. A. White, *Politics: The Citizen's Business* (New York, 1924), p. 122.
2. LaFollette, *Autobiography* (Madison, Wisconsin, 1913), p. 147.
3. A. F. Lovejoy, *LaFollette and the Establishment of the Direct Primary in Wisconsin, 1890-1904* (New Haven, 1941), p. 36.
4. A. O. Barton, *LaFollette's Winning in Wisconsin* (Madison, Wisconsin, 1922), p. 187.
5. LaFollette, *op. cit.*, p. 282.
6. Barton, *op. cit.*, p. 410.
7. LaFollette, *op. cit.*, p. 369.
8. *Ibid.*, pp. 162-163.
9. F. C. Howe, *Wisconsin, An Experiment in Democracy* (New York, 1912), p. 22.

10. Russell B. Nye, *Midwestern Progressive Politics* (East Lansing, Michigan, 1951), p. 282.
11. *LaFollette's Weekly Magazine* (March 2, 1912).
12. Walter Johnson, *William Allen White's America* (New York, 1947), pp. 196-197.
13. A. T. Mason, *Brandeis: A Free Man's Life* (New York, 1947), p. 78.
14. Ellen Tourelle, editor, *The Political Philosophy of Robert M. LaFollette* (Madison, Wisconsin, 1920), p. 145.
15. Edward Doan, *The LaFollettes and the Wisconsin Idea* (New York, 1947), p. 78.
16. *LaFollette's Magazine* (March 1917) (Armed Ship Bill speech).
17. *Ibid.*
18. *Ibid.*
19. Tourelle, *op. cit.*, pp. 242-243.
20. F. L. Holmes, *Badger Saints and Sinners* (Milwaukee, 1939), p. 519.
21. K. C. MacKay, *The Progressive Movement of 1924* (New York, 1947), p. 87.
22. *Statement and Platform of Robert M. LaFollette, Independent Progressive Candidate for President of the United States,* July 4, 1924.
23. LaFollette, Belle C. and Fola, *Robert M. LaFollette* (New York, 1953), I, 690.
24. F. A. Ogg, "Robert M. LaFollette in Retrospect," *Current History* (February 1931), p. 690.
25. R. T. Ely, *Ground Under My Feet* (New York, 1938), p. 211.
26. *Ibid.*, pp. 217-218.
27. R. H. Jackson, *Address on Robert M. LaFollette,* June 23, 1940.

BIBLIOGRAPHICAL NOTE

Works by LaFollette

Autobiography (Madison, Wisconsin, 1913).
The Political Philosophy of Robert M. LaFollette as Revealed in his Speeches and Writings, edited by Ellen Tourelle (Madison, Wisconsin, 1920).

Works on LaFollette

Barton, A. O., *LaFollette's Winning in Wisconsin* (Madison, Wisconsin, 1922).
Doan, Edward, *The LaFollettes and the Wisconsin Idea* (New York, 1947).
Holmes, F. L., *Badger Saints and Sinners* (Milwaukee, 1939).
Howe, F. C., *Wisconsin, An Experiment in Democracy* (New York, 1912).

LaFollette, Belle C. and Fola, *Robert M. LaFollette,* 2 vols. (New York, 1953).

Lovejoy, A. F., *LaFollette and the Establishment of the Direct Primary in Wisconsin, 1890-1904* (New Haven, 1941).

Nye, Russell B., *Midwestern Progressive Politics* (East Lansing, Michigan, 1951).

III

Toward the Equality of Rights

"Yea, the voiceless wrath of the wretched,
and their learned discontent,
We must give it voice and wisdom till the
waiting-tide be spent."

William Morris, *The Day Is Coming*

6

John Brown's Legacy

ALFRED MAUND

I

WHEN I WAS A CHILD in Louisiana, John Brown and the wrathy Protestant God were inseparably mixed up in my mind. The songs "John Brown's Body" and "Battle Hymn of the Republic" had much to do with this. They appeared in the school songbooks, but the teachers would skittishly refuse to let them be sung "because some people might be offended." This censorship aroused my muddled awe, and hence the "glory of the coming of the Lord" became John Brown—a terrible *bodiless* head moving over the land, withering all it gazed upon.

After I grew more sophisticated, I assumed that John Brown had been the one who confused himself with God. He was an anti-slavery settler in Kansas who had gone berserk and had raided Harpers Ferry, Virginia, upon Orders from Above. There is plenty of support for such a view of the man. Even the *Dictionary of American Biography* (1929 edition), which uniformly tries to see the brighter side of its subjects, devotes its entry on Brown to a hooting polemic that stresses the insanity in his family and the unsoundness of his plans. He did not seem to be one who could offer precepts and inspiration to a foe of latter-day slavery.

But a chance reading of his impromptu speech to the court in Charlestown on the day he was sentenced to hang yielded these burning lines:

> Had I interceded in the manner which I admit, and which I admit has been fairly proved . . . had I so interfered in behalf of the rich, the powerful, the intelligent, the so-called great, or in behalf of any of their friends, either father, mother, sister, wife or children, or any of that class, and suffered and sacrificed what I have in this interference, it would have been all right. Every man in this court would have deemed it an act worthy of reward rather than punishment. . . .
>
> I say I am yet too young to understand that God is any respecter of persons. I believe that to have interfered as I have done, as I have always freely admitted I have done, in behalf of His despised poor, I did no wrong, but right. Now, if it is deemed necessary that I should forfeit my life for the furtherance of the ends of justice, and mingle my blood further with the blood of my children and with the blood of millions in this slave country whose rights are disregarded by wicked, cruel, and unjust enactments, I say—Let it be done.[1]

These did not seem to be the words of a crazy man. I was moved to explore further into the life of John Brown. It makes an exciting and instructive story.

II

John Brown was born on May 8, 1800, in Torrington, Connecticut, "of poor but respectable parents." His family moved to Ohio when he was five, where his father raised cattle on a frontier farm and worked as a tanner.

The Brown household was staunchly anti-slavery in sentiment. John's father was a voluntary agent for the Underground Railroad and served as a trustee for Oberlin College, one of the few institutions in the Midwest to accept Negro students. It was a pious household, too, and in his middle teens Brown went back to Connecticut, where he planned to study for the Congregational ministry. But an inflammation of the eyes cut short his school career and he returned to Hudson, Ohio, where he worked at his father's tannery.

Five years after his marriage in 1820, he moved to Richmond, Pennsylvania, where, for ten years, he prospered as tanner, land surveyor, cattle breeder, and postmaster. Not until 1834, in a letter to his brother Frederick, did he express on paper any ideas about attacking slavery:

> Since you left here I have been trying to devise some means whereby I might do something in a practical way for my poor fellow-men who are in bondage, and having fully consulted the feelings of my wife and my three boys, we have agreed to get at least one Negro boy or youth, and bring him up as we do our own,—viz., give him a good English education, learn him what we can about the history of the world, about business, about general subjects, and, above all, try to teach him the fear of God. We think of three ways to obtain one: First, to try to get some Christian slave-holder to release one to us. Second, to get a free one if no one will let us have one that is a slave. Third, if that does not succeed, we have all agreed to submit to considerable privation to buy one. . . . I have for years been trying to devise some way to get a school a-going here for blacks, and I think that on many counts it would be a most favorable location. Children here would have no intercourse with vicious people of their own kind, nor with openly vicious people of any kind.[2]

This project, if Christians in free states set to work in earnest, would "operate on slavery like firing powder confined in rock," he said. But it is hard not to see in this plan a middle-class missionary-society zeal of the sort that worries about teaching Hottentots the doctrine of Original Sin. Nothing came of it.

Then ensued lean and heartbreaking years for Brown in his financial ventures. In 1835 he moved to Portage County, Ohio, where unsuccessful land speculation left him penniless two years later. He wandered the country, dealing in race horses, cattle, and sheep, but with little success. In 1842 he wound up bankrupt amid a welter of litigation. In this troublous time a harder piety imbued his attitude toward slavery. His son, John Brown, Jr., recalled a family gathering at which his father

> after spending considerable time in setting forth, in impressive language, the hopeless condition of the slave, . . . asked who of us were willing to make common cause with him in doing all in our power to "break the jaws of the wicked and pluck the spoil out of his teeth. . . ." Receiving an affirmative answer from each, he kneeled in prayer, and all did the same. This posture in prayer impressed me greatly as it was the first time I have ever known him to assume it. After prayer he asked us

to raise our right hands, and he then administered an oath . . . [which] bound us to secrecy and devotion to the purpose of fighting slavery by force and arms to the extent of our ability.[3]

In 1846 Brown moved to Springfield, Massachusetts, to embark on a career as wool merchant that ended in failure and more bitter litigation four years later. Here he became more familiar with the leading abolitionists and met Frederick Douglass and other Negro leaders. In 1848 Brown settled his family among a colony of Negroes in North Elba, New York. The land for this settlement, high in the Adirondacks, had been given by the wealthy abolitionist Gerrit Smith. But like other projects of a utopian cast, North Elba was not a success. Hostile neighbors, a harsh, unfamiliar climate, poor farming soil, and isolation depleted enthusiasm and resources. But, according to Oswald Garrison Villard, Brown's best biographer, the presence of the Negroes in the mountains furthered Brown's thinking about the possibility of guerrilla warfare in the southern Appalachians with a force of freed slaves.

In 1849, because he felt that "some of the principal manufacturers are leagued together to break us down" in the selling of wool, he sailed for England and the Continent in search of new markets. There, as he asserted in later years, he made special visits to various famous battle sites.

After the passage of the Fugitive Slave Law in 1850, Brown recruited forty-four Negro men and women in Springfield into the "United States League of Gileadites" for the purpose of resisting slave-catchers. In his "Words of Advice" to them he urged that they go about armed and "Let the first blow be the signal for all to engage; and when engaged do not do your work by halves; but make clean work with your enemies, and be sure you meddle not with others. . . . Your enemies will be slow to attack you after you have once done up the work nicely. . . ."[4] The league is not known to have engaged in any action, but Brown put his injunctions to the test of steel later.

In 1854 three of Brown's sons migrated to Osawatomie, Kansas, to aid the free state forces in the bitter "squatter sovereignty" contest with the slave states. According to federal legislation authored by Stephen Douglas, the status of slavery in Kansas and Nebraska would be decided by the vote of the majority of the settlers. Both North and

South were rushing in emigrants, and from the neighboring slave state of Missouri "Border Ruffians" were making periodic sallies to disrupt Kansas elections and to terrify the anti-slavery camp.

When his sons set out Brown wrote: "If you or any of my family are disposed to go to Kansas or Nebraska, with a view to help defeat *Satan* and his legions in that direction, I have not a word to say; *but I feel committed to operate in another part of the field*." [5] He had discussed his plan for armed attack on the slaveholding South with his family and friends for some time; it was now uppermost in his thoughts.

After hearing from his sons the tumultuous state of affairs in Kansas and of their urgent need for help, however, Brown made the first of what were to be many appeals for funds and arms from his abolitionist acquaintances and headed West. For two years he had been scratching out a living as part-time shepherd and farmer, but now he abandoned all workaday concerns. He did not go to Kansas with the intention of becoming a settler. His one-horse wagon was loaded with rifles and sabers—and some surveying equipment which he later used chiefly as a shield for spying.

The anti-slavery cause looked bleak at the time of Brown's arrival in the territory in 1855. The pro-slavery settlers were in the majority, not counting their ready reinforcements from Missouri. The federal governor, Wilson Shannon, was a pusillanimous tippler inclined toward the Southern camp. Franklin Pierce, no less a hard drinker, was President and followed the counsel of Jefferson Davis, who, as Secretary of War, controlled the federal forces in the territory. The Free Soil settlers refused to acknowledge a fraudulently elected legislature, but their own governmental body adopted such curious resolutions as a declaration "that the stale and ridiculous charge of Abolitionism so industriously imputed to the Free State party . . . is without a shadow of truth to support it." [6]

Brown and his sons took a prominent part in Free Soil affairs, including the defense of the city of Lawrence when a posse of Border Ruffians headed by Shannon were outsmarted and turned back without the firing of a shot. Here Brown received the commission of captain of the "Liberty Guards" of the Kansas Volunteers.

Five months later Lawrence was not so lucky. On May 21, 1856, despite attempts on the part of the citizenry to appease a federal marshal leading a Border Ruffian force, the city was sacked and burned.

Brown and his men set out from Osawatomie to aid the city, but when they heard it was too late they stopped to await developments. Jason Brown recalled his father saying: "Now something *must* be done. We have got to defend our families and our neighbors as best we can. Something is going to be done now. We must show by actual work that there are two sides to this thing and that they cannot go on with impunity." [7] A short time later, Brown, four of his sons, and two others set out for Pottawatomie, a pro-slavery bastion. On the night of May 24, five pro-slavery settlers, including a father and two sons, were hacked and shot to death after being pulled from their beds. Brown, it is said, did not do any of the killing himself although he directed it.

These murders, plotted in cold blood, make a hard hurdle for a sympathetic biographer. They did not bring peace or victory to the anti-slavery forces of the region; in the eyes of many, they lessened the moral supremacy the free staters had enjoyed over their foes. Only in tough-minded fashion can Brown's action be given some justification: Kansas was eventually won by Free Soil partisans because most of them were peaceful, decent settlers who persevered in the channels of lawful government. But at the moment of Pottawatomie, law and order in Kansas were in the hands of the lawless; government was by the will of distant Washington, where the influence of the Southern oligarchy was strong. The free staters could not match the brutish mien of the Southern brigands, but certainly their endurance and hope were not so saintly that they did not yearn for a hardhanded avenger. Brown, the stooped, eagle-visaged patriarch, stepped from the ranks of the people to play this role. However atrocious his deed, it may well have, vicariously, inspirited the God-fearing.

Charles Robinson, a prominent Free Soil leader, thought so. "I never had much doubt that Captain Brown was the author of the blow at Pottawatomie, for the reason that he was the only man who comprehended the situation, and saw the absolute necessity of some such blow and had the nerve to strike it." [8] Other settlers declared

that public sentiment shifted from immediate horror to general approbation. There is no doubt that Brown's name became a rallying cry
wherever anti-slavery men defended their rights.

After the killings, Brown and his men took to the brush. Two of
his sons who had no part in the deaths were captured and terribly
mistreated by Border Ruffians and federal troops before being put
in jail. Brown captured a superior force of federal troops that had set
out in pursuit of him, and the troops' rescuers lacked the nerve to
arrest him. William A. Phillips, correspondent for the New York
Tribune, wrote of an interview with Brown at this time:

> One of the most interesting things in his conversation that night, and
> one that marked him as a theorist, was his treatment of our forms of
> social and political life. He thought society ought to be organized on a
> less selfish basis; for while material interests gained something by the
> deification of pure selfishness, men and women lost much by it. He said
> that all great reforms, like the Christian religion, were based on broad,
> generous, self-sacrificing principles. He condemned the sale of land as a
> chattel and thought that there was an infinite number of wrongs to right
> before society would be what it should be, but that in our country
> slavery was the "sum of all villainies," and its abolition the first essen-
> tial work. . . .[9]

Modern thoughts these; rephrase a few terms and a tenable basis
for social action still remains. The former land speculator had come
a long way.

After a brief trip to Nebraska, Brown boldly returned to Kansas
to take leadership of a Free Soil company of raiders. On August 30
his forces were surprised at Osawatomie by about a hundred and fifty
Border Ruffians determined to destroy Brown's home settlement.
Brown directed a brilliant holding action and got the majority of his
thirty-odd followers to safety across the river. His son Frederick had
earlier been killed by the assailants' vanguard. As Brown stood on the
riverbank watching the smoke and flames of burning Osawatomie, he
told his son Jason:

> God sees it. I have only a short time to live—only one death to die,
> and I will die fighting for this cause. There will be no more peace in
> this land until slavery is done for. I will give them something else to do
> than to extend slave territory. I will carry the war into Africa.[10]

III

At the end of 1856, peace of a sort prevailed in Kansas, and Brown left for Boston to seek among his abolitionist friends funds for his deferred dream of invading the South. While his mission was represented as a plan to arm a company of men for the future protection of Kansas, the inner circle of his supporters—Gerrit Smith, George L. Stearns, Frank B. Sanborn, Dr. Samuel G. Howe, Theodore Parker, and the Reverend Thomas W. Higginson—learned his true aim and concurred in it.

The year 1857 was spent recruiting and training his company. Unluckily, Brown hired a soldier of fortune, Hugh Forbes, whom he had met in New York, as a military expert. Forbes soon became fed up with the project and devoted himself to blackmailing Brown's supporters by threatening to expose the scheme. His activities caused so much alarm that Brown was persuaded to make a trip to Kansas to throw off suspicion.

This Brown reluctantly decided to do. But before he left he assembled his company in Chatham, Ontario, a community of free Negroes, for the ratification of a "Provisional Constitution and Ordinances for the People of the United States" and the election of officers. "Whereas, Slavery, throughout its entire barbarous existence in the United States is none other than a most barbarous, unprovoked and unjustifiable War of one portion of its citizens upon another portion . . ." the preamble began.[11] But it was a fantastic document, setting up an elaborate governmental structure for the Appalachian mountain realm which freed slaves were eventually to carve out for themselves. (One of the provisos was that all confiscated property was to be owned and worked communally.) Perhaps Brown, who counted heavily on the support of the exiled Negroes in his audience, hoped to fire their imaginations in this grandiose manner. Perhaps he knew in his heart that this paper republic was the nearest he would come to molding the future with his living hands.

In June 1858, Brown returned to Kansas under the name of "Shubel Morgan." The Free Soil forces were in the ascendancy, but he was determined that no quiet should reign while slavery still existed anywhere. Hearing of the plight of a Negro slave whose wife and children were about to be sold, he led a group into Missouri on December

19 and liberated eleven slaves. A slaveowner was killed in the action. At this heinous theft of property, pro-slavery forces boiled and genteel anti-slavery people blanched. But with a price of $3250 on his head, and dodging mobs and posses all the way North, Brown escorted his charges 1100 miles to the safety of the Canadian border, traveling 600 miles of the distance in covered wagons in the dead of winter.

To indicate how Brown again was ahead of popular sentiment: Tabor, Iowa, long an Underground Railroad station and previously headquarters and arms depot for Brown, passed a resolution which declared "we have no Sympathy with those who go to Slave States, to entice away Slaves, & take property or life when necessary to attain that end." [12]

Then came Harpers Ferry. On July 4, 1859, "I. Smith & Sons," cattle buyers, rented a small farm on the outskirts of that federal arsenal town situated at the juncture of the Potomac and Shenandoah rivers. The company assembled—eventually seventeen whites and five Negroes—and were cooped up in an attic until October 16, when their chief decided to strike. This long delay Brown attributed to financial difficulties and to the wait for more men. But it is possible that, when his Great Plan assumed the unwieldy dimensions of reality, this chronically ill, rapidly aging warrior knew, out of the scarring wisdom of bleeding Kansas, its lack of chance. He delayed to steel his will for what could only be an ultimate, all-exacting gesture of protest.

For, as Villard points out:

> The general order detailed the men who were to garrison various parts of the town and hold the bridges, but beyond that, little had been mapped out. It was all to depend upon the orders of the commander-in-chief, who seemed bent on violating every military principle. Thus, he had appointed no definite place for the men to retreat to, and fixed no hour for the withdrawal from the town. He, moreover, proceeded at once to defy the canons by placing a river between himself and his base of supplies—the Kennedy Farm—and then left no adequate force on the river bank to insure his being able to fall back to that base. Hardly had he entered the town when, by dispersing his men here and there, he made his defeat as easy as possible. Moreover, he had in mind no well-defined purpose in attacking Harper's Ferry, save to begin his revolution in a spectacular way, capture a few slaveholders and release

a few slaves. So far as he had thought anything out, he expected to alarm the town and then, with the slaves that had rallied to him, to march back to the school-house near the Kennedy Farm, arm his recruits and take to the hills. Another general, with the same purpose in view, would have established his mountain camp first, swooped down upon the town in order to spread terror throughout the State, and in an hour or two, at most, have started back to his hill-top fastness.[13]

As if to make sure his gestures were understood, in the event he and his party perished, Brown left behind at the farm all his correspondence dealing with his plans. Had he managed to escape from Harpers Ferry these documents would have in all probability led to his capture.

Again, putting symbolism ahead of strategy, Brown, at the start of the march, sent a detachment five miles out of Harpers Ferry to the home of Colonel Lewis W. Washington, a great-grandnephew of George Washington. Here the colonel was made to deliver up to a Negro in the group a sword that had belonged to the first President.

Then, after thirty hours of fighting that was intermittently barbarous and ceremonial, but always undirectioned and hopeless, Brown was captured at daybreak, hacked down by bayonet-wielding marines in the fire-engine house in which he had become trapped. Beside him were the bodies of two of his sons, one dead and one dying. The commander of the marines was a Colonel Robert E. Lee.

The alarm about the attack had been spread sooner than Brown anticipated. He refused to leave the town the morning of the 17th despite pleas to do so from his men. Then Virginia militia arrived to block off escape routes over the rivers. The rest was only a mopping-up operation.

As at Pottawatomie, public reaction quickly moved from incredulous horror to partisan appraisal. He became the covert champion of the law-abiding North, which heretofore had waged a defensive struggle against slavery. The expansionist South, with its flamboyant professional soldiers and politicians, had had all the heroes. On the other hand, the South, nervous in a collapsing economic system, saw Brown as the harbinger of war. So immediate was this interpretation that the governor of Virginia assembled a huge military guard for Brown's hanging, not so much to prevent rescue attempts or violence as to gather the state's militia for training purposes and to impress the nation with its might. Other Southern states began mustering arms and men. Soon the trigger-happy atmosphere prevailed that led to the firing on Fort Sumter.

Brown, only slightly bothered by his wounds, defended his deed against charges of insanity or vainglory with amazing skill and energy. When his lawyers, at the trial which began October 25, attempted to enter a plea of insanity, Brown rejected the move, saying,

> As I have remarked . . . insane persons, so far as my experience goes, have but little ability to judge of their own sanity; and if I am insane, of course I should think I know more than all the rest of the world. But I do not think so. I am perfectly unconscious of insanity, and I reject, as far as I am capable, any attempt to interfere in my behalf on that score.[14]

After he had been sentenced to die, he categorically refused to participate in any rescue attempt. "I am worth inconceivably more to hang than for any other purpose."[15] He gave lengthy and cogent interviews to all factions and hoped that this unusual opportunity for "faithful plain dealing" with leading Southerners had left them "not entirely misimproved."[16] His brave and touching letters to his family and friends were widely printed.

On December 2, as Robert E. Lee and "Stonewall" Jackson—and John Wilkes Booth—stood at arms in the vast company that was to escort him to the gallows, the bearded "visionary" scribbled one last note: "I John Brown am now quite *certain* that the crimes of this *guilty land: will* never be purged *away;* but with blood. I had *as I now think: vainly* flattered myself that without *very much* bloodshed; it might be done."[17]

IV

But is the Civil War to be considered John Brown's legacy? Could we not view the violence of Brown's life as accidental, a part of the context of his frontier time? (He resolutely professed he had never personally killed any man, and once declined a direct bead on the slayer of his son Frederick.) If the force of arms he advocated is modulated to mean a determination that will not shrink at the prospect of physical conflict, his true greatness is more easily inspected.

In the last analysis, Brown was not a theorist, a strategist, or a leader. He had no program, no training, no tact. He had only the dynamic belief that ethical issues were human issues and the boldness of mind to see that metaphysical conflicts were human conflicts. At the time of Brown's coming of age there was no doubt about the moral iniquity of slavery; there was no doubt that the Southern oligarchy formed a threat to republican institutions. But the existing political and economic structure made it expedient to localize one's morality and republicanism. Abolition bowed to the sanctity of property rights and practiced what it preached with pious prudence. At first, Brown, with his scheme for a school for begged or bought slaves, and his North Elba venture, followed this frictionless pattern. Then, becoming disillusioned with an economic system that deified "pure selfishness," he moved—a penniless, aging man beyond all thought of personal advantage—to bring the terminology of "virtue" into debate with its opposite doctrine. Not in words, which could be erased or shouted down, but in action.

The drama he enacted, as selfless hero, engrossed its spectators— Northern and Southern—on each of its stages, because its "lines" were the unspoken, combative implications of their respective philosophies. And because Brown portrayed these implications truly, the withdrawal of "men of principle" from association with him amounted, all the same, to a choosing of sides and a cleavage of the precarious unity of Slave and Free. He made "clean work" of defining thesis and antithesis; the imperfections of the synthesis must be laid to the souls of others.

John Brown was not a unique phenomenon. "Crazed, embittered failures" such as he have been lethal misfits in every moribund, oppressive system, be it in textile mill, merchant ship, graduate school, or nation. Their moldering bodies form the nightmares of masters; from their bones come pikes for slaves.

NOTES

1. Quoted in Oswald Garrison Villard, *John Brown* (New York, 1910; new edition, 1929), pp. 498-499. All subsequent quotations are

taken from this book (the 1929 edition), which is considered the definitive work on Brown.

2. *Ibid.*, pp. 43-44.
3. *Ibid.*, p. 46.
4. *Ibid.*, p. 51.
5. *Ibid.*, p. 79.
6. *Ibid.*, p. 104.
7. *Ibid.*, p. 151.
8. *Ibid.*, pp. 169-170.
9. *Ibid.*, pp. 221-222.
10. *Ibid.*, p. 248.
11. *Ibid.*, p. 334.
12. *Ibid.*, p. 385.
13. *Ibid.*, p. 427.
14. *Ibid.*, p. 507.
15. *Ibid.*, p. 496.
16. *Ibid.*, p. 547.
17. *Ibid.*, p. 554.

BIBLIOGRAPHICAL NOTE

Works on Brown

DuBois, W. E. B., *John Brown* (New York, 1909).

Ehrlich, Leonard, *God's Angry Man* (New York, 1932; reissued 1941).

Karsner, David, *John Brown, Terrible Saint* (New York, 1934).

Sandborn, F. B., *Life and Letters of John Brown* (Boston, 1885).

Villard, Oswald Garrison, *John Brown* (New York, 1910; new edition, 1929).

Warren, Robert Penn, *John Brown, The Making of a Martyr* (New York, 1929).

7

John Peter Altgeld: Governor
for the People

RUSSELL FRASER

I

It was 1869 when Altgeld went West. In Chicago, which lay
along his route, the palace cars of George M. Pullman were building,
Marshall Field was engrossing his millions, men like Swift and Armour
were making of their city hog butcher to the world. More flamboyant,
if not so pregnant with success, was the agitation of anarchist and
socialist, born of the failure of 1848 when radicals by thousands fled
the Old World to seek freedom in the New. They found it the province
of Cyrus McCormick, spelled out by the *Tribune* of Joseph Medill,
girt round by a resurgent Know-Nothing Party which proclaimed,
amid riots: "Put None But Americans On Guard."

John Peter Altgeld did not tarry in Chicago. His youth—he was
just twenty-one—his consciousness of great expectations, were those
of America itself, trekking westward, eager for a hazard of new
fortunes, expressing, in a popular song, its faith that "Uncle Sam is
rich enough to give us all a farm!" For intangibles like social justice

Altgeld cared not at all; what he sought was material success. In this he was the child of his parents, who had left southern Germany in 1848 not as embattled revolutionaries but rather as ambitious peasants. The boy John Peter, born on December 30, 1847, they took with them, to a farm near Mansfield, Ohio.

Altgeld's childhood was a round of hard labor, dominated by a father who beat his children with a more than perfunctory zeal. It was a time, moreover, of hatred for Catholics and foreigners: when John Peter was eight or nine, patriotic citizens of nearby Louisville and Cincinnati shed the blood of foreigners in their midst. Perhaps the circumspection which marked his first years in public life derived from that conviction of apartness which early and indelibly was impressed on the boy. Later he came to rejoice in it: "It was the crowd on one side and John Peter Altgeld on the other."

In 1857 a memorable decision in the case of Dred Scott, escaped slave, was handed down by Chief Justice Roger Brooke Taney, once, in Andrew Jackson's day, a fiery radical, now, full of years and honor, impeccably conservative. The pattern was already familiar. In 1861 Major Anderson hauled down the flag at Fort Sumter, and the War Between the States was a fact. Altgeld was sixteen when, in 1864, he joined the Ohio Home Guards. In the swamps of Virginia, under the command of Ben Butler, he fell ill of "Chickahominy fever." Many in his regiment died. He himself escaped narrowly. But the fever was to plague him all his life.

With the end of his service he came back to Ohio, enrolled in the high school at Mansfield, despite his father, whose horizon had contracted to the bounds of Richland County. There followed further study at Gailey's "select seminary" at Lexington. Equipped with a certificate Altgeld began teaching, in Woodville, at the age of nineteen. Among his colleagues was Emma Ford, daughter of a well-to-do Ohio merchant. Altgeld proposed marriage. Her father rejected him: he was too poor. Not one to whimper, he threw up the job he had held for two years and, with ten dollars in pocket, headed West.

Chicago he inspected and eschewed for St. Louis, the city of Carl Schurz. Literally penniless, he got work in a chemical plant, but left it to labor for the railroad at Fort Scott, Kansas. There his fever recurred; his life again was in doubt. When able to walk, he moved on once more, to Iowa, he thought, for his health. His tramp ended in Savannah, Missouri. There, working on farms, teaching school, he

won back his strength. At night he read law. By 1871 he had advanced
to the bar. A year more, and he was city attorney. But if his rise was
phenomenal, it was marked by nothing more than a zeal for self-
advancement. The cases he fought were conventional enough. In his
conduct of them he gave no hint of the crusader. Indeed in one case
he decided that under the law a Negro woman was "property" still.

It was the Granger revolt that brought him his first elective office.
Throughout America the fantastic corruption of the Grant administration had spurred liberals to renewed activity. In 1872, under the leadership of Horace Greeley, a dissident Republican party had been
formed. It was beaten badly at the polls. In 1873, on the collapse of
the banking house of Jay Cooke & Sons, the farmers in desperation
turned to their Granges, made of them a power for reform. When the
governor of Minnesota himself declared, "It is time to take these robber
corporations by the scruff of the neck and shake them over hell!"
Altgeld listened in earnest. The angels of reform were stirring the
pools of society,[1] and he, a political adept, would fish them. Bolting
the Bourbon Democracy, Altgeld set up as People's candidate for
prosecuting attorney of Andrew County, Missouri. He was elected.
Yet the job proved irksome. Within eleven months he had tendered
his resignation, turned back, this time for good, to Chicago.

The city to which he came had been gutted four years earlier by
the Great Fire. But the fire that ravaged it in 1875 was a hatred for
"communists," for alien creeds. Said Joseph Medill: "Judge Lynch
is an American by birth and character. The Vigilance Committee is
a peculiarly American institution. . . . Every lamp-post in Chicago
will be decorated with a communistic carcass if necessary to prevent
wholesale incendiarism." [2] Altgeld was no incendiary. Aloof from
politics now, he sought work as a lawyer. So poor was he at first
that he had to borrow money to have his boots half-soled. He persevered. In 1877 he returned to Ohio, married Emma Ford. It was a
measure of his increasing success. The same year witnessed America's
first major clash between capital and labor, and the beginnings of government by injunction. A general strike gripped Chicago, federal
troops intervened, nineteen strikers were killed. The Citizens' Association presented to the city "a Gatling quick-firing gun which could
sweep a street from side to side and mow down a thousand men in
a few seconds." [3]

But if these events were of moment to Altgeld, he gave no sign. He was dabbling in real estate with what money he had saved. Uncommonly shrewd, uncommonly acquisitive, he was very soon a wealthy man. In time he possessed holdings worth a million dollars, the famous sixteen-story structure in downtown Chicago called Unity Block. His was the classic American story, and not Collis P. Huntington nor Pierpont Morgan himself worked harder to give it substance. At the age of thirty he had won his way from rags to riches, had established a footing among those who were nourished on the Dead Sea fruit of "Our primary social adjustment . . . a denial of justice . . . [which allows] one man to own the land on which and from which other men must live," a subtle alchemy which extracts "from the masses in every civilised country the fruits of their weary toil." [4] Altgeld's allegiance was given, as yet, to the evils arraigned by Henry George in *Progress and Poverty*.

Perhaps it was partly childlessness that led Altgeld back to politics. "Other men," he said, "have their children. Politics is my recreation." When asked, in later years, why he risked so much money in the Unity Block, he replied, "Because I have no children. I have to create something, and so I am creating buildings." [5] As late as 1901, when his manual on *Oratory* was published, he called it his newborn child. His entry into the recreation that was politics in Chicago coincided with the first election of Grover Cleveland in 1884. Altgeld himself was nominated by the Democracy for Congress, and though he failed of election, his showing, in a strong Republican district, was impressive. His record was not. The resurgence of labor, hard on the disastrous strikes of 1877; the hold of socialism on working people, never since so secure; the hangings of the Molly Maguires in the Pennsylvania coal fields; and the "Strike of the Millionaires against the Miners" at Spring Valley, Illinois—these dramatic events seemed not to move him. Even the diatribes of the press against "foreign scum," which grew daily in scurrile violence, did not evoke a protest.

On the day of his nomination for Congress, however, there was published a book which gave indication of change. For in *Our Penal Machinery and Its Victims,* Altgeld bore witness to the correlation of poverty and crime. "The great multitudes annually arrested . . . are the poor, the unfortunate, the young and the neglected." The victims of law enforcement are recruited *"from among those that are fighting an unequal fight in the struggle for existence."* [6] And with this perception went a more than pious humanity, a championing of the underdog. From the sheer goodness of heart revealed in that book might come an urge to reform the abuses decried there. But the reformer was scarcely fledged before an event of terrible magnitude begot in him questionings far more intense. This was the Haymarket tragedy of May 4, 1886.

II

Chicago was ripe for such a disaster. Agitation among workers for the eight-hour day excited all the venom of the press, the hysteria of business, the rash mutterings of an anarchist minority. On May 3rd, at McCormick's reaper works, these volatile elements were fused: a clash between union men and scabs was joined by police, who shot to death two of the strikers. The *Arbeiter-Zeitung* of anarchist August Spies called for revenge. A mass meeting to denounce the atrocity was scheduled on May 4th in Haymarket Square. But the crowd proved disappointingly slim, the speakers even-tempered. If there were those who hoped for violence they must have been chagrined: by ten in the evening the orderly gathering had begun to disperse. It was then that Chief Bonfield, at the head of almost two hundred police, gave his order to march on the crowd. Sam Fielden, anarchist, was protesting the peaceable nature of the meeting when the Haymarket bomb was thrown. In the carnage that followed, the police fired on each other. One of their number was killed on the spot, six were mortally injured, sixty-seven bore wounds. The fatalities of the workers were never counted.

Chicago surrendered its intellect until the tragedy was played out. A vigilante group of respectable citizens was led by John Barton Payne, who years later was to lead the American Red Cross. Raids were staged in working-class districts; *agents provocateurs* did their devious work. On May 27th indictments were returned against thirty-one anarchists, eight of whom eventually stood trial. Of these only two had been present at the bombing. July saw the trial, a hideous travesty of justice, presided over by Judge Joseph Gary. The verdict was foreordained: death by hanging for seven of the defendants, fifteen years' imprisonment for the eighth. Appeals for justice proved fruitless; appeals for mercy were cried down by men like Marshall Field. John Peter Altgeld took part in neither.

On November 10th, Governor Oglesby commuted to life the sentences of Fielden and Schwab. Defendant Louis Lingg chewed dynamite in Cook County jail, scrawling in his blood: "Long live anarchy!" On November 11, 1887, the four condemned men were marched, hooded and handcuffed, to the scaffold.

August Spies said, "There will come a time when our silence will be more powerful than the voices you strangle today!"

George Engel cried, "Hurrah for anarchy!"

Adolph Fischer said, "This is the happiest moment of my life!"

Albert Parsons said, "Will I be allowed to speak, O men of America? Let me speak, Sheriff Matson! Let the voice of the people be heard!" [7]

The identity of the bomber was never discovered.

"Capitalism," wrote the *Workmen's Advocate,* "speaks of the legal murder of its victims as the last act in the tragedy." [8] But Altgeld had yet to be heard from. It was he who was to write the last act. To his friend, labor leader George Schilling, he said, "I want to do something, not just make a speech. . . . I want power, to get hold of the handle that controls things. When I do, I will give it a twist!" [9] To make a beginning he stood in 1886 as Democratic-United Labor candidate for judge of the Superior Court of Cook County. With his election he began to speak out. A first public statement on labor had been the radical demand for compulsory government arbitration of disputes. There followed, first, his recognition that "it is the duty of society to take care of its indigent"; then a demand for social legislation to meet the evil of sweatshops. [10] Renewed attacks on the "socialistic, atheistic, alcoholic European classes" [11] who made Chicago their rendezvous provoked at last from Altgeld "The Immigrant's Answer." The publication in 1890 of the first volume of *Live Questions,* a collection of his papers and addresses, underscored his new position. The *Tribune* remarked it by calling him communist. It was signal proof that he had arrived. When in 1891 he gave up his judgeship to take control of the Unity Block, his was a Fabian withdrawal from politics.

The Democratic Party insured his return by putting him forward for governor of Illinois. Essaying the role of folksy good fellow, he canvassed the state as no other candidate before him had done. The abuse of his enemies he wisely ignored. Politics he did not: and surely it was a rare politician who was able to effect a working alliance of Lutherans, Catholics, and labor. The expenses of his campaign—

amounting to $100,000—he bore himself. Grover Cleveland, by contrast, was indebted to Wall Street, and with eager subservience he repaid the creditors who gave him his second term in the White House. His collateral was the government of the United States.

III

In 1892 Altgeld rode in triumph to Springfield, the first foreigner born, the first resident of Chicago, to be chosen governor. Before he could take office his health broke down; nonetheless he attended his inauguration. So great was the throng that acclaimed him that not even Vice-president-elect Adlai Stevenson could fight through it to shake Altgeld's hand. His first months in office were little distinguished. Ambitious to be Senator, he showed himself a liberal spoilsman. But when a Negro was lynched in Decatur, in 1893, the governor issued a state proclamation that still bristles with his wrath. The shooting of strikers at Lemont, soon after, inspired a report in which Altgeld put the blame on the employer.

His liberal supporters were not thereby appeased. They had helped elect him governor in the belief that he would pardon the three survivors of the Haymarket trial. He had bestirred himself thus far not at all. So Clarence Darrow, holding no office, came to Springfield and said, "I and the others see no excuse for waiting!" Altgeld replied, "Go tell your friends that when I am ready I will act. I do not know how I will act, but I will do what I think is right." [12] He meant that. His was the position of his fellow Illinoisan, Abraham Lincoln, roundly denounced by liberals like Greeley for holding back emancipation of the slaves. Lincoln waited his time, and so did Altgeld. He was convinced that a pardon would kill him politically. Issue it, he said, and "I will be a dead man!" [13] He began to amass evidence on the case, wavering all the while between ambition and—his phrase—"the polestar of duty." [14]

Then in 1893 Judge Gary, who had conducted the trial, wrote an article, cruel and self-damning, on "The Chicago Anarchists of 1886." Judge Gary's position was brutally simple: the anarchists, so justly punished, were animated only by "envy and hatred of all people whose condition in life was better than their own." [15]

Altgeld was convinced. On June 26, 1893, he issued the pardon. He said, "As to the Senatorship, no man's ambitions had a right to stand in the way of performing a simple act of justice." [16] It was not the pardon itself, but its character, which made him the most hated man in America. For, scorning to plead mercy as his reason—the easy and unexceptionable way—he arraigned the shocking bias of jury and judge. The jury, he showed, was chosen not by chance, as the law demanded, but by a bailiff who said coldbloodedly, "Those fellows are going to be hanged." Defense challenges for cause were peremptorily overruled. A prospective juror stated, "I believe what I have read in the papers; believe that the parties are guilty." [17] Judge Gary passed him. The evidence against the defendants was of a piece with the proceedings under which they were tried. Thus the protest of Sam Fielden, "We are peaceable," was but an example of sly deception, was in fact the signal for the throwing of the bomb.

All this and more Altgeld revealed, and so brought on himself a stream of execration to which his age affords no equal. The respectable citizens who had advocated clemency united in deploring his message of pardon. They could have countenanced mercy, but not an indictment of their class and the juridical props which sustained it. The press called Altgeld "wild-haired demagogue," "jetsam," "apologist for murder," "the Nero of the last decade of the nineteenth century." The *New York Times,* pharisaically sober, suggested that he was insane. And in truth the idea must have been more than plausible. How else was the *Times* to construe such intractable courage? But the most fatuous comment was made at a dinner of Harvard alumni by Robert Todd Lincoln, corporation attorney. Said the son of the Emancipator: "It is for you Harvard men to stand firm in the midst of such dangers in the republic." [18]

If John Pardon Altgeld, as his enemies called him now, believed that his career was at an end, he undervalued both himself and the people. For the summit of his power was yet to be attained. He reached it in the midst of economic depression and the most terrible struggle that had ever wracked his party. When Grover Cleveland returned to Washington in 1892, it was as the hope of farmers throughout the South and West, caught up already in what came to be called the "Panic of '93." In Chicago on Labor Day, Altgeld assured the workers that "no one will starve." [19] He was hard put to fulfill his promise. The following year saw the tragicomic march of Coxey's Army of the Commonwealers of Christ. More serious was the mineworkers' strike, with its wake of violence in Illinois. But dwarfing this and all else was the great Pullman boycott.

IV

It began on May 11, 1894. Did George Pullman's workers protest a cut in wages? Pullman closed the shops. Did a temerarious committee seek discussion with him? The committee was fired. The strike was on. Now it happened that a majority of the workers belonged to the American Railway Union, the most brilliant child of Gene Debs. And the ARU, if young, was already a power. It had just beaten, in strike, the Empire Builder James J. Hill, of the Great Northern Railroad. On June 12th, sitting in convention, it requested that Pullman submit to arbitration. Pullman said, "There is nothing to arbitrate." On June 26th, the first anniversary of the Haymarket pardon, the union voted to boycott Pullman cars. Soon ranged against it was the illegal General Managers' Association, representing the twenty-four railroads serving Chicago, and pledged to resist the boycott. Damaging, too, was the refusal to cooperate of the railroad brotherhoods and the AFL, convinced that caution is the better part of valor. And yet the boycott was an overwhelming success. The strike was in fact won, when the railroads and the federal government connived at the last moment to break it.

The scheme seemed a good one. All trains, irrespective of traffic, would haul Pullman cars. The workers, incited to stop them, would be stopping the United States mails as well. Still, there was little violence; for the most part, the mails did get through. It was then that Attorney General Richard Olney, one of the most notable railroad lawyers in America, and counsel to members of the GMA itself, intervened. To his special assistant at Chicago, chosen literally by the roads, Olney wrote, "I feel that the true way of dealing with the matter is by a force which is overwhelming and prevents any attempt at resistance." [20] Accordingly, Assistant Attorney Walker was empowered to draw an injunction which declared the boycott illegal. The judges before whom the injunction was brought helped first to revise it, then mounted the bench to make it law. Nor was even this deemed sufficient. Federal troops were required, to insure that the union be smashed.

Governor Altgeld, in Springfield, aware that the strike threatened private property, moved with exemplary success to protect it. The militia was less murderous, under his command, than it might otherwise have been; it was also more efficient. Yet Cleveland, without consultation, ordered federal troops to Chicago. It was the greatest insult ever delivered to the governor of a sovereign state.

Altgeld's protests served only to evoke from the press new tirades against "this lying, hypocritical, demagogical, sniveling Governor of Illinois." [21] The arrival of the troops—on Independence Day—effected something more: the violence it was supposed to have quelled. Hundreds of freight cars soon blazed in the city, fired, as Cleveland's own commission hinted later, by the railroads themselves. Thirty-five hundred men—"thugs, thieves and ex-convicts," [22] on the word of the chief of police—were deputized as agents of the federal government, though armed and paid by the strike-bound employers. To make the cup full to overflowing, Debs and his lieutenants were arrested for contempt and conspiracy. Theirs, by an ugly irony, was the first prosecution under the new Sherman Anti-trust Law. Of course the strike was broken.

Altgeld, however, was not done with Pullman and Cleveland. The former he struck at first, on receiving an appeal for aid from the starving citizens of Pullman's model town, where rent gouging was the rule, and a clause in every lease enabled the management to be rid of "undesirable tenants." The refusal of Pullman to alleviate the hunger of his workers prompted Altgeld to go to the people. Money poured in. His personal triumph he followed by forcing the abolition of the company town and by exposing Pullman as a tax evader and defrauder of the state.

And this was but a start. His biennial message to the legislature in January 1895 he fashioned into an indictment unrivaled from the beginnings of the Republic. Investigation of labor troubles must be made compulsory. The government must abandon laissez faire for a policy of active intercession. The federal courts must cease their corrosion of "the personal rights of the citizen." The public must learn to recognize "the marked feature of this age": the preying of unrestricted capital, "the large concerns swallowing the small ones." It must turn its eyes from the straw man of anarchy and see whence the real danger comes: "from that corruption, usurpation, insolence and oppression that go hand in hand with vast concentration of wealth." The Pullman strike he reviewed with ruthless cogency, focusing attention on its one most significant aspect: government by injunction, "a very great convenience to corporations." He was indeed a new kind of executive.[23]

When the United States Supreme Court declared unconstitutional a tax on incomes, Altgeld assailed the decision. The burden on the producing classes is thereby made heavier, he said, "and the whip has made a new welt on their backs, but what of it? In fact, what are they for, if not to bear burdens and to be lashed?" The Court's approbation of the jailing of Debs bore out Altgeld's conjecture that it would, doubtless, "have other opportunities from time to time to solidify our institutions and to teach patriotism by coming down with terrific force upon some wretch whose vulgarity and unpatriotic character will be proven by the fact that he is poor." [24]

And now it was time to go after Cleveland. The President's action in demonetizing silver seemed, to the embattled Democracy, an act of utter betrayal. A Southern farmer represented all his fellows when he wrote, "With a few million Airs contracting the money in use to be able to buy too dollars worth of property with one dollar, this is no longer A free country." [25] Out in Kansas, Mary Elizabeth Lease advised her hearers to "stop raising corn and begin raising hell!" [26] The greatest furor since abolition days was in the making. On the ashes of Grange and Greenback parties arose the Farmers' Alliance, whose populist movement numbered two million men, whose banner proclaimed the struggle between the people and big business. Said Henry Demarest Lloyd, "Monopoly is business at the end of its journey. It has got there. The irrepressible conflict is now as distinctly with business as the issue so lately met was with slavery." [27]

Altgeld, embracing free silver, joined the conflict. "Clevelandism," he said, "is the slimy offspring of that unhallowed marriage between Standard Oil and Wall Street." [28] He determined to drive it from the Democratic Party. A first step was the calling of a special convention in Springfield to consider the currency question. Altgeld and silver emerged victorious. Silver conventions followed in other states, all of them emulating Illinois. When Altgeld arrived at the Democratic convention of 1896 in Chicago, he, whom the Haymarket pardon had supposedly killed, was the most powerful man in his party.

What he did at Chicago was to return the Democracy from the

house of Cleveland and Tilden to that of Jackson and Jefferson. The convention was his. He ruled it. He wrote the platform. He outmaneuvered the politicians: "Those prudent, cautious, wise gentlemen who have to consult the tin roosters every morning to see what their convictions should be during the day." [29] He read Grover Cleveland from the party. And had he been by birth an American, as assuredly he was in all his being, he would have received the nomination himself.

That honor was given to William Jennings Bryan, the Boy Orator of the Platte, who captured the delegates with an unforgettable speech: "Having behind us the producing masses of this nation and of the world, supported by the commercial interests, the laboring interests, and the toilers everywhere, we will answer . . . demands for a gold standard by saying . . . *You shall not press down upon the brow of labor this crown of thorns, you shall not crucify mankind upon a cross of gold!*"

Altgeld himself did not want to stand again. His health was gone, his personal fortune largely dissipated. Yet, caricatured as an anarchist, he was made the chief target of the campaign. The strenuous Theodore Roosevelt refused to shake his hand, "Because, sir, I may at any time be called upon to meet the man sword to sword upon the field of battle." [30] Altgeld could not choose but run. Though grievousiy ill, he stumped hard for Bryan. At Cooper Union, where Lincoln had preceded him, he sat on the platform with Henry George and listened to the chant of the crowd: "We love you for the enemies you have made!" [31]

But Cleveland helped sap Democratic strength by placing in the field a "goldbug" slate. Mark Hanna shook his barrel, crammed full with the biggest fund ever spent on an American election. William McKinley, Jr., was kept out of sight on his porch in Canton, Ohio. And the Democrats were beaten.

What the people feared, said Tom Johnson, soon to be mayor of Cleveland, "was not free silver—but free men!" [32] Altgeld was more charitable: "The time was too short to educate the public." [33] Denied by his successor the privilege of a farewell address, he left Springfield, an old man at forty-nine.

Defeat did not close his public life. Though all his property was lost except a heavily mortgaged home, though the Unity Block itself passed to the control of an unscrupulous banker, he continued to exert himself politically. When young Carter Harrison, whom he had made mayor of Chicago, began to traffic with the money power, Altgeld ran against him as an independent candidate in 1899. Despite his defeat, he dominated the Democratic convention at Kansas City in 1900. Again it was Bryan and free silver, with the addition of a plank against imperialism which Altgeld supplied. But good times were at hand. Free silver was dead. And imperialism was not to be stayed. McKinley prayed for guidance—and took the Philippines. In the year of Bryan's second defeat, the stock market had its biggest day in history. America had entered a new era. Altgeld's day was done.

He continued to the end a crusader, battling monopoly as the law partner of Clarence Darrow. His last case was the defense, on March 11, 1902, of a hackmen's union against an injunction. That night he went to Joliet, to protest the Boer War. "Wrong," he said, "may seem to triumph. Right may seem to be defeated. But the gravitation of eternal justice is toward the throne of God. Any political institution which is to endure must be plumb with that line of justice." [34] As he left the stage he was stricken with a cerebral hemorrhage. Early the next morning he died.

V

His could have been a wholly different story. For he was, in his beginnings, fired with the same ambition, gifted with the same financial acumen, as the robber barons whom he fought. He came to perceive, not in theory but in sober fact, that *The Cost of Something for Nothing*—as his last book was called—is "moral death." [35] His perception derived first from a desire to cleave to the right. He was, in high degree, the good man. His goodness, moreover, was informed with a critical intelligence, the absence of which would have made for but another savorless, if altruistic, millionaire. Intelligence and rectitude created the reformer. And the inevitability with which Altgeld responded to duty makes of his biography a work of art. His life was a continual progress.

It is possible, amid the color and excitement that surround his tenure as governor, to lose sight of his solid achievement. Yet he has had few peers in the business of getting things done. The University of Illinois he built from an insignificant college to a ranking institution of higher learning. He forced through the first good-behavior parole law in the

Middle West, enacted a tax on inheritance, reformed the civil service. He successfully regulated the sweatshop and child labor. He brought factories under inspection, and limited to the eight-hour day their employment of women. Labor disputes were subjected to arbitration; employers were bridled, who for years had evaded taxation. He gave to Chicago its fine system of parks. And the poor of his state did literally come unto him.

The platform he wrote in 1896, concerned, as he said, with "the people's welfare vs. corporate aggrandizement," [36] was embodied in the New Deal program of 1932. His fight against government by injunction became the fight of a generation of liberals until, with the passage of the Norris-LaGuardia Act, victory was won. And if, in later years, a Democratic President, wielding the injunction and deploring it the while, has helped to reverse that victory, the spirit of Altgeld continues to animate those who have resumed his struggle.

He was indeed a reformer, but he was also a politician, and the reforms he inaugurated would never have been carried through had it not been for his political astuteness. He knew, though ardent liberals often do not, that the walls of Jericho are not really brought down by a trumpet, that Gideon's army is not summoned by rhetoric alone. And so like Lincoln before him and Franklin Roosevelt after, he mastered the art of politics, which is the art of the possible. August Spies on the scaffold may be a more dramatic figure, but to Altgeld, the assiduous collector of statistics, the culler of votes, is owed a greater debt.

Not the least portion of his legacy is the clarity with which he examined an issue, the candor that marked his statement of it. To those who talked plausibly of "the lesser evil," who would oppose to the threat of Republicanism a Democratic Party only less conservative, only less mendacious, he replied, "It is the Clevelands, the men who put up respectable fronts, who are the real dangers." [37] He would have no commerce with them, and if the struggle he precipitated helped temporarily to balk his party of a victory that would have been without substance, his vindication was the greater victory of Wilson's New Freedom, of Roosevelt's New Deal.

The grave dress of government—old clothes upon old sticks to scare a bird!—beguiled him not at all. Supreme Court judges wore black gowns, he suggested, "to impress the people with their infallibility.

Now as these gowns are not very thick, and as some people might be able to see through them and be unpatriotic enough to question the justice of having to bear the burdens of government while the rich escape, and as there is danger that some of these men may doubt the infallibility of the court, would it not be well to have each judge wear two gowns for a while, until the storm blows over?" [38]

But what most compels admiration for Altgeld is his passionate integrity. He lived in a gilded age when "the price-current of an honest man and patriot" jingled in the pockets of a Harriman or Hill; when for every Vanderbilt who would see the public damned, a dozen of Conklings and Crokers arose to hurry the enterprise forward. There was another America: that of Thoreau, who knew that the perception and performance of right separates the diabolical in man from the divine; of Garrison, who would not equivocate, nor excuse, nor retreat, and who would be heard; of Phillips, to whom man was ever more valuable than money. From that America Altgeld derived. As a young and impecunious lawyer he ordered from his office a client whose case he found tainted. As the chief executive of his state he vetoed, in the teeth of unparalleled opposition, and the offer of a half-million dollar bribe, the Eternal Monopoly Bills of traction baron Charles T. Yerkes. When asked if it were good policy to issue the Haymarket pardon, he said, "It is right!" [39] He lives to posterity because of his rectitude then. For once to every generation comes a moment to decide, a time, in the phrase of Ecclesiastes, to speak. The hanging of John Brown in 1859, the execution of the Haymarket martyrs, and that of Sacco and Vanzetti were such moments. Our time has had its moment, enjoining, not less than these others, a decision on all who have shared it. What is the price-current of an honest man and patriot today?

Altgeld must have pondered the question when, thinking to palliate his declaration of pardon, he asked the old liberal, Lyman Trumbull, to request it. And Trumbull, perhaps in fear of his lucrative law practice, refused. Altgeld stayed the course.

NOTES

1. In the phrase of the *Chicago Tribune,* November 22, 1875, quoted in Harry Barnard, *Eagle Forgotten: The Life of John Peter Altgeld* (New

York, 1938), p. 47. Barnard's book is the best recent study, and the source of much of the material in this chapter.

2. *Chicago Tribune,* November 23, 1875, quoted in Barnard, *op. cit.,* p. 45.

3. I. Seymour Currey, *Chicago: Its History and Its Builders, A Century of Marvellous Growth* (Chicago, 1912), II, 377, quoted in Barnard, *op. cit.,* p. 56.

4. Henry George, *Progress and Poverty* (Everyman's Library, New York and London, 1913), p. 389.

5. To George A. Schilling, who recounted Altgeld's words in an interview with Harry Barnard, May 1935. Adolf Kraus, *Reminiscences and Comments* (Chicago, 1925), pp. 107 ff.; Barnard, *op. cit.,* pp. 64, 147.

6. *Live Questions, Including Our Penal Machinery and Its Victims* (Chicago, 1890), p. 168.

7. Henry David, *The History of the Haymarket Affair* (New York, 1936), p. 463. This is the best and fullest account, and the source of the description of the tragedy in this chapter.

8. *Ibid.,* p. 474.

9. Schilling to Barnard, May 30, 1935; Barnard, *op. cit.,* p. 118.

10. *Live Questions,* pp. 75, 78 ff.

11. *Chicago Tribune,* May 5, 1886, quoted in Barnard, *op. cit.,* p. 132.

12. Clarence Darrow, *The Story of My Life* (New York, 1932), pp. 100 ff.; Barnard, *op. cit.,* p. 184.

13. Darrow, *op. cit.,* p. 101; Barnard, *op. cit.,* p. 185.

14. Barnard, *op. cit.,* p. 186.

15. *The Century Magazine,* XLV, No. 6 (1893), 809; Barnard, *op. cit.,* p. 195.

16. Suppressed Schilling letter to *The Public;* Barnard, *op. cit.,* p. 204.

17. *Ibid.,* pp. 220 ff.

18. *Ibid.,* pp. 246, 241, 262, 244, 248; *Chicago Tribune,* May 26, 1895; *New York Times,* June 28, 1893; *Chicago Tribune,* June 29, 1893.

19. *Live Questions,* II (Springfield, Illinois, 1894), 298; Barnard, *op. cit.,* p. 273.

20. Henry James, *Richard Olney and His Public Service* (Boston, 1923), p. 47; Barnard, *op. cit.,* p. 287.

21. *Chicago Tribune,* July 7, 1894; Barnard, *op. cit.,* p. 299.

22. Eugene V. Debs, *The Federal Government and the Chicago Strikes* (Chicago, 1910), p. 12; Barnard, *op. cit.,* p. 312.

23. *Live Questions* (Chicago, 1899 edition), pp. 919 ff., 933-937; Barnard, *op. cit.,* pp. 333 ff.

24. *Chicago Tribune,* April 18, 1895; *Live Questions* (1899), pp. 464 ff.; Barnard, *op. cit.,* p. 338.
25. James A. Barnes, *John G. Carlisle* (New York, 1931), p. 429; Barnard, *op. cit.,* p. 346.
26. Harry Thurston Peck, *Twenty Years of the Republic* (New York, 1906), p. 452; Barnard, *op. cit.,* p. 346.
27. Charles A. Madison, *Critics and Crusaders* (New York, 1947), p. 348.
28. *Live Questions* (1899), pp. 467-469; Barnard, *op. cit.,* p. 350.
29. *Live Questions* (1899), pp. 585-590; Barnard, *op. cit.,* p. 365.
30. Henry F. Pringle, *Theodore Roosevelt* (New York, 1931), p. 164; Willis J. Abbott, *Carter Henry Harrison, A Memoir* (New York, 1895), pp. 177 ff.; Barnard, *op. cit.,* p. 386.
31. Barnard, *op. cit.,* p. 383.
32. Tom L. Johnson, *My Story* (New York, 1911), p. 109; Barnard, *op. cit.,* p. 393.
33. *Live Questions* (1899), p. 691; Barnard, *op. cit.,* p. 394.
34. *Chicago American,* March 12, 1902; Barnard, *op. cit.,* pp. 434 ff.
35. *The Cost of Something for Nothing* (Chicago, 1904), p. 132.
36. *Chicago Times-Herald,* November 3, 1896; Barnard, *op. cit.,* p. 388.
37. Barnard-Schilling interview; Barnard, *op. cit.,* p. 322.
38. Barnard, *op. cit.,* p. 338.
39. William H. Hinrichsen, "Illinois Giants I Have Known," *Chicago Inter-Ocean,* March 16, 1902; Barnard, *op. cit.,* p. 214.

BIBLIOGRAPHICAL NOTE

Works by Altgeld

Our Penal Machinery and Its Victims (Chicago, 1884; reprinted in *Live Questions,* I, and in 1899 edition).
Live Questions, I (Chicago, 1890); II (Springfield, Illinois, 1894); Volumes I and II together, with supplementary material (Chicago, 1899).
Oratory: Its Requirements and Its Rewards (Chicago, 1901).
The Cost of Something for Nothing (Chicago, 1904).

Works on Altgeld

Barnard, Harry, *Eagle Forgotten: The Life of John Peter Altgeld* (New York, 1938).
Browne, F. F., "Altgeld of Illinois," *National Review* (London), XXVIII, 452.
Browne, Waldo, *Altgeld of Illinois* (New York, 1924).

David, Henry, *The History of the Haymarket Affair* (New York, 1936).
Lindsay, Nicholas Vachel, "The Altgeld Temperament," *The Public* (May 24, 1912).
Masters, Edgar Lee, "John Peter Altgeld," *American Mercury,* IV (February 1929).

Unpublished Material

Altgeld Collection, Illinois State Historical Society, Springfield.
Baugh, Russel Hugh, "The Attitude of John Peter Altgeld Toward Problems of Labor," master's thesis, University of Wisconsin, 1930.
Wish, Harvey, "The Governorship of John P. Altgeld," doctor's thesis, Northwestern University, 1936.

8

Vito Marcantonio: The People's Politician

RICHARD SASULY

A FRIEND ONCE PROPOSED to Vito Marcantonio that he write his autobiography. He demurred. Another friend proposed a biography, and Marcantonio shrugged off that idea too. But when someone suggested a title, "Tribune of the People," Marcantonio stiffened and interjected sharply:

"Naw, call it 'The People's Politician.'"

He was a politician, in all respects. He talked politics, thought politics, and spent a lifetime among politicians. He had a professional's skepticism about amateurs. Yet he stood quite alone among his own kind. This in itself was an exceedingly rare thing in a breed which generally stands in mobs or herds or at least in clumps and clusters. When he died suddenly of a heart attack on a New York City street on August 9, 1954, he had been out of office nearly four years. In the last years of his life, therefore, he suffered great frustration. Nevertheless—and this is the essence of his story and the proof of uniqueness—he refused to change his opinions when they became unprofitable. Apparently he was unable to do so.

145

Marcantonio served seven terms in Congress. For the greater part of those fourteen years he was regarded as the most radical member of the House of Representatives. As such he underwent some ferocious attacks. The press and a multitude of organizations opposed him in his city, New York. In the Congressional elections of 1950, liberals in various parts of the country heard themselves called "Reds" because they had associated with him on some issues. With all this, on August 10, 1954, the day after his death, a series of Marcantonio's former colleagues rose in the House of Representatives to eulogize him. All dissociated themselves from his politics, and all went far beyond the conventions of praise for the dead.

Representative Emanuel Celler, Democrat of New York, praised Marcantonio for his "great courage and determination—a determination as firm as a rock you hold in your hand and a courage as fierce as lightning." [1] Democratic Congressmen Eugene J. McCarthy of Minnesota, Eugene J. Keogh of New York, and John Blatnik of Minnesota all noted that Marcantonio had worked tirelessly for his constituents, that few Congressmen were "his equal as a parliamentarian and floor strategist" and that he was "a man who honored his word." Representative Arthur G. Klein, Democrat of New York, after apologizing to the Speaker of the House for being "somewhat overcome by emotion," said that Marcantonio was his friend and that he loved him although "in complete disagreement with his political views." Finally, one of the extreme right-wingers in the House, Representative Clare Hoffman, Republican of Michigan, said: "He was so far to the left that I could not go along with his views. Perhaps I was too far to the right. However that may be, no Member of the House, so far as I know, ever doubted his sincerity, ever failed to recognize his ability or his effectiveness."

Outside of Congress, some judgments were harsher. Reinhard H. Luthin pulled all the criticisms together in a section on Marcantonio in his book *American Demagogues*.[2] Some of Luthin's critique is simply invidious personal description. Marcantonio's friends might be astonished to read in Luthin that "His face was grave and he seldom smiled. Only occasionally did he joke." However, it must be said that a great deal in Luthin is straight from the record. For example, he points out that Marcantonio came to Congress as a Republican, that he sought many different party designations along the way, and that he made his last race in 1950 as an American Laborite attacked by all other parties. Marcantonio supporters have always made the same observation, regarding this not as a sign of demagoguery but as the way in which a resourceful fighter clung to his principles without caring for party labels. Evidently the same record can yield different readings. In Marcantonio's case, the record is full, unique, and deserves its own reading.

I

Vito Marcantonio was born on December 10, 1902, in the East Harlem section of New York City. Throughout his life he never lived more than a few blocks away from his birthplace. In a speech in the House of Representatives in 1939 he referred to himself as "one who was born in the slums, who was raised in the slums, and who still lives in the slums." [3] For a man active in national affairs and known internationally as well, he traveled amazingly little. He liked to talk about someday visiting the village in Italy where his people came from; he told a fanciful story of how a bronze bell rang in Picerno whenever he won an election. But he never went to Europe or anywhere else outside the continental United States except Puerto Rico. If he ventured out to Chicago, say, for a political convention, he seemed uncomfortable.

Washington and New York were the two cities in which he felt he belonged. In Washington he clung stubbornly to a few paths from Capitol Hill to one or two restaurants, to one or two hotels, and to the homes of a few friends. But he did indeed know his own part of his own city. He knew East Harlem house by house and floor by floor. He knew New York politics in the whole and in the particular, clique by clique and deal by deal. And he knew the Capitol in Washington, and what was going on in it, and understood it as few politicians have.

When he finished grammar school, according to Marcantonio's own story, he and one other neighborhood boy were the only ones in their class to move on to high school. The other boy, he said, dropped out before the end of the first year. It was too far to go across town and their friends laughed at them. East Harlem at that time was one of the slums in which Italian immigrants had settled. It borders on the Negro section of Harlem. Like other Italo-American districts it was accused of being a breeding ground of gangsters. Certainly it was true that crimes were committed in these slums as in all other slums. Perhaps it was the bedrock of Marcantonio's politics that he charged that the principal crimes were committed *against* the people in slums. Certainly it was also true that some of Marcantonio's schoolmates served jail terms. He took them on their own merits, as most of his neighbors did. Throughout his life he remained an important figure in the Italo-American community, and this was an obvious element in his political strength.

Marcantonio did finish at De Witt Clinton High School and went on to the New York University Law School. His talents were quickly recognized. He was chosen to make a speech before a high school assembly which Fiorello La Guardia happened to attend. La Guardia was already a leading politician in the Italo-American community. Before Marcantonio was through with law school he had helped organize support for La Guardia, becoming, in fact, one of La Guardia's chief assistants when the older man was East Harlem's Congressman during the 1920s. In 1930 Marcantonio went into the United States Attorney's office. In 1932 he helped organize the Fusion ticket which won the mayoralty election of 1933 for La Guardia. And the next year, as La Guardia's heir apparent, he was elected to Congress for the first time. He was then just under thirty-two years old.

In the 1936 election Marcantonio suffered defeat by a narrow margin. He won the seat back in 1938 and then held it through five successive elections. In 1950 he lost to a coalition of all the newspapers and practically all the political parties. He did not run in 1952. He was preparing to run again at the time of his death in 1954.

II

Probably the most common single description of the nature of Marcantonio's politics is contained in the newspaper cliché, "fiery left-winger from East Harlem." He certainly came from East Harlem. He was fiery enough, though it is remarkable how unembellished his major speeches are and how plainly facts are made to demonstrate their own logic. And he was, by his own description, a "left-winger" or a radical, but one very much in his own pattern.[4] The pattern needs description.

Marcantonio spoke warmly of Franklin D. Roosevelt in the postwar years, but in the New Deal period he had never been close to the White House. On the basis of program, Marcantonio could now be called an advanced New Dealer. The fact is, however, that he was never an organizational Democrat, and his career demonstrates that organization as well as program shapes politics.

Like La Guardia before him Marcantonio came to Congress as a maverick Republican. Except that the Nebraska prairies are worlds apart from the slums of East Harlem, it would be easy to say that Marcantonio also started in the pattern of George Norris. Marcantonio's one defeat between 1934 and 1950 came in 1936, the year of the New Deal's greatest sweep. When Marcantonio came back in 1938, the American Labor Party had been organized and from that time on he considered himself primarily a Laborite. Until the passage of the Wilson-Pakula Law in 1947 in New York, a device aimed specifically at him, Marcantonio entered Republican and Democratic primaries at will and won them more often than not, thus greatly augmenting his American Labor Party vote. But he designated himself a representative of the ALP. As early as 1939 he began referring to himself as a one-man Congressional delegation.[5]

Without exception, on every domestic issue which came up during his Congressional career, Marcantonio took the most strongly pro-labor or left-wing position in the House. From time to time he had a few allies. None of the Congressmen whose positions most closely paralleled his—John Bernard of Minnesota, Jerry O'Connell of Montana, Hugh DeLacey of Washington, or Leo Isaacson of New York—lasted more than one term. And Marcantonio often made common cause with a few other liberal Democrats. However, he maintained organizational relations at least as closely with Joe Martin and the House Republicans as with Sam Rayburn and the Democratic Congressional leaders. It should be noted here that Marcantonio was extraordinarily effective in Congress in part because his colleagues regarded him as one of them, not as a radical outsider in their midst. They liked him personally, and they respected his skill as a practicing parliamentarian.

If Marcantonio was a socialist he did not say so. He assuredly was no Marxist, and the truth seems to be that he devoted relatively little serious thought to problems which had no political solutions that he could see. That is to say, he practiced politics—people's politics, to paraphrase his own remark—within the orbit of party organization and election to office. He did not think of himself at all as a social theorist or teacher.

All this can be illustrated well enough from Marcantonio's first term in Congress. In a debate in the House on June 29, 1935, he talked about "radicalism" as directly as he ever had occasion to do in later years. He said:

> . . . if it be radicalism to smash, to abolish, and to surgically eradicate these [private utility] companies which have been throttling the life of America and siphoning out the life blood of American consumers, then . . . I am a radical.[6]

Unemployment was the key domestic issue in those years. Remarks made in 1935 or 1936 might well sound incendiary today after ten years in which the moderate Right has dominated American life. Actually what Marcantonio had to say about unemployment in Congressional debate on a relief appropriation on April 30, 1936, clearly reflected a leftist position but was hardly insurrectionary. He said the "unemployed are victims of an unjust economic and social system which has failed."[7] He talked about the possibility of the unemployed "producing for use instead of for profit" and added that "we are bound to come to it sooner or later." In that same debate he clashed sharply with Democratic leader John McCormack of Massachusetts—something he was to do often in later years. McCormack defended what Marcantonio considered an inadequate relief bill by saying it was better than what the Republicans had done. Marcantonio retorted: "Is the gentleman proud of being just a little better than Hoover?"[8]

Thirteen years later, in the 81st Congress beginning in 1949, Marcantonio plagued majority leader McCormack continually. The Democrats had captured nominal control of Congress along with the election of Harry Truman in November 1948. The Democrats won with labor support. Labor's chief stake was repeal of the Taft-Hartley Law. The Administration leaders, however, quickly adjusted themselves to the idea of limited changes in the law and as it happened did not succeed in carrying out even that program. Marcantonio goaded the majority, arguing for outright repeal and then pressing for action of some sort. In the crucial debate, with McCormack lagging, Marcantonio virtually took on the function of floor leader for the pro-labor Congressmen, with the reluctant assent of Speaker Sam Rayburn of Texas. In the House restaurant the next day his colleagues jokingly greeted Marcantonio as the new majority leader.

Similarly Marcantonio pursued the leadership of both parties on the critical issues of civil rights for Negroes. He borrowed a tactic (probably not consciously) from George Norris. Norris, as a Congressman half a century before, had dogged Speaker Joe Cannon with a procedural resolution which would break the dictatorial power of a few majority leaders over House affairs. Norris kept the resolution in his pocket day after day until the one moment came when a parliamentary situation made it possible for him to get the resolution through. In the same way Marcantonio stalked the House leaders with an amendment, applicable to any bills involving federal spending, which would bar segregation in the area affected by the bill. At least once he forced passage of such an amendment, and he kept the issue constantly before the Congress.

Marcantonio early became the chief spokesman in the House for the Puerto Ricans who had begun to settle in his district, and he also argued for Puerto Rico's right to independence. In time, as poverty in Puerto Rico and jobs on the mainland sped the migration, wild charges were made that Marcantonio was himself bringing in Puerto Ricans to win their votes. Actually, his support of the Puerto Ricans cost him some votes among older settlers in his district who resented the intrusion of the poverty-stricken newcomers.

Over a period of sixteen years, therefore, Marcantonio acted as a spokesman for labor and the minorities more clearly and sharply than anyone else in Congress. And yet—in his last years in office, his only labor support came, sometimes reluctantly and almost surreptitiously, from the group of unions expelled from the CIO in 1949. The explanation of this seeming paradox is not very difficult to find, and it tells more about the nature of Marcantonio's politics.

III

Without doubt, manipulation of the Communist issue contributed most to Marcantonio's isolation and defeat after World War II.

It is a matter of record that Marcantonio, from first to last, took an absolute position on the indivisibility of civil liberties. He very early stated that "the defense of the civil liberties of communists is the defense of the civil liberties of all," [9] and he stood on this position without moving from it. After 1950, among other civil liberties cases he handled, he acted as counsel in one of the major cases affecting the Communist Party.

In the House, Marcantonio acted as floor leader in nearly every fight against restrictive legislation. He led the unsuccessful fights against continuation of the House Un-American Activities Committee. And he appeared before the committee as counsel for at least one witness who refused to deny or confirm Communist Party membership.

With all this, Marcantonio was continually accused of being—variously, according to the source of attack—a "Communist dupe," a "Communist-line Congressman," or occasionally an outright "Communist." In reality Marcantonio himself, while defending the right of others to political privacy, made no secrets about himself, publicly or privately. He stated emphatically that he was not a Communist. He told associates repeatedly that, as an officeholder with a specific program, he intended to state this before any Congressional body if asked. In the prewar years, when he became the president of the International Labor Defense, often charged with being a red front, he publicly specified that he was doing so on the basis that the organization was not Communist.

At the same time, aside from his defense of Communists' rights in the abstract, Marcantonio associated with Communists in varying degree. Communists on occasion came to his office; he made it a point that this be done as openly as possible. For a number of years he had cordial relations with some officials of the Communist Party. Among his associates were many leftists of different kinds. It is a fact that, in the last years of his life, particularly from 1952 on, the conflicts between him and the Communist Party became acute and nearly continuous. However, this did not alter his own position; at the time of his death he was still one of the counsel for the Communist Party in the Subversive Activities Control Board case.

Probably Marcantonio could have stood off attack on all the domestic issues, including even his absolute stand on civil liberties. But he went the last step of the way and took on the brunt of attack from all agencies of government, all respectable organizations, and the entire press. He opposed United States foreign policy from the beginning of the cold war.

In 1940 and 1941 he had opposed United States entry into World War II. After the Nazi attack on Soviet Russia on June 22, 1941, he said he thought the nature of the war had changed, and from then on he supported the war. It may be noted that he waited until October 16, 1941, before delivering a major speech in the House in which he announced his turn.[10] Commenting on this delay, Marcantonio's hostile critic Reinhold Luthin said, in his book *American Demagogues:* "For several months [after June 22] Marcantonio held his pacifist position. There were rumors around New York that he would be repudiated by the leftists now that the 'imperialist' war had suddenly become a 'people's' war. But Marc swung into line. . . ."

In a general way, Marcantonio's stand on foreign policy did follow the course taken at this point by the Communist Party. He himself never quibbled about this. He did angrily deny that he had ever argued for any national interest other than American.[11] The only truly debatable point—as in all cases where the attempt is made to prove connection by parallel views—is this: Did Marcantonio stubbornly insist on doing what he personally thought right on each issue, even when this required him to stand alone? Or, did he take directives from some other source, in this case, for better or worse, from Communists? Such questions can never fully be answered, which reflects the curious blight spread by the argument of parallelism. In Marcantonio's case some partial answers do suggest themselves. His colleagues in the House, like his personal friends, had no doubts about his independence. Temperamentally he was as unlikely as a man could be to follow other people's lead. And, on the foreign issues as on the domestic ones, his position had an underlying consistency throughout his seven terms in Congress.

Marcantonio's position on foreign affairs came out clearly in one of his earliest Congressional speeches—on April 24, 1935, in connection with a Navy Department request for money for gunboats. Marcantonio said the gunboats were to carry out "our naval policy to protect China against Communism."[12] Hearings on the bill, he said, "do not indicate how many ships we have in China protecting China from Chinese Communism, and also, incidentally, from rebellions. We are determined that China can no longer have a rebellion of its own. . . . Nobody will say that we need [the gunboats] to protect the Standard Oil interests or other commercial interests. Of course not. They always give us a holier than thou defense."

He concluded the speech by asking that the gunboats be brought home—including at this point a rather cool reference to President Roosevelt and Secretary of State Cordell Hull—and said:

> I am not interested in making China safe from Communism. I am not interested in protecting sellers of religion or sellers of products. I am not interested in those who go to China for huge profits. They take the profits; let them take the risks. I am interested in minding our own business and protecting the American youth by keeping out of war.[13]

He opposed the Korean War; as much as any single issue this cost him his seat in 1950. Yet he refused to modify his position and at the end he was convinced his stand on the war would win him more votes in the future than he had lost.

Toward the end of the Korean War, he picked up and endorsed the Indian peace proposals perhaps as soon as anyone in the country, certainly while the proposals were still being attacked by both belligerents. Though it is of course worse than futile to try to project any man's position into the future, it is at least interesting to note that Marcantonio's last conspicuous act in foreign affairs pointed toward the neutralist bloc.

IV

The nature of Marcantonio's politics was unique among Congressmen in his time. He practiced politics in a unique way too.

A considerable organizing feat placed the Progressive Party on the ballot in most states in 1948. Regulations have been made more stringent since then, and it is difficult to see how any but major parties could place candidates before the voters on a wide scale nationally today. In any case, this rare opportunity in 1948 netted Henry Wallace 2 percent of the vote for President. By 1952, the Progressive Party vote was down among the splinters of Socialist Labor, Socialist Workers, and Vegetarians. It was doing well in the states where it received one-half of one percent of the vote.

Seen against this background, Marcantonio's power to win votes seems all the more amazing. In the 1949 election for mayor of New York—the office he probably wanted more than any other—he ran against William O'Dwyer and Newbold Morris. He was running with little money and no major party support for one of the handful of most important elective posts in the country. He received 356,626 votes, about 14 percent of the total. In 1950, when he ran again for Congress, he had been under continuous fire in New York for years. The shadow of the Korean War fell over the election campaign. Marcantonio could no longer enter Democratic and Republican primaries. The American Labor Party, his sole political vehicle, had been founded by labor, but all the major unions in the city had left it. Redistricting had added some of the richest sections of the city to his home base in East Harlem; in the new areas he had little hope of winning votes. With all this he was beaten, but he won more than 40 percent of the vote cast, in the face of solid Democratic, Republican, and Liberal party opposition.

The facile explanation often heard was: "Marc has his own machine." Curiously, his defeat in 1950 revealed that he had practically no machine at all. His strength lay in a particular kind of intimate relationship with the people of his district which had been maintained over the years and was as much part of the routine of his life as eating.

He rarely missed a vote or an important debate in Washington. But he always rushed back to New York—often several times a week. He maintained offices in two parts of his district. There, throughout the weekends and sometimes on other days, he talked to an unbelievable number of constituents. He sometimes saw literally hundreds in a day— tens of thousands in the course of a Congressional session. He heard complaints, listened to problems, prevented evictions, took care of kids in trouble.

Marcantonio was not a robust man and he suffered from diabetes. Nevertheless he had a seemingly endless capacity to drive himself. No one ever found him too tired to see constituents who needed his help. After 1950, the people kept on coming to his offices. In fact, they continued to come for a year after his death. He could do less for them after he was out of office, but his name still meant something in city bureaus, and the people continued to fill his headquarters waiting to talk to him.

Marcantonio was a completely professional politician. That is to say, he had no illusions. He maintained easy conversational relations with men he knew to be crooks and stumblebums. He knew all the mechanics of getting out and recording a vote. He was unprofessional in only one respect: he did not capitalize on his services to constituents;

he never made service to a constituent contingent on a political service to himself. He did not even use his list of visitors to build up the captains he needed to man a campaign. Until 1948 he controlled a certain amount of patronage as a result of having won Democratic or Republican nominations. After 1948 he lost the patronage, but maintained some relationships with both Democratic and Republican leaders who had in the past received patronage. Beyond this, his lieutenants were mainly personal friends.

When Marcantonio decided to run again in 1954, he no longer had even the American Labor Party as a vehicle. He resigned his state chairmanship of the ALP late in 1953, after nearly two years of continuous conflict within the organization. What difference this would have made in a campaign is of course impossible to say. He thought his chances were good. The coalition against him was less popular. He thought that many more people had now come to his position on the Korean War. Some of the newspapers in the city agreed with his estimate. Even hostile observers were impressed by the sight of some ten thousand people who jammed the streets around his home for his funeral.

However, it remains a fact that at the time of his death he was a politician out of office. And since his political capacity was so unusual, it might be argued that his career demonstrated the futility of independent, radical politics.

Marcantonio himself rejected this argument furiously. The argument consumed much of his time after 1952. The essence of the dispute went back to the 1948 campaign. In the spring of 1948, several developments greatly encouraged organizers of the Progressive Party which included, of course, the American Labor Party in New York. In a special election in a Bronx Congressional district, an American Labor Party candidate, Leo Isaacson, won a three-way race. In California, enough valid signatures had been obtained to put the Progressive Party on the ballot, in the face of a law which it was thought made this virtually impossible. Nationally, it was evident that Henry Wallace would run for President on the Progressive Party ticket, and he drew large crowds wherever he spoke.

Given any opportunity, Marcantonio generally cocked his hat at a jaunty angle, both figuratively and literally. He now talked jokingly of the day when he would be Speaker of the House—that is, when the Progressive Party would be the majority. He pointed out that his delegation had already doubled. At the time, the statement, though made jokingly, struck no one as outrageous. In April 1948, sober professionals in both major parties thought Wallace might get five or even six million votes.

· When Wallace drew only two percent of the vote, some of the Left argued that the Progressive Party campaign should never have taken place. Instead, it was said, the Left should have tried to influence the Democratic Party, essentially from within Democratic organizations. Marcantonio was openly scornful of leftist amateurs who talked about "influencing" a party which despised them, abused them, banned them, and would surely try to hunt them down and cast them out if they entered it. He in turn was accused of being a die-hard who failed to understand the nature of "coalition" politics. He had practiced politics involving coalitions for many years, but since he sought coalitions only where he thought they could be had, his were called "deals." He argued that it was indeed necessary and possible to influence the Democratic Party, but the period from which he drew the most parallels was the decade of the 1850s when the Republican Party was established. He saw a new organization coming out of sections of the Democratic Party, just as the Republican Party took shape in part from remnants of the Whigs. By 1952 he had long since stopped thinking the Progressive Party itself was the vehicle for expansion, but he thought it could still play the role played a century before by, say, the Free Soilers.

The argument ended, for Marcantonio, after the 1953 mayoralty campaign in New York. He resigned from the American Labor Party after that election. During the campaign, he repeatedly charged that some in the American Labor Party did not support their own mayoralty candidate, Clifford T. McAvoy, but tried to throw what influence they had to the Democrat, Robert F. Wagner. He also charged that the Communist newspaper, the *Daily Worker,* had tried to persuade the ALP toward this course. Wagner himself, incidentally, took enough notice of this dispute on the Left to issue a statement, couched as violently as possible, denouncing the Communists and any tender of support by them. The *Daily Worker* denied that such an offer had been made.[14]

Behind the conflicting local issues—and these were many, complex, and angrily fought—were several issues of national scope. The debate, of course, took in more than Marcantonio and his immediate followers and their opponents in the ALP. It included by and large a community of leftists, sometimes vaguely called "progressives," though clearly the term is loose. The community is and was very small by Western European standards, but it approximates what would have been the backbone of a popular front. In terms of ideas it grouped for the most part around such points as these: clear-cut defense of civil liberties, strong support of the civil rights of minorities, support of social welfare legislation, and a free hand in criticizing United States foreign policy, beginning with Greek-Turkish aid and the Marshall Plan. The ideas thinned out and became unclear in two directions: public ownership and foreign policy. Little was said about public ownership though it appeared that most of the people involved favored it. On foreign policy, once past the criticisms of the State Department, further orientation became vague. The dividing line between the so-called progressive community and the New Deal sections of the Democratic Party lay mainly in this area. And the charge was repeatedly made, of course, that if only the right to criticize United States official policy was actually practiced, then, inferentially at least, the other side in the cold war, the Soviet side, was being supported.

It is curious that within this small community both the left and right wings seemed to agree that the 1948 campaign had been a mistake. And the assumption here was that it could not have succeeded and therefore the same energies should have been expended within Democratic organizations. The Marcantonio position held that not only was it right to have launched the Wallace campaign and the Progressive Party, but that coalitions, or deals, with the Democrats could only be had on the basis of some showing of strength. An unstated assumption lay behind this argument too: that the fault in 1948 and after lay not in the launching of a party, but in the kind of party that was organized and the kind of policies it pursued. In the post-mortems, the effect of Harry Truman's veer to the Left for campaign purposes was often cited. So far as can be seen, the possibility of some other kind of progressive party was not explored.

This was the shape of a debate which was interrupted by Marcantonio's death in 1954. For that year, he planned a completely independent campaign. As for the broader issues in the years beyond, the questions hung in air, asked but unanswered—and they still do. His own contribution to an answer lies in his career. He used his energies as intensely as possible within his lifetime. He demonstrated how deep a mark could be made by the force and integrity of a single people's politician, working intimately with the people he represented.

NOTES

1. *Congressional Record,* Vol. 100, No. 154; this statement and the following are on pages 13175-13176.
2. Boston, 1954.
3. Annette T. Rubinstein and associates, editors, *I Vote My Conscience: Debates, Speeches, and Writings of Vito Marcantonio* (New York, 1956), p. 109.
4. *Ibid.,* p. 54.
5. *Ibid.,* p. 106.
6. *Ibid.,* pp. 53-54.
7. *Ibid.,* p. 78.
8. *Ibid.,* p. 77.
9. The statement in the text, which the writer has often heard made by Marcantonio, is elaborated at Rubinstein, *op. cit.,* p. 479.
10. Rubinstein, *op. cit.,* pp. 139-145.
11. *Ibid.,* p. 145.
12. *Ibid.,* pp. 47-48.
13. *Ibid.,* p. 48.
14. *Daily Worker,* October 21, 1953; *New York Times,* October 22, 23, 1953.

IV

For the Brotherhood of Workers

"There—
beyond sorrow's seas,
sunlit lands uncharted.
Beyond hunger,
beyond plague's dark peaks,
marching of millions' imprint!"

Vladimir Mayakovsky, *Left March*

9

The Achievement of Debs

BERT COCHRAN

I

AMERICAN SOCIALISM, David Karsner once wrote, began in Woodstock jail.[1] What he was referring to was Debs's conversion to socialism while serving a six-month prison sentence at Woodstock, Illinois, in 1895 for violating a court injunction issued in the course of the American Railway Union strike against the Pullman Company. Debs had been an important official of the Brotherhood of Railway Firemen and well known in labor affairs. But the Pullman strike gave him national prominence, and when he came out of jail he was a revered figure. In his campaign for the Presidency in 1900, he put socialism on the map.

Eugene V. Debs can unquestionably be considered the spiritual father of the Socialist Party which was formally founded in Indianapolis in 1901, and which stood at the forefront of American radicalism for the next twenty years. There is no question that he was the most popular and effective socialist figure ever to appear in America. No one in his time, or since, has even remotely approached him in his impact on the American people. He struck a spark wherever he went, and was the

163

only American left-wing leader around whom a *personal legend* grew up, in the manner of famed rebels of old. Is he simply to be admired and honored as a colorful personality and America's first great socialist apostle, or is there, beyond that, something in his life and work that can guide those of us who are seeking to recreate American socialism as a mass movement?

Debs has often been compared to Lincoln. John Swinton, a celebrated newspaperman, for a time chief editorial writer of the *New York Times,* heard Debs at Cooper Union in 1894, and was reminded of the speech he had heard in the same hall more than three decades earlier when Abraham Lincoln came out of the West seeking the Presidential nomination. "It seemed to me that both men were imbued with the same spirit. Both seemed to me as men of judgment, reason, earnestness and power. Both seemed to me as men of free, high, genuine and generous manhood. I took to Lincoln in my early life, as I took to Debs a third of a century later." [2]

This comparison was very widely held and disseminated in and out of the socialist movement, and even Debs partially accepted it. The truth is that there was a certain similarity between the two men, but it was of a strictly limited and narrowly circumscribed character. Both were very tall and lanky in appearance. They had the informality, displayed the tolerant manner, and exuded the democratic spirit of Middle Westerners of an earlier day. They were both self-taught, and empirical and practical in their approach. And both possessed to a large degree virtues highly admired by the American people: generosity, courage, and independence. They even resembled each other in a more personal way in their attitude of chivalry and courtliness to the point of prudery toward women, coupled with occasional flashes of coarseness where their male associates or boon companions were concerned. They both had great natural eloquence; but here, as we come to the domain of their intellectual and political equipment and outlook, the comparison abruptly breaks off.

Lincoln had far superior literary gifts, and was the possessor of a beautiful style, but he was by no means an electrifying speaker, and his addresses are primarily pieces of written eloquence. Debs, in his earlier years, was often florid and sentimental in expression, and even at his height sometimes rambled, or got lost in sonorous generalities. But he was one of America's most gifted orators. He lifted audiences out of their personal preoccupations; he communicated his earnestness, his conviction, his humor, his love for his fellow man; he fired men and women with a vision of a new brotherhood that was possible, that was coming. Lincoln became a nationally revered figure only after he had been apotheosized. Debs became a cherished leader while under the barrage of disapprobation in high places and the slanders of a hostile press.

It is unnecessary here to attempt a judgment as to the comparative abilities and greatness of the two men. The one rose to the highest office in the land and directed its affairs in the midst of civil war. The other remained for his whole life a leader of a minority movement. But as public figures the two revealed themselves dissimilar in essentials.

As a politician, Lincoln was shrewd and cagey, a compromiser and a diplomat. As President, he followed a cautious, dilatory policy; he tried to run a revolutionary war with legalistic methods, and was pushed into every one of his far-reaching positions only by overwhelming pressure of events. If Lincoln had been a political leader in a less tempestuous period, he might have emerged as a personality of the Henry Clay variety.

In contrast, Debs's passionate nature made him utterly contemptuous of political trimming, and incapable of practicing it. After serving one term as a Democrat in the Indiana state legislature, he became thoroughly disgusted with the corruption and logrolling of capitalist politics, and resolved never to seek public office again. He could not see labor bettering its conditions by this path. After throwing himself heart and soul into building the Brotherhood of Railway Firemen into a sizable organization, and being instrumental in starting most of the other rail Brotherhoods, he found each craft undercutting the other to the advantage of the railroad companies. As soon as he determined that solidarity could not be achieved under the old craft setups, he unhesitatingly chucked his union career, turned his back on the Brotherhoods, and set out to organize the railroad workers into an industrial union. When the government moved in to smash the victorious ARU strike against Pullman, and Debs realized that simple unionism was not enough to emancipate the workingman, he began to seek for the solution in the same honest and courageous fashion that he had done before. Once convinced that socialism was the answer, he devoted himself to the cause without hesitation or thought of self.

Thus, when we penetrate beneath the surface, the differences between

Lincoln and Debs become striking and palpable. Of course they lived in different times and represented different classes and causes. But Debs in 1860 would have been an abolitionist, whereas Lincoln in 1900 would have been, at the extreme, an Altgeld. In truth, it would be far more accurate to liken Debs to Wendell Phillips, despite the dissimilarities of the two men in personality and background.

II

In the decline suffered by American radicalism in recent years, Debs's writings are all but forgotten, and on the rare occasion when his name is mentioned nowadays it is always to emphasize that he was a kindly, generous, and lovable man. When, in 1948, Debs's writings and speeches were republished, Arthur M. Schlesinger, Jr., was selected to write the introduction, in which he made Debs out to be a kind of pioneer Rooseveltian New Dealer.[3] Max Eastman had previously sentimentalized Debs as a saintly old man.[4] As Lenin once wrote, during their lifetime great revolutionists are persecuted and slandered. After their death, attempts are made to convert them into "harmless icons."[5] Debs has not escaped this fate.

He was not simply a kindly and lovable man, with a gift for speech-making. Had he been only that, or chiefly that, he probably would have mounted the pulpit, and ministered in a minor way to the small, faithful flock of his congregation. But Debs combined an overwhelming sympathy and sense of comradeship for his fellow man with the burning zeal and uncompromising resolve of the indomitable revolutionist. When a minister visited him in his cell while he was serving time in Atlanta prison for his opposition to World War I, Debs told him he didn't believe Christ was meek and lowly at all, but an agitator who went into the temple with lash and knout and whipped the oppressors of the poor. It was for this they nailed his body to the cross, not because he told men to love one another. "That was a harmless doctrine," Debs said. "But when he touched their profits and denounced them to their own people, he was marked for crucifixion."[6]

Debs not only was a revolutionist; he was completely conscious of what was involved when he chose that road. "Hold Your Nerve" was the significant title of an article he wrote for the *Appeal to Reason* in 1907, in which he talked about the revolutionist's way of life. "Ferdinand Lassalle, the brilliant social revolutionist, once said that the war against capitalism was not a rose water affair. . . . It is rather of the storm and tempest order. . . . All kinds of attacks must be expected, and all kinds of wounds will be inflicted. . . . You will be assailed within and without, spat upon by the very ones that you are doing your best to serve, and at certain crucial moments find yourself isolated, absolutely alone as if to compel surrender, but in those moments, if you have the nerve, you become supreme." [7]

When Debs put on his first Presidential campaign in 1900 he was already forty-five years old. For the next eighteen years, until he was sent to jail for his Canton speech, he went up and down the country spreading the socialist message as no man ever had before, spending the better part of his life on the lecture platform, sleeping in day coaches and cheap hotel rooms, hastily gulping down restaurant meals between appointments. Once he hit his stride, he talked to big audiences everywhere. Thousands traveled miles to hear and see the famed agitator. His 1904, 1908, and 1912 Presidential campaigns pushed the socialist challenge onto the public arena with increasing urgency and effectiveness. The 1908 campaign, with its "Red Special," is still talked about by old-timers. Debs spoke for sixty-five consecutive days from six to ten times a day. A week in advance of his scheduled Hippodrome speech in New York City ten thousand tickets had been sold, and the night of his appearance they were being hawked for five dollars apiece in front of the hall. Debs polled almost a million votes in 1912, and many of the newspaper commentators admitted that but for the extraordinary competition of Theodore Roosevelt's "Bull Moose" party the socialist vote might have been doubled.[8]

Eugene Debs preached a militant class-struggle brand of socialism. He was a champion of fighting industrial unionism and, in the initial days of its formation, lent his efforts to building the IWW. As a lecturer and agitator, and for many years as chief editorial writer for the *Appeal to Reason*, he was in the forefront of every important labor battle of that period, whether it was a strike, a free speech contest, an organizing campaign, an election, or the defense of a framed labor organizer.

One illustration will convey the flavor of his language, the hard-hitting policy, and the militancy of the tone employed in those stirring days. After the Ludlow massacre of 1914, when the militia raked the tent colony of miners with machine-gun fire, murdering two women and eleven children, Debs stated in the *International Socialist Review:*

> The time has come for the United Mine Workers and the Western Federation of Miners to levy a special monthly assessment to create a Gunmen Defense Fund. This fund should be sufficient to provide each member with the latest highpower rifle, the same as used by the corporation gunmen. . . . If a thief or thug attacks you or your wife and threatens to take your life, you have a lawful right to defend yourself and your loved ones, even to the extent of slaying the assailant. . . . Rockefeller's gunmen are simply murderers at large, and you have the same right to kill them when they attack you that you might have to kill the burglar who breaks into your home. . . . It remains to be said that we stand for peace, and that we are unalterably opposed to violence and bloodshed if by any possible means, short of absolute degradation and self-abasement, these can be prevented. We believe in law, the law that applies equally to all and is impartially administered, and we prefer reason infinitely to brute force. But when the law fails, and in fact, becomes the bulwark of crime and oppression, then an appeal to force is not only morally justified, but becomes a patriotic duty.[9]

III

Debs was the most influential single leader through the two decades when socialism constituted an important movement, and he was generally accepted as its main spokesman. The Socialist Party was divided into right and left wings from its earliest days, and Debs was always associated with the left. Yet, almost from the time of its formation up to America's entrance into World War I, the Socialist Party began drifting to the right, until it was dominated by a middle-class leadership of lawyers, preachers, editors, and lecturers. Under their influence it was steadily being transformed into a mild-reform, office-seeking type of organization. The Milwaukee "sewer socialists" became the symbol, for many, of what the party stood for. At the 1912 convention, just six months before Debs's greatest campaign triumph, Hillquit and Berger and the other party officials crushed the left wing, and soon afterwards drove its leader, Haywood, and thousands of his followers, out of the party. How explain the anomaly that socialism's leading spokesman had so little influence inside his own party?

Here we come to a peculiar side of Debs's makeup. Some of the very qualities which made him the irresistible personality that he was, conspired to make it impossible for him to assume the burdens of party organization leader. Soon after his conversion to socialism, he got involved in the factionalism and caucus maneuvering which marked the early struggles of the Social Democracy of America (the forerunner of the Socialist Party) and in the subsequent fusion negotiations with the split-off group of the Socialist Labor Party, which finally resulted in the formation of the Socialist Party. Temperamentally, Debs had no stomach for this jockeying and internal squabbling. He felt it was beneath him and would reduce him to petty shysterism. Apparently he made up his mind in those early days to stay out of all these internal conflicts and keep himself free to do his big work. He thereafter went to such extremes that for twenty years he never participated in a party convention, never ran for or held a party position, never attempted to line up members behind his views, and never took part in the left wing's organizational deliberations.

Debs had his own office at Terre Haute, owned his own publishing company (directed by his brother), and pretty much ran his own show. Undoubtedly, he felt that in a party where every state organization had autonomy, and all the important socialist papers and magazines were privately owned and controlled, his speeches, election campaigns, and articles were as important in setting actual socialist policy as any pronouncements made by the National Committee. And up to a point he was probably correct. But this individualistic mode of operating had severe limitations, even in the prewar Socialist Party, as experience was to prove.

The left wing's conflict with the party leadership smoldered for a number of years. By 1909, the revolutionary socialists had got a big shot in the arm with the sensational IWW victory at McKees Rocks, Pennsylvania. Displaying new confidence as a result of the rising swell of progressivism and radicalism in America, they reasserted themselves against the reformists with growing assurance. From 1910 to 1912, the battle between the two factions raged up and down the party. As in previous years, Debs was associated with the left wing in a general sort of way, but he participated in none of its activities, had no organizational relations with its leaders, and limited himself to occasional pronouncements in the party press. But this proved none too happy an arrangement either for Debs or the other left-wingers.

For one thing, the revolutionary socialists were deprived of the considerable support that Debs could have swung behind their faction had he been so disposed. Moreover, by abdicating as a political leader in this matter, he was able to exert little influence in shaping the character of the left wing. And this was a pity, because the revolutionary elements were then sidetracked by syndicalism and by mistaken notions about "direct action." They could have been straightened out by Debs, who had a better feel of the American labor movement, and a superior understanding of the all-round nature of the political struggle for socialism. For Debs was one of the very few prominent Socialists who consistently steered clear of both opportunist and syndicalist misconceptions. But since he kept himself aloof, the struggles between the two factions developed along the lines of reformism versus a revolutionary socialism vitiated by syndicalism.

Debs never bothered to attend the 1912 convention, for which the right wing had sharpened its factional knife to destroy its opponents. But just a short time prior to the convention, he published an article in the *International Socialist Review* entitled "Sound Socialist Tactics." [10] It was a splendid article in many ways, far superior to the thinking of the left-wing leaders. But, in the concrete situation in the party at the time, it was like an announcement that the great Debs was washing his hands of both factions, and in effect therefore made it easier for the right wing, which was the stronger side and the aggressor in 1912, to cut down its rival. The close to a million votes that Debs rolled up that year was no adequate compensation for Haywood's being clubbed out of the party and approximately forty thousand left-wingers dropping out in disgust.

The same criticism can be made of Debs in relation to the new left wing that arose in the war period. Its leader, Charles E. Ruthenberg, begged Debs to come to the emergency St. Louis convention in April 1917, and help in the fight, but Debs flatly turned him down. His explanation was a characteristic one. He said that he had stated his views and now it was up to the delegates to make their own decisions. [11] Debs half rationalized his conduct into a theory of skepticism of "leadership," which he vaguely equated with the middle-class leadership of the Socialist Party, and into a belief that in some unspecified way it was up to the rank and file to save the situation. He said in his Canton speech: "I never had much faith in leaders. I am willing to be charged with

almost anything, rather than to be charged with being a leader. I am
suspicious of leaders, and especially of the intellectual variety. Give
me the rank and file every day in the week." [12] Debs had worked in
organizations all his life, and he knew that they could not be operated
on the basis of pure anarchism. This attitude, however, reveals the
fear of giving any officialdom too much power, lest it be misused—a
fear that was highly prevalent among radicals in prewar America.
This was not just soap-boxing on Debs's part. In 1912 he had written:
"I confess to a prejudice against officialism and a dread of bureaucracy.
I am a thorough believer in the rank and file, and in *ruling* from the
bottom up instead of *being ruled* from the *top down*. The natural
tendency of officials is to become bosses." [13]

In the light of postwar developments, the fears of the prewar militants
cannot be said to have been groundless. But Debs certainly did not
have the solution. His proposal for a rotation of officials—a popular
Wobbly nostrum is too unrealistic to warrant discussion. If the semi-
military organization that the Communist movement developed at a
later date is not the answer, certainly it cannot be said that the mad-
house that was the organizational setup of the prewar Socialist Party
was the answer either.

At any rate, with his instinct for the trends among American
workers, and for the right approach, Debs might have given the new
generation of left-wingers some sense of reality about postwar America, and cured them of many of their romantic revolutionary hallucina-
tions. But his responsibility by this time was at a bare minimum, as
he was now an old and sick man, and he had been in jail while some of
the important party developments were transpiring.

IV

In recent years, Debs has been criticized from a different point of
view. William Z. Foster and others have found fault with the great
agitator for his dual unionism, his opposition to a labor party, and his
underestimation of the Negro question,[14] arguments which Ray Ginger
repeats in his excellent biography of Debs, *The Bending Cross*. With
the exception of the last point, the criticisms are, I think, not well taken.

Left-wingers of various persuasions are pretty much agreed today
that it is ineffective for radicals to walk out of the established unions

in order to set up ideal and pure unions for the workers, that such a policy leads to the self-isolation of the Left and gives capitalist-minded labor leaders an unchallenged control over the unions. The criticism used to be especially applicable to this country, where for many years strong tendencies existed among radicals to form arbitrarily pure socialistic unions without any reference to the actual trends in the labor movement. Two classic examples of such conduct were De Leon's Socialist Trade and Labor Alliance of 1895 and the Communist Party's Trade Union Unity League of 1929.

But this does not mean that a suprahistorical law ordained that all developments had to occur within the AFL and the Railroad Brotherhoods, which during most of Debs's active life were woefully small and weak. The Western Federation of Miners was organized independently of the AFL and was a very effective union. The Amalgamated Clothing Workers developed outside of the AFL and remained independent for many years. As a matter of fact, the CIO, while originating inside the AFL, launched its crusade for industrial unionism as an independent movement, and in opposition to the AFL.

It is more than doubtful that Debs can properly be criticized for having abandoned the Railroad Brotherhoods and launching the American Railway Union in 1893. The organization was not the dream child of some radicals but rather the product of the actual experiences of the railroad workers. It was headed by some of the most prominent rail unionists of that period. And proof of its validity was the fact that in a year's time the ARU had more members than all the Brotherhoods put together. It is true that the railroad corporations, in alliance with the courts and the United States army, managed to destroy the union after the Pullman strike. But that cannot be considered an argument against its formation, any more than the loss of the steel strike of 1919 is an argument against the calling of the strike and the attempt to unionize the industry at that time. The 1919 strike prepared the way for the next and successful attempt.

The founding of the IWW in 1905 by left-wing socialists is a more debatable proposition. But even this is not the clear-cut mistake that Ginger imagines it to be. The AFL had a membership of less than a million and a half in 1905, and was moreover bound by a gentleman's understanding with the National Civic Federation to confine itself to the thin stratum of skilled crafts, thus in effect abandoning the mass of unskilled workers. It is by no means established that an independent industrial union movement might not have prospered at that time. Where Debs, Haywood, and the other left-wingers erred was in their equation of industrial unionism with revolutionary politics, making the IWW into a red revolutionary organization with all the trimmings. The IWW might have had mass appeal as a straightforward movement for modern unionism, but as a cross between a union and a revolutionary party its appeal was decidedly limited. This was the common mistake of all left-wingers of this period, which Debs came partially to realize after a while, especially when the IWW took a turn towards anarcho-syndicalism. He then returned to the position he had promulgated in earlier years. After his break with the IWW, he wrote: "I would encourage industrial independent organization, especially among the millions who have not been organized at all, and I would also encourage the 'boring from within' for all that can be accomplished by the industrial unionists in the craft unions." [15]

The labor party criticism has the appearance of an attempt mistakenly to transplant the conditions and problems of the present to those of Debs's day. From 1901 to World War I, the Socialist Party was the biggest labor political organization on the scene. The isolated attempts of some local unions here and there to form local labor parties represented diversionary movements from the mainstream rather than possibilities of organizing the labor political movement on a broader basis. The question would have presented itself as a practical problem to the SP only if Gompers and his associates had decided to organize a labor party. But the national AFL leaders clung obdurately to the old-line parties. In the circumstances, Debs is to be commended rather than condemned for his political course.

On the Negro question, the Socialist Party is open to strong condemnation. The party sucked up the prejudices of middle-class America and was rife with Jim Crow attitudes. Debs fought these chauvinistic manifestations with his customary vigor, but he believed that it all reduced itself to the labor question. He did not understand the responsibility of socialists to champion the specific fight for Negro equality.[16] This was the one important phase of the struggle he ignored.

V

Of course, Ginger's criticisms, mistaken or otherwise, are predicated on acceptance of Debs as a big political leader. But Debs's right-wing opponents maintained that he was no leader at all. As the party's internal struggles grew fiercer, the officials got the word around that his heart was bigger than his head. Debs was too popular with the rank and file to be openly attacked, but along the grapevine the word was spread that he was just a glorified soap-boxer. When Heywood Broun wrote, "Debs was never the brains of the party," [17] he was voicing the conviction of the official leadership and the general feeling of the Eastern intelligentsia. That Debs was no scholar or original thinker was undeniable. That he had neither the training nor leisure for extensive research or theoretical study was equally true. Without a doubt, there were many on the Rand School staff who had read more books than he, and could deliver more erudite lectures on Marxian economics or philosophy.

But Debs held firm to Marxist *principles* throughout his life as a socialist, which could not be said of the Rand School scholars and theorists. Beyond that, he had a profound knowledge of the American labor movement, and an uncanny instinct for what was right. Despite his individualistic habits and his aloofness from inner-party conflicts, he undoubtedly was the national spokesman of American socialism in its halcyon period. His tactical sense was exceptionally keen, his kinship with the American worker was extraordinarily close and sensitive, and he understood better than anybody else the meaning and content of a broad, all-national, political struggle for the minds and hearts of the American people. He was the first to blaze the trail for industrial unionism. He was the first to raise the standard against the prosecutions of William Haywood, Fred Warren, and the McNamara brothers. He crowned his work with the dramatic demonstration against the war, first in his Canton speech, and again in the courtroom. "Big Bill" Haywood was certainly his equal as a revolutionary fighter. But Haywood let himself get detoured into the stagnant backwaters of anarcho-syndicalism, and thereby lost his opportunity to play the role of a national political leader. Debs saw more clearly, and clung to his position through all the difficulties and vicissitudes of the struggle.

The peculiar type of leadership exercised by Debs resulted from the interaction of a number of factors, other than just his personal idiosyncrasies and limitations. If the latter alone had been involved, Debs might conceivably have formed a bloc with several others who possessed qualities and abilities that he lacked, and in that way have given the party a more rounded and stable leadership. The Socialist Party, however, from its foundation in 1901 up to the final split in 1919, was never a homogeneous party, but a bloc of two basically antipathetic factions pulling in opposite directions. They lived inside one organization, which, moreover, housed dozens of side-factions, groups, grouplets, cliques, and what-not, each with its own special interpretations and notions of socialism, ranging from Christian utopianism to bizarre forms of ultra-leftist purism. The numerous privately owned papers, all pitching their own special creeds, added to the general confusion and disorganization.

The chaotic situation inside the party was a reflection of the immaturity and inexperience of the working class in the country. Through most of the years of its glory, the SP was riding the crest of the wave of populism and progressivism that was sweeping America (halted only by the war, and then broken by the postwar prosperity). But this progressivism was of a nebulous character, and was composed of many diverse currents. Debs was therefore confronted with the problem of how to keep the revolutionary program and maintain contact with the masses who were not yet revolutionary.

These are the circumstances which conditioned Debs's prewar type of leadership and probably reinforced his special personal traits. This mode of operation is certainly no abstract ideal. But it had superb achievements to its credit, and it was not as simple a matter to improve on it as the left-wingers of the 1920s seemed to think. With all of their faults—and they had many—the Debs days are still rightly talked about as the best period of American radicalism.

The movement has passed through many experiences since Debs's time. Many valuable new things have been learned as well as many valuable old things unlearned. This is not the place for a critical examination of Communism, which was the mainstream of American radicalism in the '30s and '40s. It is also vain to recommend Debs's specific traits of personality, which in any case cannot be transmitted or adopted by others at will. And the America of the witch hunt and H-bomb is a considerably changed country from the one Debs knew, and it demands a different kind of organization. But his conception of a broad struggle for socialism, undominated by machine politics, opportunism, or bureaucratism, retains its validity. And it can further be avowed that some of Debs's incomparable virtues which captured the American imagination 'will be sought again in the socialist leaders to come, and that the chords which he struck in the American heart, of human solidarity and the passion for honesty, straightforwardness, and fair play, will have to be struck again if a new emancipatory movement of national proportions is to be called forth.

NOTES

1. *Current History Magazine,* June 1924.
2. John Swinton, "Lincoln, 1860—Debs, 1894," in *Debs: His Life, Writings and Speeches* (Girard, Kansas, 1908), p. 502.
3. *Writings and Speeches of Eugene V. Debs,* with an introduction by Arthur M. Schlesinger, Jr. (New York, 1948).
4. Max Eastman, *Heroes I Have Known* (New York, 1942).
5. N. Lenin, *The State and Revolution* (New York, 1921), p. 7.
6. David Karsner, *Debs, His Authorized Life and Letters* (New York, 1919), p. 10.
7. *Appeal to Reason,* March 23, 1907.
8. "The Socialist Vote in the U. S.," *The Chautauquan,* January 1913.
9. *International Socialist Review,* September 1914, in *Writings and Speeches of Eugene V. Debs,* pp. 383-386.
10. "Sound Socialist Tactics," *International Socialist Review,* February 1912, in *Writings and Speeches of Eugene V. Debs,* pp. 350-357.
11. Ray Ginger, *The Bending Cross* (New Brunswick, New Jersey, 1949), p. 342.
12. Canton speech, June 16, 1918, in *The Debs White Book* (Girard, Kansas, 1919), p. 5.
13. "Sound Socialist Tactics," *op. cit.,* p. 355.
14. William Z. Foster, *The Railroaders' Next Step* (Chicago, 1921); *History of the Communist Party of the United States* (New York, 1952), pp. 97-104.
15. "Sound Socialist Tactics," *op. cit.,* p. 356.
16. Karsner, *op. cit.,* pp. 32-33.
17. Heywood Broun, *It Seems To Me, 1925-1935* (New York, 1935), p. 37.

BIBLIOGRAPHICAL NOTE

Works by Debs

Debs: His Life, Writings and Speeches, with a biography by Stephen M. Reynolds (Girard, Kansas, 1908).
The Debs White Book (Girard, 1919).
Walls and Bars (Chicago, 1927).
Speeches by Eugene V. Debs, with a critical introduction by Alexander Trachtenberg (New York, 1928).
Writings and Speeches of Eugene V. Debs, with an introduction by Arthur M. Schlesinger, Jr. (New York, 1948).

Works on Debs and Related Subjects

Coleman, McCalister, *Eugene V. Debs, A Man Unafraid* (New York, 1930).

Egbert, Donald Drew, and Persons, Stow, editors, *Socialism and American Life,* 2 vols. (Princeton, 1952).

Ginger, Ray, *The Bending Cross* (New Brunswick, New Jersey, 1949).

Karsner, David, *Debs, His Authorized Life and Letters* (New York, 1919).

Karsner, David, *Talks with Debs in Terre Haute* (New York, 1922).

Kipnis, Ira, *The American Socialist Movement 1897-1912* (New York, 1952).

Madison, Charles A., *Critics and Crusaders* (New York, 1948).

Quint, Howard H., *The Forging of American Socialism* (Columbia, South Carolina, 1953).

10

William Haywood and the Syndicalist Faith

CARL E. HEIN

He is the embodiment of the Sorel philosophy, roughened by the American industrial and civic climate, a bundle of primitive instincts, a master of direct statement. He is useless on committee; he is a torch amongst a crowd of uncritical and credulous workmen. I saw him at Copenhagen, amidst the leaders of the working-class movements drawn from the whole world, and there he was dumb and unnoticed; I saw him addressing a crowd in England, and there his crude appeals moved his listeners to wild applause. He made them see things, and their hearts bounded to be up and doing.[1]

THIS UNEMBELLISHED COMMENTARY on Haywood by someone who viewed him in the perspective of international socialism is one that Haywood himself, with qualifications, might have accepted. Like Debs, "Big Bill" always felt closer to the workers than to their formal leaders. He disliked the need for the "pie-cards" of payment for union office, and his faith in an untrammeled industrial democracy led him to deny on occasion that any leadership prevailed in a strike except

179

that supplied by the workers themselves. The workers, not their leaders, would find the way to the new society.

Louis Adamic described Haywood as "the toughest fighter the American labor movement has yet produced":

> . . . Bill Haywood was a he-man, a man of elemental force, with the physical strength of an ox, a big head and a tremendous jaw; hard, direct, immensely resistant, impatient of obstacles, careless, violent, ready and fit to deal blow for blow; a boozer; a son of the Rockies, risen, as he put it himself, "from the bowels of the earth," to grope his way through years of misery and economic injustice to Socialism. . . .[2]

I

William Dudley Haywood was born in Salt Lake City in 1869. His father was of an old American family—"so American that if traced back it would probably run to the Puritan bigots or the cavalier pirates," as Haywood put it disparagingly.[3] His mother, of Scotch-Irish parentage, was born in South Africa. Her family had been attracted by the gold fever of California and migrated to America, but traveled only as far as Salt Lake City. Haywood's father had made his way West from Iowa as a youth and met his future wife in Salt Lake City.

Haywood lost an eye as a boy while carving on a slingshot, and treatments at Salt Lake City could not cure the damage. But this injury at the age of nine did not prevent him from going to work in the same year in a mine at Winnemucca, Nevada. His formal schooling thereafter was haphazard, but he acquired his first knowledge of trade unionism from Pat Reynolds, an Irish fellow worker who had been a member of the Knights of Labor. Reading of the Haymarket riot in the newspapers, the youth talked over its meaning with Reynolds. The social question was already raised in his mind.

Following his mining apprenticeship at Winnemucca, Haywood took on a number of other mining jobs. He married Nevada Jane Minor, and in his twenties he followed the varied careers of cowboy, miner, and homesteader, with residence in Nevada and Utah. His marriage with Nevada Jane was not a happy one. She had been injured as a girl by a throw from a horse. In the early years of their marriage he attended his ill wife carefully, and she bore him two daughters. But he became estranged from her as she gradually immersed herself in Christian Science and became an invalid.

By 1896 Haywood found work in the Blaine mine in Silver City, Idaho, where he joined the aggressive Silver City local of the Western Federation of Miners as a charter member. The next decade saw the WFM engaged in a struggle with the mine operators in clear-cut class war. Haywood assumed prominent leadership in this struggle, a period in American labor history unparalleled in its violence.

II

The Western mining scene around the turn of the century contained some of the strongest manifestations of untamed American individualism. It was a region which still recalled the frontier environment, with sporadic outbreaks of six-gun justice and vigilantism. Farmers and townspeople were not yet numerous enough to soften or obscure the issue between the mine operators and the miners.

The class war in the West derived from the rise of the nonferrous mining industries which mushroomed after the 1870s. Gold, lead, silver, and copper mining towns sprang up all over the mountain states. Conflicts developed initially as a consequence of the raw laissez-faire competition among mine operators to keep costs low. The Coeur d'Alenes struggle had a special significance in that it led directly to the formation of the Western Federation of Miners.

In 1887 the leading employer in the Coeur d'Alenes district of northern Idaho, the Bunker Hill and Sullivan Company, reduced the daily wage of the miners. The miners walked out, and the company restored the former wage. Having won this first skirmish, the men formed the Miners' Union of the Coeur d'Alenes, a federation of the workers in the area. In 1891 the operators countered by forming the Miners' Protective Association, and three months later shut down all the mines in the district. Blaming high freight rates for the shutdown, the association offered to reopen the mines if the miners would accept the original wage reduction. The union refused and the operators brought in strikebreakers. Some four hundred determined miners then forced almost three hundred non-union men to leave the county. The operators, blocked on the local level, turned to the governor.

The governor requested the Secretary of War to send federal troops, and the War Department sent General Carlin to the Coeur d'Alenes. Carlin brought back the deported strikebreakers and proceeded to punish the workers by placing known union men in a bull pen or stockade where they were maltreated and starved. Eighty-five of them were charged with contempt of court. Twelve of the leaders received sentences of four to eight months in the Ada County jail, and union men were fired. The military had established the open shop.

The defeat in the Coeur d'Alenes caught the Western miners up sharply, and they raised a clamor for a unified miners' organization. In May 1893, a convention of forty delegates from the metal-mining camps of Colorado, Montana, Idaho, and South Dakota met at Butte, with the aim of organizing the miners, millmen, smeltermen, and engineers throughout the West.

The Western Federation of Miners, one of the most militant unions in American history, began with a meliorative economic program: prohibition of child labor, payment in money instead of company scrip, a wage compatible with the dangers of employment, and opposition to employment of private guards around the mines. In the next decade, the WFM became transformed into a revolutionary organization as it met the recalcitrant mine operators in head-on struggle. A determined union met equally resolute employers, and the resulting strife attained at times the level of civil war.

In 1901 Haywood was elected secretary-treasurer of the WFM, an office he held for six years; at the same time he joined the newly founded Socialist Party. At the convention of the WFM in 1901, the delegates endorsed socialism and the cooperative commonwealth. In his new job Haywood edited and wrote articles for the *Miners' Magazine,* the journal of the WFM, managed union finances, and spent many after-office hours in organizing the smelter workers in the area around Denver. He found himself at the heart of the looming conflict with the mine operators. The opening gun sounded in the Telluride district of southwestern Colorado.

Early in 1901, the Smuggler-Union coal mine in the Telluride district under its manager Arthur Collins introduced the "fathom system" of mining, tantamount to piecework. The miners in the WFM local saw in this an attempt to destroy the eight-hour day already won by the union. On May 1, 1901, the union struck the mine, and Collins in turn began to import strikebreakers. The Telluride local, under the capable and aggressive leadership of Vincent St. John, later one of the best-known leaders of the Industrial Workers of the World, sent a committee of twenty-five armed union miners to the mine to meet the strikebreakers. Deputy sheriffs supporting the strikebreakers fired on the committee and a striker was killed. The infuriated union miners gathered, some 250 in number, and armed with Winchesters laid siege to the mine buildings. After a fire-fight of two hours, the deputies and strikebreakers were forced to surrender.

The union miners then took possession of the Smuggler-Union and forced the strikebreakers to leave the county that afternoon. The sheriff asked Governor Orman for troops, but Lieutenant Governor David M. Coates, a former union leader, insisted that a commission first be sent to investigate the need for troops. The commission advised against sending troops. The manager of the mine was obliged to grant full recognition to the union and to modify some of the worst features of the fathom system. By the end of 1901, all the mine operators in the Telluride district had come to terms with the union. To cap the violence of the strike, Arthur Collins, the manager of the Smuggler-Union, was murdered by a shotgun blast from an unknown assailant. The local authorities tried to place the blame on St. John and other WFM leaders but the effort failed for want of evidence.

The Telluride episode showed the mine operators that they needed to secure their political front. The neutrality of the state government had permitted the balance of power to slip over to the union. Two years later the operators had mended this fence, and with the state government partisan to their interests they turned their energies to the destruction of unionism in Colorado.

In the spring of 1903, leading businessmen launched the Citizens' Alliance of Denver to unite all classes in resistance to unionism. Other Citizens' Alliances blossomed in the mining towns, and their vigilante activities supplied the authorities with a strong auxiliary. From 1903 to 1905, the war between miners and operators reached its height in Colorado. On the one side, the embattled unions of the WFM; on the other, the Associated Citizens' Alliances, the Colorado Mine Owners' Association, and the state and judicial power centering in the person of Governor Peabody. General Tom McClellan, of the Colorado militia, described the military principle used in the struggle with his celebrated statement: "To Hell with the Constitution . . . we are following the orders of Governor Peabody." [4] The union finally lost any recourse to conventional legal defense.

The issues in the battle were the eight-hour day and the very existence of the WFM in Colorado. The main front was the gold mines of Cripple Creek and Colorado City, with minor fronts at Idaho Springs, Telluride, and the smelters in Pueblo. Deportation of strikers, calling up state militia and federal troops, terrorization of miners in their homes and in jail, the now-familiar bull pens, were common appurtenances to the battle. The entire state was aflame, and the enraged miners on occasion resorted to their Winchesters. It was a classic school for syndicalism.

Haywood was everywhere—setting up union stores to feed the miners and their families, encouraging the district locals, organizing strike strategy. Along with other union officials, he was a marked man to the omnipresent deputy sheriffs. "Big Bill," not one to suffer intimidation, often went armed. Attacked by a group of deputies right in the streets of Cripple Creek, Haywood had to shoot, and he wounded a deputy severely. A decade later, during the hard-fought Lawrence strike in Massachusetts, he remarked that it seemed like a pink tea compared to the raw warfare in Colorado.

Though the WFM in the end was defeated in the strike, the union held together and managed to retain the eight-hour day in some areas. Haywood, from the storm center, could appreciate with bitterness the line-up of the forces of "law and order" with the employers. But he emerged with an unshaken respect for the courage and tenacity of the common miner, who resisted the operators in the face of intimidation, manhandling, deportation, even death. Of the WFM he could say: "The membership was now being tested in the crucibles of Telluride, Denver, Cripple Creek, wherever the strikes were on. The ore was proving to be of high grade."[5]

III

During the bitter conflicts in Colorado, the WFM had received only lukewarm support from the AFL and John Mitchell's United Mine Workers. A widespread feeling developed among the miners of the West that the entire American working class must be organized along industrial lines. The national convention of the WFM in 1904 instructed the executive board of the union to take appropriate steps. Initiated by the WFM, some thirty invitations were sent to union leaders and Socialists, and in January 1905 a secret organizational meeting was held in Chicago. Charles H. Moyer, president of the

WFM, John O'Neill, and William Haywood represented the Western miners. In attendance were Eugene Debs, Mother Jones, William Trautmann, Frank Bohn, Daniel De Leon, Lucy Parsons (widow of the Chicago anarchist), and other leading Socialists. Haywood was elected permanent chairman, and the delegates voted to hold a founding convention.

On June 27, 1905, some two hundred delegates assembled at Brand's Hall in Chicago. Delegates represented the WFM, the dominant group; the Socialist Party; De Leon's Socialist Trade and Labor Alliance; and smaller unions at odds with the AFL or the Railroad Brotherhoods. As chairman, Haywood opened the convention by asserting that it was the "Continental Congress of the working class," and proceeded to score the AFL leadership equally with capitalists:

> The American Federation of Labor, which presumes to be the labor movement of this country, is not a working-class movement. There are organizations that are affiliated . . . with the A.F. of L. which . . . prohibit the initiation of . . . a colored man; that prohibit the conferring of the obligation on foreigners. What we want to establish at this time is a labor organization that will open wide its doors to every man that earns his livelihood either by his brain or his muscle. . . .
>
> When the corporations and the capitalists understand that you are organizing for the express purpose of placing the supervision of industry in the hands of those who do the work, you are going to be subjected to every indignity and cruelty their minds can invent. You are also going to be confronted with the so-called labor leader, the man who will tell you and other workers that the interests of the capitalist and the workingman are identical. I want to say that a man who makes that assertion is a worse foe to the working-class than is D. M. Parry or August Belmont.[6]

Haywood was nominated for the presidency of the new organization, but he declined. Just having been re-elected secretary-treasurer of the WFM, he felt his primary duty lay there.

At the ratification meeting following the convention, Haywood summed up the case for industrial unionism by pointing out that the gains of union labor had been made at the expense of the unskilled and the unorganized:

> I do not care a snap of my finger whether or not the skilled workers join this industrial movement at the present time. When we get the

unorganized and the unskilled laborer into this organization the skilled worker will of necessity come here for his own protection. As strange as it may seem to you, the skilled worker today is exploiting the labor beneath him, the unskilled man, just as much as the capitalist is.[7]

The convention adopted the name "Industrial Workers of the World." The preamble of its constitution emphasized the class struggle and advocated independent political action on the part of the workers.

Even at the first convention factionalism began to manifest itself. Conflict developed between the political Socialists on the one hand, and the unionists, mostly from the West, on the other, who favored direct economic action as the road to socialism. The implicit hostility was tempered somewhat by the trial of Moyer, Haywood, and Pettibone for the murder of Frank Steunenberg, and the IWW closed ranks to support the defense of the accused.

Frank Steunenberg had been elected governor of Idaho on the Populist ticket in 1897 with the support of labor. On the occasion of the great strike in the Coeur d'Alenes district in 1899, Steunenberg had requested the aid of federal troops. President McKinley sent several companies of troops, and miners by the hundreds were imprisoned in bull pens. Steunenberg, who had been a member of a printers' union, evoked the special hatred of the Idaho miners, to whom he became a symbol of betrayal. Following his term of office, he became a sheep rancher.

On December 30, 1905, Steunenberg was killed by a bomb attached to the gate outside his home in Caldwell, Idaho. The next day, Harry Orchard, a member of the WFM, was arrested and confessed to the murder. He made his confession to James MacParland, head of the Pinkerton detective agency in Denver—the same MacParland who had figured in the Molly Maguires case in Pennsylvania in the '70s. Orchard immediately implicated the WFM leadership. On February 12, 1906, charges were filed against William Haywood, Charles Moyer, president of the WFM, and George Pettibone, a Denver merchant and former blacklisted miner, friendly to the WFM. Extradition papers for the trio were secretly signed by Governor Gooding of Idaho, based on Orchard's claim that the three men had been present at Caldwell as accomplices in Steunenberg's murder. Haywood, Moyer, and Pettibone were arrested at night and taken to the penitentiary at Boise with no chance to challenge the extradition.

The three men were indicted for murder; Orchard was indicted on a separate charge. The "kidnapping" of the accused aroused a widespread protest from American labor, and contributions for the defense poured in. Eugene V. Debs, profoundly affected, wrote his famous front-page editorial in *Appeal to Reason:*

> There have been twenty years of revolutionary education, agitation, and organization since the Haymarket tragedy, and if an attempt is made to repeat it, there will be a revolution and I will do all in my power to precipitate it. . . .
>
> If they attempt to murder Moyer, Haywood, and their brothers, a million revolutionists at least will meet them with guns.[8]

Parades were held throughout the country. In Boston some fifty thousand workers streamed through the streets chanting:

> If Moyer and Haywood die, if Moyer and Haywood die,
> Twenty million workingmen will know the reason why.

The defense hired Clarence Darrow, the noted criminal lawyer, as chief counsel, and he was assisted by E. F. Richardson, the attorney of the WFM. The special prosecutor in the case was William E. Borah, recently elected to the Senate by the Idaho legislature, assisted by James Hawley, a former governor and attorney for the WFM in the '90s. Hawley, Haywood ironically noted, had been the defense lawyer for the Coeur d'Alenes strikers in 1899.

Under interrogation, Haywood impressed the court with his sincerity and directness. Witnesses shook Orchard's testimony at crucial points. Darrow exposed Orchard as an unreliable degenerate, and concluded the defense with an eleven-hour peroration in which he attacked the "vultures of Wall Street" and traced the struggle of the WFM for social justice. The jury voted Haywood's acquittal. Moyer's case was dismissed, and Pettibone was freed later.

IV

Haywood's imprisonment of more than a year paralleled the critical beginnings of the IWW. He had kept in close touch with developments while in prison, but he was restive under the routine. "I felt the work of a lifetime was being torn to shreds. The peace and quiet of the jail was dispelled. . . . I was in prison, and every letter, every article that I read bearing upon this disruption increased my restlessness under restraint." [9]

The second IWW convention took place in his absence in Chicago in September 1906. A fight broke out in earnest between the revolutionary radicals and the "conservatives," in which the former were triumphant. Of crucial importance to the IWW was the position of the WFM. In a referendum vote the WFM membership had emphatically rejected paying contributions to the extremist IWW. The West was clearly becoming more conservative. Haywood, in jail, approved the policies of St. John and his radical supporters. By 1908, the WFM had withdrawn, Moyer maintaining that the time was not yet ripe for a drive for industrial unionism. The WFM further declared that it was severing relations with Haywood. Haywood himself never personally withdrew from the WFM; this repudiation depressed him, and for a time he drank heavily.

With the withdrawal of the moderate Sherman faction and the WFM, the final dispute in the IWW shaped around the DeLeonite socialists, who favored fighting capitalism through political education of the workers, and the radical or direct action group, supported by Haywood and St. John. De Leon's sensibilities were particularly shocked by the representatives of the "overall brigade" at the 1908 convention at Chicago. Mostly migratory workers, they had traveled from the Pacific Coast to Chicago in freight cars, holding meetings at towns along the way. Their refrain, "Hallelujah! I'm a Bum," echoed at the convention. The direct action group, supported by the overall brigade, gained the upper hand at the convention and expelled De Leon on the technicality that he was representing a union which was not his own.

With De Leon out, the convention proceeded to eliminate the political clause from the preamble of the constitution and to emphasize industrial unionism. The revised preamble read in part:

> The working class and the employing class have nothing in common. There can be no peace as long as hunger and want are found among millions of working people and the few, who make up the employing class, have all the good things of life. . . .
>
> It is the historic mission of the working class to do away with capitalism. . . . By organizing industrially, we are forming the structure of the new society within the shell of the old.[10]

Haywood nonetheless lent his enthusiastic support to Debs's Presidential campaign of 1908. He joined Debs for part of the way on the famous "Red Special," the chartered train on which Debs toured the country. The Socialist vote of 1908 only approximated that of 1904, but Haywood felt the campaign had great educational value. And now Haywood took up the work of the IWW in earnest. In the coming years, as general secretary-treasurer, Haywood became identified with its rough-and-tumble championing of the humblest groups in American society: the migratory, the Negro, the foreign, and the generally unskilled workers. No AFL unions deserted to the IWW, and the WFM remained aloof. Scorning socialist politicians after De Leon's expulsion, the IWW followed its turbulent and independent career in the East, West, and South.

V

The years with the IWW saw the maturation of Haywood's syndicalism, or "revolutionary industrial unionism," as he and other Wobblies preferred to call it. Haywood pointed out that syndicalism in European practice was based on the coordination of existing craft unions, whereas the IWW favored the organization of workers along industrial lines already extant. The difference, however, doubtless lay more in structure than in spirit. Both the European and American movements showed a predilection for terms like the somewhat vague "direct action," and the "general strike." The IWW also paid lip service at least to "sabotage," but its leaders denied that this implied violence, or that it meant anything more than withholding efficiency on the job in return for poor pay. To avoid misunderstanding, the IWW forbade the use of the term in 1917. But the major emphasis always lay on industrial unionism, through which the new society would readily emerge "from within the shell of the old."

Syndicalism fitted in with Haywood's own proclivity for action. Its doctrines could not be watered down by theorists, they remained clear and pragmatic. The IWW could not be controlled by politicians and could not serve to moderate revolution. It would not come to contractual terms with employers and thus it incurred their fear and hatred. Haywood always strongly opposed formal contracts with employers. He often stated that the WFM had enforced a minimum wage and the eight-hour day without a single written agreement. At Copenhagen in 1910, when informed that one Danish typographical union had a nine-year contract with the employers, Haywood inquired "why the workers didn't sign up for ninety years . . . while they were about it, thus eliminating the class struggle from their span of life!" [11]

Since IWW officials were generally incorruptible and could not be used as a mediating agency between the workers and their employers, they were often subjected to ruthless treatment by the authorities. Distrust of union officialdom prevailed not only among the IWW rank and file, but among their secretaries and organizers as well. Haywood's own faith rested with the workers, and he never discouraged the almost anarchic democracy which prevailed throughout the IWW. His aphorism, "Industrial Unionism is Socialism with its working clothes on," [12] reflected the sentiments of most Wobblies.

During the formative years of the IWW, Haywood served on the national executive committee of the Socialist Party. But he became more and more aware of the drift to opportunism within the party, and was highly critical of the influence of Victor Berger and Morris Hillquit and the prevalence of middle-class leaders. At the national convention in Indianapolis in 1912, Haywood was abruptly expelled from the Socialist Party and thousands of left-wingers followed him out. American socialism and syndicalism had formally parted ways.

The IWW launched its great organizing drive in the West. Here the issue centered around the "free speech" fights. The migratory workers in the lumbering, construction, railroad, and farming industries suffered from malpractices by employment agencies, which often sold jobs that proved nonexistent when the men reported for work. Agencies and foremen on the job frequently ganged up to hire then fire the workers when they reported, in order to split the job fees. Efforts to obtain redress from the local authorities usually proved futile, and the IWW moved in to combat this manifest injustice.

The IWW demanded the right of making street speeches to enlist casual labor. In 1908, it opened a speaking campaign in Spokane with the slogan "Don't Buy Jobs," conducting street meetings near the employment agencies and the workers' lodging houses. This was the only contact the IWW had with the workers, who were under constant surveillance by foremen while on the job. Then the city council of Spokane passed an ordinance forbidding street speaking: the IWW defied it. When one speaker was arrested, another took his place. Roving sympathizers and IWW affiliates helped out. The jails got crowded and the city deputized a hundred extra persons. Taxpayers protested the cost of keeping the prisoners, and the city officials were finally forced to concede IWW demands: the freeing of prisoners and the right to sell IWW literature. The right of free speech was tacitly conceded by the authorities.

In the next few years, free speech fights ensued throughout the West, notably at Missoula, Fresno, Walla Walla, and San Diego. The most vicious fight of all, accompanied by considerable violence, occurred at San Diego in 1912. Public protest persuaded Governor Hiram Johnson to appoint a special investigator to look into the disturbances. The investigator, Colonel Harris Weinstock, included in his report that IWW organizers and sympathizers

> had been arrested by the police . . . and without being charged with a violation of law and many of them without being guilty of a violation of law, had been taken out of the city . . . for a distance of twenty-two miles and there subjected to an inhuman beating by a body of men, part of whom were police officers, part constables, and part private citizens.[13]

Governor Johnson defended the Weinstock report as substantially correct, but vigilante activity continued. And months passed before the IWW held its first undisturbed meeting in San Diego.

The IWW at one time or other appealed to several millions of migratory workers in the Western states. Though its membership fluctuated widely, it maintained itself successfully in the 1910s and refused to succumb. An intimate observer said:

> This tenacity of life comes because the I.W.W. is not only incapable of legal death, but has in fact no formal politico-legal existence. Its treasury is merely the momentary accumulation of strike funds. Its numerous headquarters are the result of the energy of local secretaries. They are not places for executive direction of the union as much as gregarious centers where the lodging house inhabitant or the hobo with his blanket can find light, a stove, and companionship. In the prohibition states of the West, the I.W.W. hall has been the only social substitute for the saloon to these people.[14]

The IWW moved dramatically into the East in the McKees Rocks strike in Pennsylvania. Early in 1909, the Pressed Steel Car Company of McKees Rocks introduced a system of wage payment by which all workers on a car were classified as gangs and their earnings based on the total output of the gang. If the car was not completed, the whole gang went unpaid. This, with other grievances, led to a walk-out in July. In August the IWW offered leadership under William Trautmann, and a local was formed. Haywood spoke at Newcastle and raised money for the workers. Violence reached its height when the state militia was sent in, and eleven lives were lost. The management finally surrendered and conceded the workers' demands all along the line. The militancy of the workers had carried the day, but the IWW had supplied badly needed leadership. It could now view with great hope the possibility of industrial organization in the East.

Around 1900 the unskilled textile workers in the East reflected a multitude of national backgrounds. The AFL approached the unionization of these foreign-born workers timidly, and soon gave up its efforts completely. A strike broke out in Lawrence, Massachusetts, in 1912, when the American Woolen Company began a general reduction of wages on January 1. The unskilled workers, already living on subsistence wages, had no alternative. The strike spread to other mills in New England, and by the middle of January some 25,000 workers were out. They asked the IWW to direct the strike, and Haywood arrived at the end of January and took charge. He spoke at innumerable meetings in Lawrence and surrounding mill towns, raising funds and making constant appeals to the strikers to hold out. To prevent scabbing, an endless picket line was set up around the mills. The mill operators finally capitulated, and a general wage raise was announced throughout New England, which benefited 250,000 workers. The Lawrence strike marked the greatest victory of the IWW. As Haywood put it, however, ". . . it was a sweeping victory for the workers. Hours of labor were reduced, wages were increased from five to twenty per cent. . . . The strike had been a magnificent demonstration of solidarity." [15]

The Lawrence strike represented the high-water mark of the IWW, and fired the hopes of American socialists and industrial unionists. But the victory did not begin a trend. In 1913, large-scale strikes in the silk mills at Paterson, New Jersey, and in the rubber factories at Akron, Ohio, ended in defeat. Haywood took a leading part in both strikes, pushing himself remorselessly, though he was suffering from ulceration of the stomach. He lost eighty pounds during the struggle, and in 1913 took a brief trip to Europe to recover.

The IWW had found it impossible to hold together the multinational unskilled workers in the East. It had failed to build a permanent organization. Following the collapse of the Paterson and Akron strikes, the IWW accelerated its organization in the West. Due to the increasing scarcity of labor, it was able to increase its membership in 1915 and 1916 as Allied war orders poured in. But the involvement of the United States in the war placed the IWW in a uniquely vulnerable position.

VI

The patriotic fervor which swept the country released popular feelings which were easily channeled by employers against the IWW. The IWW took its stand on the war from the formulation of the Lenin socialists at the Zimmerwald conference in Switzerland in 1915, and formally declared its opposition:

> With the European war for conquest and exploitation raging and destroying the lives, class consciousness and unity of the workers, . . . clouding the main issues . . . , we openly declare ourselves the determined opponents of all nationalistic sectionalism, or patriotism, and the militarism preached and supported by our one enemy, the capitalist class. We condemn all wars, and for the prevention of such, we proclaim the anti-militarist propaganda in time of peace, . . . and, in time of war, the General Strike in all industries.[16]

In opposing the war, the IWW was universally portrayed by the press as unpatriotic. Incongruously, it was accused of both pro-Germanism and Bolshevism. Criminal syndicalism laws passed by the states led to the indictment of most of its leaders by the end of 1917, and its treasury was depleted by drains for legal defense.

In September 1917, full-scale raids were carried out by agents of the Department of Justice on IWW headquarters throughout the country. Tons of equipment and records were confiscated. At the end of September Haywood was arrested in Chicago and charged with obstructing the war effort, on an indictment of five counts. With fellow Wobblies, he was placed in the notorious Cook County jail, amid dirt, disease, and general squalor. After six months, he was released on bail in the spring of 1918, his health deteriorated through a diabetic condition.

Haywood's trial with one hundred other Wobblies began on April 1, 1918, in the Northern District of Illinois. The judge was Kenesaw Mountain Landis. George F. Vanderveer, a former IWW counsel, handled the defense. John Reed described the prisoners:

> . . . I doubt if ever in history there has been a sight just like them. One hundred and one *men*—lumberjacks, harvest-hands, miners, editors; one hundred and one who believe that the wealth of the world belongs to him who creates it, and that the workers of the world shall take their own.[17]

Haywood was on the stand for four days. He recounted the experiences of the labor movement in the West and East. He pointed out that the IWW had not expelled members who had joined the army, but he asserted his opposition to the war:

> . . . I don't want the jury and I don't want these defendants to get the idea that I am in favor of war. I am very much opposed to war, and would have the war stopped today if it were in my power to do it. . . . I hope, if it be necessary, that every man that is imbued with the spirit of war will fight long enough to drive the spirit of hate and war out of his breast.[18]

The verdict was no surprise. Haywood received twenty years in Leavenworth and a fine of $30,000. Ninety-seven men received sentences ranging from one to twenty years with fines ranging as high as Haywood's.

From Leavenworth, Haywood was let out on bail for the second time, in the fall of 1919. He returned to the Chicago headquarters to conduct a fund-raising campaign for the defense of other IWW prisoners. Contributions came in generously—from liberals and socialists, from eminent persons in the learned professions, from trade unions. But active solicitation of funds led to difficulty. Haywood commented:

> The government was not content with its bitter persecution for alleged violation of war measures, but everything possible was done to prevent us from raising funds for our defense. Appeals that we sent through the post office or the express companies were confiscated and destroyed. Our speakers were arrested. Meetings were broken up.[19]

Haywood traveled throughout the West, at considerable personal peril, addressing meetings and raising funds. In Omaha, the hall where he was to speak was raided, and a mob picketed his hotel. But in Seattle he addressed large meetings, and he noted with satisfaction the pile-up of war materials and supplies destined for the counter-revolutionary Kolchak forces in Siberia; union longshoremen had refused to load them.

Back in Chicago, with his case on appeal to the United States Supreme Court, Haywood talked of the improbability of a favorable decision. Some of his friends importuned him to leave the country. Haywood had developed strong communist sympathies and was becoming convinced that the workers' hopes lay in Russia. In the spring of 1921 he jumped bail, and with a forged passport secured passage to Europe on the *Oscar II,* the former Ford peace ship. He arrived in Moscow in time for the May Day celebrations of 1921 and received warm greetings from the Russian crowds and from Lenin.

His life in the Soviet Union contrasts with his stormy career in the American labor movement. He was placed in charge of the Kuzbas coal-mining colony in the Donets basin, but shortly thereafter returned to Moscow. After 1923, Haywood resided at the Lux Hotel in Moscow, writing articles for the Soviet press and working on his autobiography. In 1927 he married a Russian office worker. In the spring of 1928 he suffered a stroke in Moscow, and died on May 18. Following his earlier request, his ashes were divided: half were buried in the Kremlin, the other half in Waldheim Cemetery beside the Haymarket victims, whose fate had first prompted his interest in socialism.

Ralph Chaplin fulfilled a request made by Haywood that he visit his wife, Nevada Jane. When Chaplin visited her briefly in Denver before Haywood left for Russia, she said to him: "I thought the world of that man, but nothing meant as much to him as the labor movement. For it he gave up his God, his country, his wife and two children— everything." [20]

The ruggedness of Haywood's character tended to obscure his tender feelings for the poor and the forgotten in a society given to deifying success. He profoundly appreciated the beauty of the American West and the promise of his country, but he measured their value only as they could be shared by all. During most of his mature life he never knew the meaning of the common legal security assured most ordinary citizens. He accepted the terms of conflict willingly and courageously, sustained by his vision of the new society.

NOTES

1. J. Ramsay MacDonald, *Syndicalism: A Critical Examination* (Chicago, N.D.), pp. 36-37.
2. Louis Adamic, *Dynamite: The Story of Class Violence in America* (revised edition, New York, 1934), pp. 135-136.
3. Haywood, *Bill Haywood's Book* (New York, 1929), p. 7.
4. *Ibid.*, p. 140.
5. *Ibid.*, p. 154.
6. *Ibid.*, p. 181.
7. *Ibid.*, p. 187.
8. *Appeal to Reason,* March 10, 1906, quoted in Ray Ginger, *The Bending Cross* (New Brunswick, New Jersey, 1949), p. 247.
9. *Bill Haywood's Book,* p. 205.
10. Quoted in Paul F. Brissenden, *The I.W.W.: A Study of American Syndicalism* (2nd edition, New York, 1920), pp. 251-252.
11. *Bill Haywood's Book,* p. 233.
12. *Ibid.*, p. 158.
13. Quoted in John R. Commons and associates, *History of Labor in the United States,* 4 vols. (New York, 1918-1935), IV, 241.
14. C. H. Parker, *The Casual Laborer* (New York, 1920), pp. 114-115.
15. *Bill Haywood's Book,* p. 253.
16. *Ibid.*, p. 294.
17. Quoted in Ralph Chaplin, *Wobbly: The Rough-and-Tumble Story of an American Radical* (Chicago, 1948), p. 224.
18. *Bill Haywood's Book,* pp. 321-322.
19. *Ibid.*, p. 312.
20. Chaplin, *op. cit.*, p. 289.

BIBLIOGRAPHICAL NOTE

Works by Haywood

Bill Haywood's Book: The Autobiography of William D. Haywood (New York, 1929).
With Frank Bohn: *Industrial Socialism* (Chicago, 1911).

Works on Haywood and the IWW and Related Subjects

Adamic, Louis, *Dynamite: The Story of Class Violence in America* (revised edition, New York, 1934).
Brissenden, Paul Frederick, *The I.W.W.: A Study of American Syndicalism* (2nd edition, New York, 1920).
Brooks, John Graham, *American Syndicalism: The I.W.W.* (New York, 1913).
Chaplin, Ralph, *Wobbly: The Rough-and-Tumble Story of an American Radical* (Chicago, 1948).
Commons, John R., and associates, *History of Labor in the United States,* 4 vols. (New York, 1918-1935).
Dowell, Eldridge F., *A History of Criminal Syndicalism Legislation in the United States* (Baltimore, 1939).
Gambs, John Saké, *The Decline of the I.W.W.* (New York, 1932).
Ginger, Ray, *The Bending Cross: A Biography of Eugene Victor Debs* (New Brunswick, New Jersey, 1949).
Jensen, Vernon H., *Heritage of Conflict: Labor Relations in the Non-Ferrous Metals Industry up to 1930* (Ithaca, 1950).
MacDonald, J. Ramsay, *Syndicalism: A Critical Examination* (Chicago, N.D.).
Parker, C. H., *The Casual Laborer* (New York, 1920).
Saposs, David J., *Left-wing Unionism* (New York, 1926).
Veblen, Thorstein, *Essays in Our Changing Order* (New York, 1934).

11

Daniel De Leon: The Rise of Marxist Politics

DAVID HERRESHOFF

WHILE THE DEBS CENTENNIAL OBSERVANCES in 1955 showed that a wide range of American radicals and liberals count Debs among their progenitors, the marking of the De Leon centennial in 1952 had disclosed, in contrast, that there are no claimants to the De Leonist mantle outside the Socialist Labor Party. American radicals, however, live with the heritage of De Leon almost as much as they do with the heritage of Debs. They are stronger for his insights and weaker because of his faults and blunders. Had De Leon never lived, today's American radicalism would be different than it is—for better and for worse. And tomorrow's radicalism, if it is to be an intellectually serious movement, will be unable to blanket him with condemnation or consign him to memory-hole oblivion; it will need to strike a true balance of his work.

Daniel De Leon was so completely absorbed in politics that it would appear plausible to see him simply as the embodiment of his own version of the Marxian doctrine. But no mortal, of course, can be absolutely the incarnation of an idea, the word made flesh. De Leon's roots were Caribbean, Latin American and, at least in part, Jewish. He was born in 1852 to Salomon and Sara De Leon in the Dutch colony of Curaçao, a semi-arid island forty miles off the coast of Venezuela. At fourteen De Leon was sent to Europe for schooling, first to Germany and afterwards to the Netherlands. When he returned to the New World in 1872 after six years of European study, it was not to the West Indies but to New York City. He was the first Latin American intellectual to make his home in our political metropolis and to dedicate his talents to the cause of American socialism.

In the early years of his life in the United States De Leon maintained an active interest in Latin American political affairs. The first political cause to win his support was Cuban independence. In its behalf he collaborated with a group of Cuban revolutionary exiles who put out a paper in New York. Gradually De Leon's interests shifted from émigré politics to domestic, and from the cause of an oppressed people striving for national independence to the cause of an exploited class struggling for social emancipation. In 1886 he worked in Henry George's mayoralty campaign, and in 1888 he joined the Knights of Labor. A reading of *Looking Backward* drew him into Edward Bellamy's "Nationalist" movement in 1889. Within a year he went over to Marxism.

From 1876 to 1899—years of deepening involvement in politics for De Leon—he was a student and teacher at Columbia University. He took a law degree with honors in 1878 and in 1883 won a prize lectureship in international law which he held for six years, abandoning it when Columbia's administration refused to promote him to a full professorship. For the remainder of his life he was at the disposal of his party. He brought to the socialist movement matchless resources of scholarship and admirable native endowments of intellect and nerve. Although harsh and intemperate in political argument, he never flaunted his learning or patronized his unschooled comrades.

For twenty-four years, from 1890 to 1914, De Leon strove to make the Socialist Labor Party the spokesman of the American working class in fact as well as in name. A vigorous and able man, he molded his party into a propaganda group which has survived the four decades since his death, firmly convinced that it alone represents the interests of the working class and that the solutions to the problems of socialism in America are provided in his writings. The merits of these convictions have long ceased to be a matter of public controversy. Fifty years have elapsed since the SLP first protested that a "conspiracy of silence" prevented its message from reaching the ears of the people. The cause of the SLP today is undoubtedly lost.

De Leon's writings, despite the fate of his organization, continue to deserve the attention of all who care about the history and prospects of American socialism. A definitive study of them has yet to be written, but it is possible here to review briefly De Leon's thought on three problems of continuing interest: the transition from capitalism to socialism, America's role in the international revolution, and the building of an American Marxist party. Such a sampling of De Leon's intellectual legacy can perhaps afford a preliminary gauge of his stature as a socialist thinker and politician.

I

De Leon's view of the socialist revolution is forcefully presented in "The Preamble of the IWW," written in 1905 as an exposition of the principles of the Industrial Workers of the World. The revolutionary party, De Leon argues, cannot accomplish its mission if it permits the capitalists to monopolize the elections. The party must participate in campaigns, but electioneering is not its sole activity. Without the support of militant, class-conscious unions a socialist victory at the polls would quickly transform itself into a defeat. Confronted with a hostile or indifferent union movement, a socialist government—unable to use the machinery of the capitalist state for socialist ends—would find itself helpless in the face of capitalist control of the economy. The capitalists would easily wreck such a socialist government.

The need, then, is for a two-pronged attack on capitalism which will organize the workers into industrial unions while simultaneously striving to win a socialist electoral victory. When the revolutionary party wins its majority, it will immediately vest authority in the unions and dissolve itself and all other existing political institutions. Any other course, in De Leon's view, would be a betrayal of socialism. "The political movement of labor, that, in the event of triumph would prolong its existence a second after triumph, would be a usurpation." [1] De Leon sees no need, at least in the United States, for an interim period of proletarian dictatorship between the working-class political victory and the flowering of the classless, stateless society.

But would not the socialist revolution encounter the violent resistance of the capitalists? Since the United States is the most civilized country in the world and the workers are the bulk of the population, the path of the revolution here, in De Leon's opinion, will most likely be rational and peaceful. The massive organization of the American workers will simply cow the capitalists. To support this contention, De Leon draws contrasting character sketches of the European and American ruling classes:

> Look across at Europe. The feudal spirit still prevails there in an important respect, as a consequence of the continued prevalence there of large chunks of feudal institutions. In Europe, even the capitalist class is feudalized, let alone the surviving feudal heads. . . . there is one vice that the feudal lord is substantially free from. That vice is *cowardice*. Valor is the burden of the songs that rock their cradle; valor is the theme of the nursery tales to which they are raised. . . . Take as a type the semi-crazy, semi-crippled Emperor of Germany. He will fight whatever the odds. In Europe a peaceful solution of the social question is out of all question. But how is the lay of the land here in America? Was it songs of valor that rocked the cradles of our capitalist rulers? . . . Daily experience, confirmed by every investigation that one set of capitalists institutes against another, tells us that they reached their present status of rulers . . . by swindle. . . . Now, then, the swindler is a coward. Like a coward he will play the bully, as we see the capitalist class doing, toward the weak because disorganized workingclass. Before the strong the bully crawls.[2]

De Leon's argument in this passage seems to proceed in part from unfamiliarity with the children's literature of the English-speaking world—a cultural legacy which is neither specifically bourgeois nor demonstrably demoralizing. His argument, moreover, rests on the premise that a parvenu oligarchy will defend its stake in society with less determination than will a "legitimate," long-established ruling class. If De Leon had foreseen the possibility that the American ruling class might acquire a Prussian, militarist spirit, that it might become "feudalized," he might have been less certain that "The complete industrial organization of the workingclass will have assured the peaceful issue of the struggle."[3] It was not De Leon but Jack London who, in *The Iron Heel,* had the dark vision of a long agony of class struggle in America. Complete organization of the workers has not been, and probably never will be, realized in a capitalist society; to suppose otherwise would be to endow them with a capacity for perfect harmony of thought and action. Freed from the dogmatic rigor of its form, however, De Leon's thought about the American transition to socialism has contemporary relevance. He has helped American radicals to understand that the more extensive the unionization of the working class and the better developed its class consciousness, the more probably will its aspirations be attained without the violent opposition of its class antagonists.

II

Describing the United States as the most developed capitalist country, De Leon concluded that "no other country is ripe for the execution of Marxian revolutionary tactics." [4] Gripped by the idea of the imminence of revolution in America, De Leon, like many others, never entertained the possibility that countries like Russia and China might be the first to begin building socialism. Even for economically advanced Germany, the prospect seemed to him dim for the early advent of the socialist revolution. In his outlook on the world, optimism about America balanced pessimism about the Old World.

In 1903 De Leon translated August Bebel's *The Woman Question*. The veteran German Marxist expressed in that book his belief that Germany would most likely "assume the leading role in the pending revolution." [5] Bebel's prediction drew from his translator a lengthy, reproving footnote. In his faulty estimate of the course of revolutions in the twentieth century, De Leon was at one with most Marxists of the time outside Russia:

. . . Germany is almost half a revolutionary cycle behind [the United States]. Her own bourgeois revolution is but half achieved . . . feudal boulders [obstruct] the path of the Socialist Movement in that country.

Still, De Leon recognizes, social development is not always compelled to follow the logical progression from slavery through feudalism to capitalism and, only then, to socialism:

The social phenomenon has been seen of an oppressed class skipping an intermediary stage of vassalage, and entering, at one bound, upon one higher up. . . . Without first stepping off at serfdom, [the American

Negroes] leaped from chattel slavery to wage slavery. What happened once may happen again. But in the instance cited above and all others we can call to mind, it happened through outside intervention. Can Germany perform the same feat alone, unaided?

De Leon's answer is that for Germany "alone possible and practicable, is the completion of the capitalist revolution, first of all." As a matter of fact feudal institutions, he argues, will have to be obliterated throughout Europe before socialist revolutions there can have any chance of success:

> Whatever doubt there can be as to Germany's ripeness, there can be none as to the utter unripeness of all other European countries with the single exceptions of France and Belgium,—and none surely as to Russia, that ominous cloud to the East . . . the masses would be mobilized from the surrounding hives of the Cimmerian Darkness of feudo-capitalism, and they would be marched convergently with as much precision and dispatch upon the venturesome leader. And what is true of Germany on this head is true of any other European country.[6]

This forecast has of course been refuted by history. Countries "half a revolutionary cycle" and more behind the United States have shown themselves ripe for revolution and are currently engaged in the work of socialist reconstruction. Classes oppressed by the heritage of feudalism have shown an ability to combine the anti-feudal revolution with the task of creating a planned economy. In "skipping an intermediary stage" of full-blown capitalism the great revolutions of the twentieth century have not found "outside intervention" a prerequisite of victory. Counter-revolutionary military intervention has not proved to be the decisive factor De Leon feared it would be. The "hives of the Cimmerian Darkness" raised the armies which decided the fate of Spain, Greece, and Guatemala, but similar armies were defeated in Russia, fought to a standstill in Korea, and barely escaped total rout in Indo-China. Most other efforts to halt revolutions through military intervention have been abortive—and Hungary may be no exception.

De Leon's pessimism about the chances of socialist revolutions outside the United States and his optimism about American revolutionary prospects were outgrowths of his belief that the country which is economically the most ripe for socialism is necessarily the country which is politically most ripe for socialist revolution. This error alone was grave enough to have doomed his effort to build an American Marxist party. But it was an error easy to make in the period between 1900 and 1914, when the socialist and labor movements were taking great strides in the major industrial countries.

III

Entering the Socialist Labor Party in 1890, De Leon quickly rose to leadership and became editor of the party's English-language paper, *The People*. By 1894 he established participation in elections as a normal part of the party's activity. A year later he launched the union policy which has been a distinguishing trait of the SLP's political character since then. He had come to believe that socialists will never succeed in reorienting the existing, non-socialist unions. Subsequently he persevered as an advocate of revolutionary unions and an inflexible foe of all socialist efforts to "bore from within" the AFL. De Leon's union policy found its first expression in the creation of the Socialist Trade and Labor Alliance. He hoped that the STLA would supplant the AFL. The new union's first fruit, however, was not the downfall of Gompers but a bitter struggle within the SLP itself between De Leon's supporters and the opponents of head-on collision with the established unions. The struggle culminated in 1899 in the expulsion of the opposition and its leaders, Morris Hillquit and Job Harriman.

De Leon regarded the split with Hillquit and Harriman as a positive accomplishment, a final step in the transformation of the SLP from a weak propaganda circle into an effective party. In the aftermath of the split he reviewed the first decade of his political work with satisfaction:

> Ten years ago, the Socialist Labor Party was a "Party" in name only. It is essential to a political party, first, that it be a pulsation of the national life . . . and secondly, that it be politically active. That which ten years ago called itself the "Socialist Labor Party," lacked both essentials. . . .[7]

This statement indicates that for De Leon the organization's size and the breadth of its influence were not the criteria of its maturity. Putting up a Presidential ticket signified for him that the SLP had become "politically active." The party became "a pulsation of the national life" in his view when it began to address itself primarily to the English-speaking majority of the population. Since the Hillquit-Harriman forces had the support of the German-American socialists around the New York *Volkszeitung,* De Leon could see his victory in the faction fight as an Americanization of the SLP. Admittedly the party in its earlier years had been a remarkably exotic formation. At the beginning of the '90s, Henry Kuhn recalls, only two members of the party's national executive committee spoke English.[8]

Convinced, as he wrote in *The People* on July 23, 1899, that "The SLP has become a Party indeed," De Leon entered the new century full of optimism. A brilliant future awaited the party, he told the delegates to its 1900 convention:

> . . . economic and political development have gone on in a way that clears the field in America as it clears it in no other country under the sun. Not only are the two capitalist parties . . . clear cut, but they have absorbed to themselves all the petty parties that sprang up four years ago and logically belong to them. During this campaign they will absorb all the other bogus parties that may yet spring up like little weeds in a forest of oaks. This development has gone on obedient to the economic development in part, but . . . it has been helped along by the action of the Socialist Labor Party itself. But for the action of the Socialist Labor Party, the political field could not possibly be as clear and as clean as it is today.[9]

It is impossible to say whether De Leon's assumption that by 1899 the SLP had become a fully developed party distorted his view of the American political scene, or whether his misreading of American reality was the major source of his illusions about the situation of the SLP. Cause and effect interpenetrate here. In any event, he imagined that SLP political activity had been an essential part of the historical process which had doomed the Populists to decline and merge with the Democrats, and that the party would beat down any rival radical movements which might arise in the immediate future. The Debs and Harriman organizations, already moving toward unity and the formation of the Socialist Party, he saw as "little weeds" destined to wither in the shade of such oaks as the two capitalist parties and the SLP. In the Presidential election of 1900 the SLP candidates received 33,382 votes, less than half the vote recorded for the Debs-Harriman ticket.

De Leon's beliefs about American development and his conviction that the SLP had become "a Party indeed" had political consequences which insured his organization's isolation from the mainstream of American radicalism. A party which is prepared to lead a revolution, he reasoned, need not occupy itself with the struggle for such lesser objectives as reforms within the framework of the capitalist system. The revolutionists of 1776, he recalled, had not written a minimum program into the Declaration of Independence. Why, then, should the revolutionists of 1900 clutter their program with immediate demands?

In accordance with this reasoning the 1900 convention eliminated from its platform twenty-one planks. The demands which were scrapped included reduction of the hours of labor in proportion to the rise of production, nationalization of mines, transport, and communications under workers' control, protection of federal and municipal workers from discharge for political reasons, conservation of natural resources, freedom of organization, jobs for the unemployed on public works, equal wages for equal work, women's suffrage, and abolition of capital punishment and the convict labor system. De Leon called the list of immediate demands "the navel string that connected the active fighting S.L.P. with the embryo S.L.P. . . . They are nonsense and they are untrue. They imply a state of things that is not to be accomplished." [10]

A concomitant if not a result of the conviction that the party had come of age was the decision to transform the party's weekly newspaper into a daily. On July 1, 1900, the *Daily People* began its fourteen years' existence. "From that time on," writes Henry Kuhn, the party's chief historian, "the life of the Party organization was dominated by the necessity of maintaining a daily paper, a terrible task . . ." [11] Kuhn, implying that the venture may have been premature, sees it as a source of much misfortune for the SLP: "Part of the membership worked like Trojans and almost bled themselves white to give support. . . . Not a few militants broke under the strain and withdrew from the fray. The S.L.P. of those days used up a good deal of human material." [12]

Meanwhile the Socialist Party was experiencing rapid growth. The founding of the IWW in 1905, while temporarily a source of encouragement to the SLP, produced no improvement in the party's situation. De Leon was not oblivious to the fact that American political development was diverging widely from the course he had charted for it in 1900. Events demanded a reconsideration of the prospects of American radicalism, of the future of the SLP, and of its relations with other sections of the left wing. De Leon faced up to the need for reappraisal. And in 1905 he expressed a cautious appreciation of Debs. "What Debs can do, I can't do, and what I can do, Debs can't do." [13]

In a more self-effacing mood he wrote on August 3, 1907, to Bill Haywood congratulating him on his acquittal in the Boise trial:

> The capitalist class . . . has, through your celebrated case, built you up for the work of unifying the movement on solid ground. Those who have been early in the struggle have necessarily drawn upon themselves animosities. However undeserved, these animosities are unavoidable; and what is worse, tend to disqualify such organizations and their spokesmen for the work of . . . unification.[14]

De Leon now saw the political situation in America as analogous to the situation in the critical years before the Civil War: "We are now again in the days when the old Republican party was organized out of the warring free-soil and abolitionist, and up to then wavering elements." [15]

A rigorous use of this analogy would have led De Leon to conclude that the revolutionary party in America had yet to be built and that the SLP was not a party in deed as well as in name. Haywood left De Leon's letter unanswered in part because "De Leon always insisted he was right. He made it impossible for any except his devotees to work with him." Haywood felt that an SLP "dominated by De Leon's prejudices . . . could not lend strength to any movement with which it became associated." [16]

The re-evaluation of the role of the SLP implicit in De Leon's letter to Haywood was never actually carried out. De Leon could not bring himself to abandon hope that the organization he had created would, through a process of organic growth, come into its own. In *As to Politics,* a pamphlet issued in 1907, he came as close as he ever would to relinquishing his faith in the future of the SLP. The pamphlet projects three hypotheses for the development of American socialism:

> How things will shape themselves—whether the clear-headed and upright elements in the Socialist Party will be able to attain control of and cleanse their own party and . . . merge in the S.L.P., or, jointly with it, perfect a new party, under a new name; of whether these clear-headed and upright elements in the S.P. will fail within their own party, be absorbed in the S.L.P. . . . or, as a third hypothesis, whether in

any event the Industrial Workers of the World will prefer to cast its own political reflex, disentangled from all annoying reminiscences of the past conflicts—"all that, forsooth, rests on the knees of the gods." [17]

The knees of the gods were evidently not sturdy enough to support the additional possibility that the SLP enter the Socialist Party for the purpose of helping the left wing win organizational control. If Debs and Haywood, it might be asked, could try to turn the helm of the SP leftward, why not De Leon as well? The question may not have troubled De Leon, but it agitated other SLP members including the party's national secretary, Frank Bohn. Together with James Connolly, Bohn struggled for SLP-SP unity from 1904 to 1908. Bohn, according to an SLP chronicler, Olive M. Johnson, wanted to supplant De Leon as editor of the *Daily People* "so as to be able to turn over the Socialist Labor Party in bulk to the Socialist Party." [18] It was discovered in 1908 that Bohn favored supporting the SP's candidates for state offices in the New York election. To make matters worse, as Kuhn puts it, "he tried to enlist other Party members in his treasonable plotting . . ." Bohn was thrown out of the party for this effort which "only a person utterly ignorant of the spirit of the S.L.P. membership could have conceived." [19] He then joined the SP; and Connolly returned to Ireland and a hero's death in the Easter Rebellion.

A remark by one of De Leon's lieutenants suggests that he never regarded the idea of SLP-SP unity with favor. "When unity was broached in 1904," observes Mrs. Johnson, "it was never a question—except in the minds of Bohn and his cohorts—of unity with the S.P., officialdom, press, and all. The hope was to interest those who were in rebellion against the officialdom and press and turn them toward the S.L.P." [20] At the request of the Second International, it is true, the SLP in 1908 passed a resolution calling for a joint conference with the SP on unity. But a unity resolution by an organization engaged in a war of extermination against proponents of unity in its own ranks could hardly have been taken seriously by the SP. The leadership of the SP did not accept the conference proposal. Mrs. Johnson explains that the SP leaders were as reluctant to face De Leon "as could possibly a fallen angel have been to face the Lord of Hosts." [21]

Speaking at a meeting of the party's national executive committee in 1908, Henry Kuhn expounded a view of unity which was to become the SLP's fixed stand on the matter:

If we of the S.L.P. permit that the further existence of our movement be continually called into question . . . we simply weaken and injure our movement to that extent. We show a lack of faith in the correctness of our position, which showing or which lack—whichever it be—tends to demoralize us and cause discord in our ranks.[22]

Disposal of the unity question virtually completed the SLP's political evolution. After the expulsion of Hillquit and Harriman, the party regime had hardened into monolithic rigidity. With the rise of the IWW, De Leon had thoroughly worked out the party's program. The growth of the SP had challenged the party's faith in its historical mission and had taken a heavy toll of its numerical strength, but De Leon and his faithful followers had defended the SLP from this threat to its life. Questioning voices continued to be heard within the party for the better part of a decade but the answers of the party were seldom in doubt.

De Leon listened to one such voice in 1913. Charles H. Chase, a member of the SLP and onetime business manager of the *Daily People,* boldly wondered why the party had so little to show for its long years of work and whether it was not acquiring a passive, millennialist attitude toward the class struggle. De Leon recognized these questions for what they were—expressions of doubt about the SLP's right to exist. His answer was to state that the party had been struggling for twenty-three years, that it was indestructible, that it was roundly hated by its foes, and that it was still busy:

These are facts, in the teeth of which flies all charge of S.L.P. supineness; and the charge is specifically refuted by the sight that greets the eye of whosoever takes his stand on the floor of the national headquarters of the S.L.P. at the head of the stairs that lead to the composing and printing floor . . . taken up to its utmost capacity with a printing plant . . . throbbing with the activity of issuing four S.L.P. journalistic publications, one of them a daily.

De Leon's argument concluded with an illustration intended to assure the skeptical Chase that the SLP was the antithesis of a sect of recluses:

Not thus did the awaiters for the return of Christ comport themselves. They fled to the seclusion of the desert, and the isolation of the columns of St. Simeon Stylites.[23]

Fortune had dealt severely with De Leon's attempt to build a movement. His Socialist Trade and Labor Alliance had been stillborn. The

IWW, which he had helped to launch, had turned against him. He had waited in vain for reinforcements from the left wing of the Socialist Party. But in the midst of adversity the *Daily People* was his sustaining joy. The daily throb of the party's presses drowned out the voices of the skeptics and belittlers. This circumstance must have irked the malicious deity who appears to have arranged the last months of the veteran socialist's life, for within a year after De Leon wrote his reply to Chase he was to be deprived of this last comfort. The *Daily People* suspended publication on February 22, 1914. "It was no easy operation," writes Mrs. Johnson, "it hurt De Leon as few other things had." [24] In the hospital then during his last illness, De Leon was at least spared from witnessing the demise of his beloved journal. For fourteen years the daily paper had been a symbol of strength, an evidence that the SLP was no mere propaganda group circle but a party indeed. Now the symbol was gone. Four months later, on May 11, 1914, De Leon was dead.

IV

De Leon was a pioneer of American socialism. Like many another pioneer, he struggled manfully with an environment which he could not master because he misunderstood it. But if time and experience have confounded much of his political legacy, it can be said that De Leon was, during his lifetime, America's most important Marxian theorist and scholar. What, then, are his living ideas?

An important thinker is not necessarily the originator of imperishable thoughts, and today's radicals will not go to De Leon in order to memorize his precepts and analyses. (Nor, let us hope, will they offer ritual obeisance to anybody else!) But if radicals read De Leon, they will find germinal ideas which invite development, amendment, and revision. And an American Marxism which neglects De Leon will not be as sturdy and independent as it ought to be. While no renaissance of De Leonism is to be expected, it seems likely that some of his thoughts about the transition to socialism and about the Americanization of Marxism will turn up from time to time—anonymously, perhaps, and in unexpected quarters of the radical movement. Anonymity would be unjust but De Leon himself, I believe, would not object to it. For although he was called a pope,[25] he was not vain: he was too completely in love with his cause, his organization, and his friends to be prone to self-love. He left a personal following which time will disperse but which, in the forty-three years since his death, has never profaned his memory.

The most admirable things about De Leon were not his original theories but his attitudes and concerns. First, he was his own man. Without being parochial, he was an independent American socialist who never kowtowed to Plekhanov, Trotsky, Bebel, Lenin, Kautsky, or any of the other luminaries of the European socialist movement of his time. In his independence of mind De Leon was superior to the bulk of American socialists and Communists of the decades since his death. Second, he had the intelligence to see that if Marxism is to take root in our soil, it has to be related to the American political tradition. It did not occur to De Leon to claim, in the manner of Earl Browder, that he was Lincoln's true heir, nor did he found any Jefferson Schools. He did, however, try to interest his followers in Benjamin Franklin's opinion that the right to private property is not sacred, and he suggested to them that James Madison, in the tenth *Federalist* paper, anticipates the Marxian theory of class struggle.[26] And when he wrote to Bill Haywood about how a mass socialist movement would take shape in this country, it was natural for him to look to the 1850s and the rise of the Republican Party for an instructive parallel.[27]

Third, De Leon was a political man, in the most serious sense of that protean term: he was a man of organization. To many this will not seem to be a virtue. Indeed, it is not always one. Devotion to an organization which has used up its possibilities, for example, is surely difficult to commend. And this is most poignantly true in De Leon's case. For in the end his dedication to his organization tarnished his essential nobility of character. His identifications with the socialist goal, with the working class, and with the SLP fused into one, and he succumbed to that special sin of a party-loyal radical: an inability to see that opponents of his party are not necessarily foes of socialism or agents of the capitalists within the ranks of the working-class movement. De Leon saw the AFL officialdom, for example, as "essentially hired men of the capitalist class,"[28] a designation which distorted reality because it implies that the union leaders could do nothing but betray the interests of the workers. His conviction that the IWW, after its repudiation of his views on political action, degenerated into a collection of bums and *agents provocateurs* was another fruit of an organizational patriotism which went beyond the bounds of reason.[29] At the same time something of De Leon's sense of discipline and party responsibility would seem to be an essential attribute of a successful socialist politician. Possessing this sense, De Leon might have been able to make up for Debs's deficiencies in organizational matters, had the two leaders been able to work together as a team; and Debs, in turn, would have been able to compensate for De Leon's lack of feel for the existing labor movement. "What Debs can do, I can't do, and what I can do, Debs can't do." De Leon's remark has the beauty of a simple truth, simply stated.

As it was, De Leon took his solitary way across the American scene with his strengths largely unused by other men and his weaknesses largely uncompensated for by the strengths of others. Yet he went with an earnestness and singleness of purpose which give dignity to his figure.

NOTES

1. De Leon, *Socialist Reconstruction of Society* (New York, 1930), p. 45.
2. *Ibid.*, pp. 54-55.
3. *Ibid.*
4. *Ibid.*, p. 43.
5. August Bebel, *The Woman Question* (New York, 1903), p. 372.
6. *Ibid.*
7. *The People*, July 23, 1899.
8. Henry Kuhn, editor, *De Leon, The Man and His Work: A Symposium* (New York, 1919), p. 4.
9. *Proceedings of the Tenth National Convention of the Socialist Labor Party* (New York, 1901), p. 300.
10. *Ibid.*, p. 93.
11. Henry Kuhn and Olive M. Johnson, *The Socialist Labor Party During Four Decades* (New York, 1931), p. 46.
12. *Ibid.*, pp. 53-54.
13. Ray Ginger, *The Bending Cross* (New Brunswick, New Jersey, 1949), p. 243.
14. William Haywood, *Bill Haywood's Book* (New York, 1929), p. 221.
15. *Ibid.*
16. *Ibid.*, p. 222.
17. De Leon, *As to Politics* (New York, 1907), p. 110.
18. Kuhn, editor, *op. cit.*, p. 126.

19. *Ibid.*, p. 63.
20. Kuhn and Johnson, *op. cit.*, pp. 83-84.
21. *Ibid.*, p. 85.
22. Kuhn, editor, *op. cit.*, p. 67.
23. De Leon, *Marxian Science and the Colleges* (New York, 1932), p. 13.
24. Kuhn and Johnson, *op. cit.*, p. 86.
25. Arnold Petersen, *Daniel De Leon: Social Architect* (New York, 1953), II, 282.
26. *Proceedings of the Tenth National Convention, op. cit.*, pp. 95-96.
27. Haywood, *op. cit.*, p. 221.
28. *The People,* January 15, 1899.
29. Olive M. Johnson, introduction to *As to Politics* (New York, 1921, 4th edition), pp. ii-iii, and Kuhn and Johnson, *op. cit.*, pp. 78-79, are typical De Leonist characterizations of the post-De Leon IWW.

BIBLIOGRAPHICAL NOTE

Works by De Leon

Socialist Reconstruction of Society (New York, 1905 ?). A lecture delivered July 10, 1905, originally entitled *The Preamble of the IWW*, now readily accessible in two editions: as a separate pamphlet (New York, 1930, with frequent reprintings) and as a chapter in *Socialist Landmarks: Four Addresses* (New York, 1952).

As to Politics (New York, 1907; 4th edition, 1921).

Two Pages From Roman History (New York, 1915). Two lectures delivered April 2 and 16, 1902.

Marxian Science and the Colleges (New York, 1932). A selection of articles which appeared in the *Daily People* between May and October 1913.

Proceedings of the Tenth National Convention of the Socialist Labor Party (New York, 1901). Contains impromptu remarks by De Leon on a variety of topics including the American revolutionary tradition, the Negro, unionism, and immediate demands.

Bebel, August, *The Woman Question* (New York, 1903). Translated and annotated by De Leon, this volume with its notes illustrates De Leon's critical and independent attitude toward a contemporary great name in the roster of European socialism.

NOTE. The above works, in my opinion, convey the essentials of De Leon's thought. An extensive bibliography is in James B. Stalvey, "Daniel De Leon," cited below. The repository for the De Leon papers is the Wisconsin State Historical Society. De Leon's writings have not been collected. The SLP occasionally reissues selections from his immense journalistic production.

Works on De Leon and Related Topics

Foster, William Z., *The History of the Communist Party of the United States* (New York, 1952).

Hillquit, Morris, *Loose-leaves From a Busy Life* (New York, 1932).

Kipnis, Ira, *The American Socialist Movement, 1897-1912* (New York, 1953).

Kuhn, Henry, editor, *De Leon, The Man and His Work: A Symposium* (New York, 1919).

Kuhn, Henry, and Johnson, Olive M., *The Socialist Labor Party During Four Decades* (New York, 1931).

Madison, Charles A., *Critics and Crusaders* (New York, 1947).

Petersen, Arnold, *Daniel De Leon: Social Architect,* 2 vols. (New York, 1941 and 1953).

Quint, Howard, *The Forging of American Socialism* (Columbia, South Carolina, 1953).

Raisky, L. G., *Daniel De Leon: The Struggle Against Opportunism in the American Labor Movement* (New York, 1932).

Stalvey, James B., "Daniel De Leon: A Study of Marxian Orthodoxy in the United States" (unpublished thesis, University of Illinois, 1947).

V

Obstacles to Radicalism

"There are some people who can't act, who go
to pieces under action, who can think straight
only when they have plenty of time and no
noise."

Vincent Sheean, *Personal History*

12

The Renegade: A Study of Defectors

RUSSELL FRASER

I

It seems to me patent that as radicals vary, one from another, so also do renegades, abjurors of the faith. I have tried, then, to tell of the different varieties: the opportunist or cuckoo bird, who knows a good nest when he sees it; the yea-sayer or chameleon, so affable and easy to titillate that he tricks himself out, with neither malice nor compulsion, in whatever dress the present fashion decrees; the overrunner or babbler, a kind of intractable bird dog, who never throws his tongue but where the scent is undoubtedly false, who, with the best will in the world, the stoutest heart, and the reddest cockade, is only to be censured in this, that he doesn't know a hawk from a handsaw, no, not even with a southerly wind. There is, last, the unalloyed, or wholly self-conscious, defector, who figures in this kingdom of the foolish and the damned as Leviathan. But because men are prone, and rightly, to cavil over words, it is requisite first to establish one's terms, to make clear the nature of defection, and the creed a defector forswears.

In 1832, Emerson gave over the ministry, unable to bear any longer the little room it afforded. Certainly, however, no stigma is his for that abrupt and dramatic withdrawal. One does not presume to label him renegade, an ugly word emblematic of treason and flight. But when Walter Lippmann, once a socialist; a protegé of Steffens; a secretary to the Socialist mayor of Schenectady; an unillusioned writer for the *New Republic* when it was young, and unillusioned; when Lippmann bates and dwindles into the supporter of Eisenhower, into the good gray columnist of thrice-weekly lucubrations in the periphrastic style, he is said to have fallen away.[1] When Upton Sinclair, polemicist, novelist of sorts, left-wing politician, valorous enough once to go to jail in San Pedro for reading publicly the Declaration of Independence, when Sinclair begins to redbait and, aesthetically rather worse, to celebrate the puerilities of that latter-day Munchausen, Lanny Budd, then a transformation occurs: not praise but derision attaches to his name.

Why is one man damned for breaking with his past, and another eulogized for it? To answer is to enter on a definition of terms. Radicalism is here affirmed to be, neither a handy surrogate for those disgruntled persons not fed at the breast of their mother, nor pleased in their choice of a father, nor yet an ardent interlude through which young romantics must travel on their way to the "real world" beyond, but rather a way of life humanitarian in the best sense, because it entails the most entire, the most reckless in point of self-interest, indeed the most fanatic, consecration to the common weal. To be a chandler today, a greengrocer tomorrow, and next week a machinist is to follow a course that may be erratic but is not of much import besides. To eschew radicalism for reaction, as did Charles A. Dana, whose progress, begun at Brook Farm, ended in the jingoism of the New York *Sun,* with its plea for the annexation of Cuba and Canada, is to compass a new fall of man. For the radical, like Shelley's Prometheus, is committed "Neither to change, nor falter, nor repent." And whether he is a cleric like Father Edward McGlynn, the New York priest who was excommunicated for political activity on behalf of Henry George, or a fervent anticlerical like Ethan Allen, of Revolutionary fame, he is·in his work essentially a secular figure, devoted to the building of the Kingdom of God upon earth, and not in some intense inane that may or may not lurk beyond it.

Blessed are those who take the sword in their hand to end the power of the Beasts; those who build towers of stone to gain the clouds, who climb the ladder to fight with the angel; for they are the true sons of man.

This, as Arthur Koestler described it in his early novel *The Gladiators,*[2] is the proper business of a radical.

It is fair to say that Emerson, forswearing one church, as his contemporary Frederick William Evans gave witness to another, embarked on no retreat, but that Evans most certainly did. For that same Elder Evans, the best-known Shaker of the nineteenth century, had once with his brother George Henry been a champion of agrarian and educational reform, had founded in 1829 the *Workingman's Advocate,* the most influential of all labor papers in its time, had demanded equal rights for women, and the abolition of slavery both in chattel and in wages, a truly revolutionary position. That he left it after 1831 for religion is to be deplored absolutely.[3] Of course there is arrogance in such an assertion, but the assertion has got to stand. Otherwise it is of no use to speak of advance or retreat. For without any standards, one can speak only of change.

Here is a further assertion: that just as a radical may be said to defect when he abandons his secular faith for a religious, so may he be called a renegade when he puts aside his idealism for what is termed practicality, when he becomes that most fatuous of all journalistic fictions, the hardheaded liberal, the reasonable progressive, who reputedly never carries reason to extremes. Disallow the point, and one is confronted with a curious assortment of heroes. There is Stephen Simpson, a follower of Andrew Jackson, a prophet before Marx in claiming for the laborer all the fruits of his labor. The leading spokesman of the Philadelphia Workingmen's Party, Simpson managed also, by 1831, to swallow as the only specific the American System of Nicholas Biddle and the Bank of the United States. His new faith he propounded, not as an honest conservative, but rather as a friend of the "children of toil" in a volume entitled *The Working Man's Manual.*[4] But then perhaps Simpson was shrewder than his radical fellows, possessed of that clearer vision attributed often to Walter P. Reuther, whose role as president of the CIO was suggestively different from the one he fulfilled when, in May of 1937, he was beaten by hoodlums in the pay of Henry Ford for attempting to organize at River Rouge.

Again, there is the case of Franklin Plummer who, leaving his native New England for Mississippi, was elected to Congress in 1828 by the small farmers of that state. A member of the Workingmen's Party, Plummer delivered, in 1834, an address before the House that is filled with considerable insight. Society, he averred, is composed of two classes, one living by labor, the other by law. But the latter class, parasitic on the first, is itself divided. Those who are out of office wring their hands at the venality of those who are in, until at last the credulous voter, rising up in his wrath, effects a reversal of roles: Tweedledum is installed in place of Tweedledee. And "the never-ending audacity of elected persons," in the phrase of Walt Whitman, goes on in the very same way. Plummer, manifestly, was too keen. He could not be duped, as most Congressmen are who talk in stentorian tones of rugged individualism—and toady to corporate wealth. He could, however, be bought, and so he was, by the bankers of Natchez in 1835.[5] But, it may be said, this early reformer understood the necessity of trimming his sails, if ever he was to make port. So Minnesota's Hubert Humphrey, steering dexterously away from the radicalism of his Democratic-Farmer Labor beginnings, from the party of Floyd Olsen and Elmer Benson, looms up in good time as the foe of all subversive, which is to say, militant, unions; as the scourge of that ubiquitous and most useful of villains, the Communist Party.

For the most part, however, radicals have been disinclined to follow so twisting a course. Rather have they balked, with William Lloyd Garrison, at the reefing of a solitary sail. With Henry Demarest Lloyd they have looked on moderation as a policy of fighting the devil without fire, and have shown a willful antipathy to "moderately cold ice and moderately hot boiling water, moderately pious Christs and moderately honest 'Old Abes.'" Neither Simpson nor Reuther, neither Plummer nor Humphrey, are really of the radical communion, whose members, so long as they remain in good standing, are never turncoats.

II

But if one concedes high merit to the radical position, he may wonder that men defect from it. A popular explanation, if somewhat too facile, would describe and dismiss all apostates with a phrase from Tom Paine: they are the summer soldiers, the sunshine patriots, who shrink, in a crisis, from the service of their country. The counterfeiters, to be sure, we have had with us always; thus the story of Robert

Goodloe Harper, which may be taken as a pattern for the many that follow in its train. A raging democrat when democracy was all the rage, Harper made himself the leading Jacobin of Charleston. Few men were more fulsome in praise of the Revolution in France. His reward was election to Congress. On arriving in Philadelphia, however, he found speedily the mote in his eye: the party of power was the party of Hamilton. Secluded in South Carolina, he had not perceived that it was so. Not a man to be embarrassed by past professions of faith, Harper went over to the Federalists. He lauded the Jay Treaty of 1795, a notorious act of abnegation to England; smiled in '96 on the candidacy of the conservatives, Adams or Pinckney; curried favor with the British and called for war with the French. When in 1798 the Alien and Sedition bills came before Congress, he backed them with all the zeal he could muster. When in 1800 the election of Jefferson threatened, he threw his support in a desperate maneuver to the sinister figure of Burr. In 1816 he was Federalist candidate for Vice-president. Alas, the prize he had earned through long and dutiful service escaped him.[6]

Fortunately for opportunism, its professors have in general been more handsomely rewarded than the unhappy Harper, who changed sides not wisely and rather too well. Consider the acumen of Henry Ward Beecher. When Elijah P. Lovejoy was murdered in Illinois for preaching abolition, Beecher was dumb as any stone. When, however, abolition had become an irresistible force, he in turn became its vociferous champion, defying the slave power from the pulpit of Plymouth Church in Brooklyn, at $10,000 a year.[7] In the generation which preceded the Civil War, John C. Calhoun, the shrewdest if not the best of Southern politicians, posed as the friend of wage workers North and West, attracting in his bid for the Presidential nomination the applause and support of leftists Mike Walsh and Orestes Brownson. With the close of the war, radicals like Thaddeus Stevens and Charles Sumner attempted to effect a Reconstruction that would abolish for all time the domination of landed capital in the South; while "radicals" like Samuel J. Tilden, Democratic monopolist, and Roscoe B. Conkling, Republican spoilsman, captured that program and delivered it up to finance capital in the North.[8] Nor were there Southerners lacking to coerce the New South; indeed, many, like Barkis, were eminently willing: men of the order of Joseph E. Brown, Alfred H. Colquitt, General John Gordon, the Bourbon triumvirs, good radicals all, who embraced Reconstruction, questioned the loyalty of those who decried it, but were in their hearts not a tenth part so radical as Robert A. Toombs, that bitter "reactionary" who fought against them and lost, because he hadn't wit enough to make his peace with the future. And if in time Southern farmers, oppressed beyond endurance, threatened to overturn the new order, their expressions of protest, the Grange, the Alliance, the populist movement, had inevitably to contend with leaders like C. W. Macune who, in 1877, flattered the ears of old-party politicians: "Now to sum up: The Alliance is a strictly white man's non-political, secret business association." [9]

In the 1930s, as trade unionism expanded, curiosities like Homer Martin flourished with it. Baptist preacher, automobile worker, union organizer, and first international president of the UAW, Martin so suited Harry Bennett, Ford's chief of police, as to evoke from that best friend of company unions the title "A sincere and honest champion of labor." Union men, infuriated at such betrayal, successfully impeached their president, in 1939, and chose in his place R. J. Thomas. Only a little crestfallen, Martin organized, in concert wth the AFL, a second union, free of "CIO dictatorship" and "cleansed of Red elements." [10] The parallel here to the subsequent cleansing of the CIO itself, to the defection of James Carey from UE and the setting up of a rival union, to the pulling down by Reuther of the moderate Thomas on charges of Red domination, is striking, if melancholy. The working out of that parallel is a fulfillment, albeit on a much grander scale, of the homely wisdom of Harry Bennett, who remarked, on pocketing the complaisant Homer Martin and so splitting the auto workers in two: "Any time I can't lick them, I'll join them."

In the 1950s the radical-turned-renegade has become excessively familiar. This suggestion respecting the opportunist may, however, be safely ventured: outright conservatism, the vehicle of Hamilton and Hoover, to cite men quite unequal in ability, is dead in the United States and unlikely to be resurrected. The conservative today mouths the slogans of the liberal, in the manner of Mussolini before he achieved full control. Huey Long, that consummate opportunist, was himself clever to see, if rash to affirm, that fascism would be fastened on America not with jackboots and truncheons but rather with the cry of reform. And the chief tyrant of our century, one remembers, was a National Socialist.

III

But men with an eye to the main chance have enlisted in every crusade, as soon as it gave promise of success. There are those, however, whose farewell to reform cannot be resolved in terms of Paine's memorable apothegm. Thus is heard the plaintive query, apropos of Steinbeck and Dos Passos, of Odets and Irwin Shaw, What has happened to our radical writers? In truth, little has happened that might not have been foreseen. A novel like *1919* proclaims on every violent page, in each meaningless incident, in every joyless character, the future course of its creator.

"Men are as the time is," said the cynical Edmund, in *Lear*. The time was just right a generation ago for *Bury the Dead* and *The Fifth Column* and *Waiting for Lefty*. It is good and exhilarating to be radical when the very air that one breathes is instinct with reform. It is good and but natural to write in such a time *The Grapes of Wrath*. But the shoddiness of that novel as a portrait of "the people," its basic lack of integrity, are the best indication that the radicalism of Steinbeck *et hoc genus omne* was only of the surface, after all.

That change which occurs when the fires die down requires no great explication. When, however, one gives ear to the themes of evasion, renunciation, and death that are heard in the land (with a little judicious promoting) he may find them expressive of a graver and more general debility that points at a failure in society itself. Consider in evidence the *hysterica passio* of that quondam reformer, John T. Flynn; the pitiful attempt to diminish the stature of Lincoln that preoccupied Edgar Lee Masters; the jeremiads of Robinson Jeffers, the maunderings of Ezra Pound. For the Pound of *Personae* was a righteous and irreverent breaker of icons who paid his disrespects to a society in which men are coerced by that "Power that compels 'em / To be so much alike that every dog that smells 'em, / Thinks one identity is / Smeared o'er the lot in equal quantities." Usury, which nourishes that society, is especially condemned: "There is no land like England / Where banks rise day by day, / There are no banks like English banks / To make the people pay." [11]

But it is simpler to see behind the practice of usury the figure of Shylock, the International Jew, who with fine impartiality directs the evil juggling of Lombard Street and Wall Street and that of their enemy, the Kremlin; simpler to rail, to give way to a blind and easing hatred, to focus that hatred on a straw man, than soberly, without passion, to arraign the system itself. Thus the strange tangents pursued by so many reformers who, troubled in mind, fail to probe the root of their trouble, but seek to allay it by fixing on some heady illusion that, unlike the morbid fantasies which have taken Ezra Pound, evokes often in those who come after a kind of admiring despair. So William Ellery Channing, for all his hatred of slavery, is content to preach "internal" reform, the gist of which is best expressed in the old labor song: "Work and pray, live on hay, / There'll be pie in the sky when you die." So does L. W. Ryckman immure himself at Brook Farm, while deploring the tendency of extramural workingmen to strike. His fellow utopian, Parke Godwin, devotes years to the panaceas of Fourier and association. Orestes Brownson, freethinker, Jacksonian radical, who would "share in the world's toil, / And, though so task'd, / Keep free from dust and soil!" helps to organize the Workies, and urges on them a policy, not of vulgar political action—the recourse of the plebs— but of pure moral suasion instead. Dana sees the worker's remedy as lying not so much in the coercion of capital by labor as in a cooperative industrial effort, cooperation likened by Thomas E. Watson to that of an earthquake with the city it swallows, or to that of the lion with the lamb: "Result: lamb soon dissolved in the gastric juice of said lion." Horace Greeley, increasingly distraught, wanders up and down the land, now exhorting to battle, now counseling retreat. E. L. Godkin, as editor of *The Nation,* strains at the brazen plundering of Republicans under Grant, swallows the respectable plundering of Democrats under Cleveland, and all the while pleads for good manners. Bryan, the Peerless Leader, declaring war on plutocracy, chases the chimera of free silver. Bellamy, atop Mount Pisgah, proclaims a magical transition to a happier day: the better part of the capitalists, he affirms in *Equality,* must accede to the popular will. Theodore Roosevelt, reform incarnate: muddleheaded, heroic, pre-eminently moral, sets out to bust the trusts (on Rosinante), and so fulfills a role like that of those weavers in England who by smashing their looms would turn back the Industrial Revolution. In the nascent labor movement there spring up, for every Gene Debs who sought to revolutionize the basis of labor, a hundred apostles of things as they are, to whom talk of a state in which workers enjoy first position is not merely nonsense, but parlously close to high treason.

I think labor people ought to stay in the labor movement. Follow Sam Gompers' philosophy. No labor party. Just have enough power so the politician will respect you. A labor party is practically everything for the labor men and nothing for the investor. It'll never work under our capitalist system—and I'm for the system.

Here, through James Caesar Petrillo,[12] speak the "practical" unionists, debunkers of theory, men who may negotiate with courage and skill, but only for a larger slice of the pie. And the end of their effort is this: the appetitive instinct is rooted in the worker as well as in the entrepreneur; the drive for less work brings with it the debasing of work—travail that one abridges or escapes as he can; the worker acquiesces in a dollars-and-cents evaluation of his labor, and hence, logically enough, of himself. How much greater is the worth of Andrew Carnegie than that of the steel puddler he employs!

IV

But false prophets are easily demolished and (after the fact) quite as easily placed. The psychology of those who give way neither from greed nor ambition nor confusion of purpose is not nearly so transparent. The trimmer, the fool, the pusillanimous man, the good-government reformer who would Turn the Rascals Out and whom Steffens lampooned as the "goo-goo," these after all are so many Aunt Sallys: it needs no special skill to unmask them. But a study of defectors from American radicalism that pretends to be more than a beadroll of names has got to grapple at last with the genuine apostates in whom there reside a certain dignity and mystery appropriate to men intelligent enough to choose, moral enough to incur condemnation, and of sufficient stature to make a crash when they fall.

Such a man was Tom Watson of Georgia, whose tale is one to make the angels weep.[13] His boyhood is history in little: of the South beyond the cities that failed to survive the Civil War. The son of a father whom the ultimate victors of that war—the Little Foxes of Lillian Hellman—made landless, a cipher, a pauper, Watson made himself a scourge to punish the grasping Northern bankers and their Southern allies. As legislator, as Congressman, he attacked the convict lease system, which gave to private persons the right to exploit penal labor; the railroads, exempt from taxation in counties whose wealth they partook of; the jute-bagging trust; the Pinkertons, a private army of strike-breaking thugs. These he fought hard—if not always with entire success. The eternal appetite of capital for war he anatomized well. The real enemies he spied out within. "I mean bad laws here at home; I mean class legislation at home; I mean overgrown and insolent corporations here at home; I mean the greed of monopolies here at home." Others were not so discerning; and the Spanish-American War finished the populist movement to which Watson gave much of his life.

The cause of the tenant farmer and the urban worker became his cause. But Republicans and Democrats cared little for either. "There is," he discovered, "a party for Caesar, a party for Pompey, but no party for Rome." Watson hammered out his answer: he would help realize the party for Rome. The Farmers' Alliance was the matrix of that party. But the Southern order and the Northern order were unable to agree. The South—or the "Plug-hats" who spoke for the South—thought it smart politics to work within the Democratic Party. And the Bourbon Democracy made a meal of the Southern Alliance.

Chagrined but instructed, Watson cut his Democratic connection to endorse the new Populist Party. He saw victory at the polls blown up with bribes and violence. He heard the governor of Georgia decry him as one who "ought to be killed." He knew of and had no power to prevent the importation of Negro voters by the wagonload from South Carolina, and the acquiescence of local police in the stuffing of ballot boxes. His seat in Congress was stolen from under him. He was not to hold another office for more than twenty-five years. This was the lesson of 1892.

The campaign of '94 underscored it: for the majority alone of Watson's victorious opponent overtopped the registration of the district. Still the People's Party waxed; the Democrats tried a new tactic. This was fusion. If the Pops in '96 would but pledge themselves to Bryan, Watson might have second place on the ticket. The agreement was concluded. The third party forbore to run an independent slate. And the Democrats nominated Sewall for Vice-president!

The humiliation Watson suffered must have few parallels in American political history. He was forced to witness and abide a great political movement—the party for Rome—go to pieces. The disintegration left its mark: "Deep down in the hearts of men who want no office and hunger for no pie, is settling the conviction that they have been tricked, sold out, betrayed, misled . . ."

In the long years that followed, Watson engrossed that betrayal.

His writings exalted the strong man: Bonaparte became "the great Democratic despot." His lectures revived the Lost Cause. Hickory Hill, his ugly but well-appointed mansion, insisted on the ante-bellum manner. His politics increasingly he rooted in vanity and whim. By 1910 he was back in the Democratic Party.

He, who very early had perceived the class basis of society, denounced others who saw it still. He, whose father had been driven from the land, turned now to champion the landlord. He, who had proclaimed the inutility of reform ("In case of blood poison, shin-plasters for surface abrasions never yet saved the patient"), instructed the socialists, in *Watson's Jeffersonian Magazine,* that only a little reform was needful, after all. Never did a Southern white man pose as a better friend of the Negro, nor more cleverly defend than Tom Watson the considerations—economic and political—which presumably imposed segregation on the South. Never did a man work with greater zeal for white supremacy, nor damn with more frenzy the chief victim of that doctrine, nor hate him more obscenely than this sometime crusader, who vowed in 1912 to defeat Woodrow Wilson as one *"ravenously fond of the negro."*

The Ku Klux Klan, resurgent around 1915, was a giant emblem of his own disordered spirit, and, like that of the Klan, his malice encompassed not only the black man but also the Catholic and Jew. The Pope was a "fat old dago"; the Jew "a lascivious pervert," incarnate in the tragic figure of Leo Frank, wrongfully convicted of the rape of Mary Phagan, and hanged by vigilantes in 1915. Watson's delight in the murder is terrible to contemplate; more terrible, however, is the corruption of feeling that fed his approbation. For Frank was not merely the "libertine Jew," Mary Phagan the violated Gentile. He was the wealthy playboy with the millionaire uncle and the mighty connections; she the working-class martyr, "only a factory girl," with "no glamor of wealth and fashion about her." This was the face which the struggle of poverty and privilege came to wear at last for Tom Watson.

V

How does one rationalize the decline of this man, and that of other radicals, themselves able and courageous, for whom he may stand? The explanation, I think, lies in this: that American critics and crusaders, with few exceptions, have been bred up and believed in that tradition of Jeffersonian liberalism which, deriving from the Enlightenment of the eighteenth century, and taking new color from the American experiment—something new beneath the sun—gave a philosophy to the early republic, a philosophy which, however vitiated by the record of the last hundred years, survives intact in the popular imagination to the present moment of history.

Crèvecoeur, the eighteenth-century Frenchman turned enthusiastic American, was a herald of the new day, the first day, in some respects, of Creation. Of his adopted country, he wrote:

> Here are no aristocratical families, no courts, no kings, no bishops, no ecclesiastical dominion, no invisible power giving to a few a very visible one; no great manufacturers employing thousands, no great refinements of luxury.

"We are," he concluded—and his legion of followers and fellow believers have ever amended: "Or could be, if only this nostrum were tried"—"we are the most perfect society now existing in the world." [14]

Here is a creed of incorrigible optimism. He who accepts it is wonderfully sustained. He who, accepting it once, discovers that it is tenable no longer, is very apt to be destroyed, to fall victim to that despair which infected the young Theodore Dreiser: "I cannot find any meaning in what I have seen—I go through life in dismay and horror."

The American writer of a century ago was not wont to despond. Indeed his faith was so pronounced as to be almost risible. So Whittier could write, of "The Poor Voter on Election Day": "My palace is the people's hall, / The ballot-box my throne!" The buoyancy of Emerson—"Let us advance and advance on chaos and the dark"—was matched and exceeded by the exaltation of Whitman, who saw his country as "the scheme's culmination." That Americans could be so utterly sanguine—"eupeptic" seems at times the better word—is traceable to the fact that America was affirmed to be unique, the working out of a plan "enclosed in Time and Space," a plan at once deific and singular. "The measur'd faiths of other lands, the grandeurs of the past," and by inference the ills those lands and that past have been heir to, "Are not for thee," insisted Whitman. [15]

A corollary of that faith is a faith in ineluctable progress, orderly (if rather mystical), democratic, but at any rate sure. The onward and upward evolutionary spiral of Darwin's American disciples [16]—John Fiske, E. L. Youmans, Asa Gray—informs the sociology of William Graham Sumner: Every day in every way I am getting better and better. Accept the myth of American uniqueness, and the view of a progress divinely appointed; agree, when that progress seems to falter, on the viability of patchwork reform, the philosophy of the new broom that sweeps clean, the reliance on "spinning-wheel and ox-team remedies" in a dynamo age; and one is spared the heinous task of applying those draconian measures, that root and branch reconstruction that are the only remedy for a system diseased in its parts. Thus accepting, thus agreeing, the American radical has tended to deprecate theory, which interprets the present in terms of the past and offers a key to the future. He has deprecated theory: arid, bookish, materialistic (thus becoming himself a mere particle in flux, the sport of those materialistic forces which theory sets out to define), and has embraced in its stead a workaday pragmatism, signalized in the slogan: More, Here, Now.

If this judgment is valid, a figure like De Leon, disbelieving utterly in the possibility of working within the system and so rejuvenating it, is seen to be an aberration. The more typical American radical is the abolitionist Garrison, who set himself a goal, achieved it, and fell silent, presumably satisfied; or the reformer Frederick Howe, who put his faith in the efficacy of Wilson's New Freedom; or the suffragist Lucretia Mott, for whom the world turned on women's rights; or even the Populist L. L. Polk, who thought to amend society by creating a third political party.

These are dissimilar figures. They have in common, however, a belief in the restorative power of reform, the belief that tomorrow will see a better day, if this canker or that is excised. And for all that Garrison was hated and very nearly lynched, and the others reviled and harassed, they partake nonetheless of that essential respectability which is the hallmark of American reform. Thus the partisans of Jefferson were not so much the enemies as the protectors of property, which the business community, under the leadership of Hamilton, would plunder and take to itself. The nineteenth-century reformers who fought the consolidation of the great corporations were not so much socialists as apostles of a real laissez faire, whose end was not the end of competition, but a restoration of competition. The agrarians who rallied round Bryan in '96 did not so much reject the capitalist system as they did the grosser spokesmen of that system, gathered then as now in the Republican Party. Tom Watson, in hortatory prose, caught well if un-selfconsciously the aspirations of the agrarian revolt: "Close no entrance to the poorest, the weakest, the humblest. Say to ambition everywhere, 'the field is clear, the contest fair; come, and win your share if you can!'"

Nor were the friends of the New Deal friends at heart of real radicalism. For the philosophy of FDR, enunciated by him in a homely analogy that begs the question it purports to resolve, was that of the liberal capitalist who, scorning alike the conservative 'program—to leave the tree of state quite untouched—and that of the radical—to chop down the tree once for all—determined rather to cut away whatever tissue was infected, to prune, but not to supplant. But the philosophy of liberal capitalism rests on the assumption that the husbandman, who is the people, can prune without let, where pruning is indicated; that the offending member will acquiesce in its own lopping off; that, in short, the diverse parts which constitute society and are properly subordinated to the whole can be maintained in a constant equilibrium, one countervailing the power of the other, none achieving a central importance.

And what if the equilibrium is broken? Is there not a tendency in any struggle for tension to be dissipated, for power to go to one pole? What if the struggle is resolved in favor of the business community? The Jeffersonians, it has been said, were defenders of personal property. But before the era of great corporate wealth, indeed as if in anticipation of it, the courts decided that a corporation was just as much a person as the meanest citizen whose independence it menaced. What this meant was that radicals, unless they were to join with the party of privilege, could champion property no longer. They had now to champion the poor, the dispossessed of the cities whom Jefferson had feared most of all. Thus the first battle.

The corporation had received the imprimatur of the courts. Might it not be rescinded? But those who fought in that faith were best described by Jack London: they were the "Machine Breakers."[17] Not understanding history they sought to repeal it. They failed, and the bitterness of many was intense. The agrarians failed, also. Creating

the People's Party, they made of it a powerful instrument for change—
and allowed William Jennings Bryan to absorb and kill it dead. They
won the reward of those practical voters who declined to vote for
Debs, for LaFollette, for Wallace: the right the people have at each
election, in the words of Henry Demarest Lloyd, "to be crucified between two thieves—who are not crucified."

Even the supporters of a liberal capitalist system only more en-
lightened, less rigid, a shade quicker to intervene in times of depression
than government had been in the past, even such cautious tinkers as
these drove a number of radicals to strip off their coats, in the manner
of Joseph, and flee. Now it used to be true that interference by government, agent of a privileged and anachronistic class, stoppered as it
could each attempt at a truly national progress. That is why Thoreau,
in 1849, beginning his essay of *Civil Disobedience,* heartily accepts the
motto, "That government is best which governs least"; amends it,
indeed, to "That government is best which governs not at all." But
times change, as attitudes also should change. Hiram Johnson of
California was not alive to that fact. His achievements, be it said, were
notable and many: as exposer of graft and corruption in San Francisco
a half-century ago; as governor of his state; as a founder in 1912 of the
Progressive Party, and that party's nominee for high office; as a Senator
who dared the perfervid patriots of 1918 by denouncing the Sedition
Act, that last flower of Wilson's New Freedom. Yet Johnson is remembered as an old, embittered relic, standing for policies quite hope-
lessly archaic even as early as 1917, when his thirty-year tenure in
Washington began. He lacked the keen perception of Lester Ward
who, in *Glimpses of the Cosmos,* saw and stated this crucial distinc-
tion: "Government under a real autocrat is the interference by one man
with the affairs of millions. Government by popularly chosen representatives is the management by society of its own affairs." As it is
wisdom to challenge the one, so is it folly to challenge the other.
Failing to share Ward's perception, Hiram Johnson, and those who
marched with him to the top of the hill, only to march down again,
ended as diminutive figures, gesticulating angrily, a goodly distance
back, shouting the slogans of Thoreau and Emerson, of Godwin and
Mill, unamended.

With respect to the New Deal, stigmatized now as twenty years of
treason, the best gloss on its demise and interment is the political

demise of Henry Wallace, perhaps the ablest Secretary of Agriculture the United States has ever had, and certainly the outstanding American progressive in the years immediately following the death of Franklin Roosevelt. For Wallace, a man once uncommonly sanguine, traveled toward the New Jerusalem along the old roads that lead nowhere at last and, mistaking his way, mistook the object of his search for a chimera.

Out of that mistake, and the bafflement consequent on it, has come titanic rage. Tom Watson is only its most poignant, and fearsome, manifestation. One thinks of another man, great also in his way who, raised in the same native American tradition, in the same Middle West, as Gene Debs, was devoted from his youth to Tom Paine, to Bob Ingersoll, and Bryan; who proclaimed himself a foe of professional religion, and of the irreligion that is Wall Street; whose oracles were "Coin" Harvey and Sockless Jerry Simpson; whose roots were in the Farmers' Alliance, the Populist Party; who might have marched with Coxey's Army.

This was Henry Ford. And from the legacy of protest into which he was born there emerges a hatred of all things that are alien, a jocular contempt for the arts, a purblind and vicious morality, a fierce hunting after scapegoats, at last a kind of fascism. Why?

Ford is not to be set down as the typical reactionary, on whom is loaded as a matter of course every species of emotional disorder. For one observes the same insensate fury, the same unhappy penchant for ranting and tears, in those radical movements which came out of the West in the decades that followed the Civil War. The agrarians suffered, and sought a personal villain. They found him in the Jew, in the "Rothschilds across the water," to whom the Central Greenback Club of Detroit attributed the hard times of 1878.[18] But anti-Semitism is not an American phenomenon. It is present in French Jacobinism; it tinges the relations of Marx himself with the Jew, Ferdinand Lassalle.[19] It takes its rise from the frustration engendered by the failure of the Left to grasp power. For a man cannot work within a hole-and-corner movement—one forever about to succeed—without becoming a prey to crankiness and the temptation to exercise his lungs. Thus the steady disintegration of Bryan, victimized by that emotionalism so popular in America, where a lump in the throat makes the whole world kin. It is the reason why Bryan, at the Democratic convention of 1924, supported the Ku Klux Klan, which derived its main strength from precisely that portion of the electorate which followed the erst-while Boy Orator, and enlisted for his war on evolution.[20]

VI

But the radicalism of the English Chartists, or that of the French Commune, was quite as genuine as any that ever flourished in America; and it was far more decisively, even terribly, quelled. Yet it did not end in the studied acquiescence of Dana, cultivating porcelains, exotic plants, and a connoisseur's taste in old wine; nor in the ragings of Joseph M. Patterson, whose identification with the *New York Daily News* is apt to make one forget the energetic socialism of his earlier years. It did not end so, because the Left in France and England, in Germany, in Italy, in Russia, succumbing to almost every infirmity of mind, has yet been spared one. It has given its allegiance to the Christian Socialism of Kingsley, and to the vulgar utopias of Cabet and Fourier,[21] who would transform the ocean into pink lemonade; it has seen its leaders beaten, for lack of decision, as Blanqui was beaten, and with him the Commune; seen them corrupted, like Ramsay MacDonald; beguiled, like Bakúnin, by the hocus-pocus of secret societies; turn patrioteer, like the German Socialist deputies in 1914; and Loyal Opposition, like Snowden and Henderson, Bevin and Attlee, thereafter. But never has it swallowed an indigenous narcotic so enervating as the American Dream. Like Bonaparte in Victor Hugo's poem, who learns by degrees of the ultimate punishment ordained by God for his sins—not Moscow nor even Waterloo, not St. Helena nor yet the jailer kings, but worse than all these (*oh, quel dernier chapitre!*): the hideous bandit with the bulky mustache, the circus rider, Napoleon III!—like Bonaparte, so America has been most exquisitely cursed. And the dream it endorses is all the more imposing for this kernel of truth: that no country is richer than our country, nor more advanced in industrial techniques. Even the leaders of industry, if not endowed with human kindness beyond their fellows abroad, have been nonetheless somewhat shrewder, less patently willing to wring the neck of the goose: witness Ford's Five-Dollar Day. Not so long ago the state of Kansas furnished the largest part of the Populist delegation in Congress; within living memory the Middle West was called the Valley of Democracy. Perhaps radio commentators call it so still. But the fact that Kansas today is Eisenhower and Schoeppel, the Middle West

Bender, Dirksen, and Lausche, is a tribute of sorts to a standard of living the American capitalist has thought it profitable to concede. Let there be no mistake: the dream *does* have substance; America *is* different, in degree if not really in kind. What European could have written of his country as Nathaniel Morton, annalist of the Pilgrims, wrote of his:

> Gentle Reader, I have for some lengths of time looked upon it as a duty incumbent especially on the immediate successors of those that have had so large experience of those many memorable and signal demonstrations of God's goodness, viz. the first beginners of this Plantation in New England, to commit to writing his gracious dispensations on that behalf; having so many inducements thereunto, not only otherwise, but so plentifully in the Sacred Scriptures: that so, what we have seen, and what our fathers have told us (Psalm lxxviii. 3, 4), we may not hide from our children, showing to the generations to come the praises of the Lord; that especially the seed of Abraham his servant, and the children of Jacob his chosen (Psalm cv. 5, 6), may remember his marvellous works in the beginning and progress of the planting of New England, his wonders and the judgments of his mouth; how that God brought a vine into this wilderness; that he cast out the heathen, and planted it; that he made room for it and caused it to take deep root; and it filled the land (Psalm lxxx. 8, 9). And not only so, but also that he hath guided his people by his strength to his holy habitation, and planted them in the mountain of his inheritance in respect of precious Gospel enjoyments: and that as especially God may have the glory of all unto whom it is most due; so also some rays of glory may reach the names of those blessed Saints, that were the main instruments and the beginning of this happy enterprise.[22]

"It was not," wrote Tocqueville aptly, of the Pilgrims, "a mere party of adventurers gone forth to seek their fortune beyond seas, but the germ of a great nation wafted by Providence to a predestined shore."

America was promises. What if the promises fail? Then the hope of that multitude, nourished on their fulfillment, sickens also, and fails. And for all that it goes unrecorded officially, such a failure leaves in those who, robot-like, continue to deny it, to pay homage to a myth that no longer jumps with reality, an indefinite feeling of loss, of displacement, as if, bereft of one world, they have never gained another. "Is it a dream?" Whitman wondered, of that American future whose prophet he affirmed himself to be. His answer is portentous: "Nay but the lack of it the dream, / And failing it life's lore and wealth a dream, / And all the world a dream." [23]

This is why America is haunted by its past. Even the great industrialists who have been the premier killers of the dream continue to salute it, to insist that it lives. So Henry Ford, who epitomized the change and the betrayal, paid his respects, in the fantasy village of Greenfield, to the husks of a past existence, surrounded himself with them, as if they were fetishes to ward off self-reproach. So Rockefeller gave millions to create again, at Williamsburg, the Colonial era, when the pattern of American life had not hardened. The stress on plebeian beginnings—the saga of rags to riches—attests further to the legend's appeal. Ford was a poor farm boy who, singlehanded, made his way to the top; Lincoln, his unique genius discounted, was the roughhewn product of the frontier, who rose from Log Cabin to White House. Even Herbert Hoover has been lately revived as the persevering son of a blacksmith. Tradition is never more insistent than when the forces which go to create it are spent.

Yet the killers of the dream cannot really be blamed, except in a moral sense. What they did, the revolution they accomplished, was in the context of an Industrial Age at once inevitable and necessary. But they, and the radicals who fought them, had been conditioned emotionally and intellectually by myths that depicted a vanished America. Thus radical and reactionary were lost. They were lost because the ideals and desires that drove them failed to square with observable fact. They made no attempt to adjust those ideals and desires. Instead, they rejected life: it was not as they would have it. But the man who rejects life so entirely must pay a forfeit. His ills are isolation, indifference, ennui. And these are not to be borne. He escapes from their pain by surrender of the intellect, by giving over to irrational conduct. It is this demon of loneliness, and the attempt to exorcise it, that have made America such peculiarly fertile ground for the renegade, the bigot, and the apostle of violence, whose violence is the solvent of frustration and despair.

NOTES

1. For a short account of Lippmann's development, see Heinz Eulau, "Man Against Himself: Walter Lippmann's Years of Doubt," *American Quarterly*, IV, No. 4 (Winter 1952), 291-304.

2. (New York, 1939), p. 343.
3. Evans figures briefly in Mark Holloway, *Heavens on Earth: Utopian Communities in America 1680-1880* (London, 1951), *passim,* and especially pp. 114 ff.
4. Simpson is treated by Arthur M. Schlesinger, Jr., *The Age of Jackson* (New York, 1945), pp. 201 ff.
5. For the story of Plummer, see Schlesinger, *op. cit.,* pp. 207 ff.
6. Harper's career forms a part of the narrative of Claude G. Bowers, *Jefferson and Hamilton: The Struggle for Democracy in America* (New York, 1925), *passim.*
7. See Paxton Hibben, *Henry Ward Beecher: An American Portrait* (New York, 1927).
8. See C. Vann Woodward, *Reunion and Reaction: The Compromise of 1877 and the End of Reconstruction* (Boston, 1951), *passim.*
9. C. Vann Woodward, *Tom Watson: Agrarian Rebel* (New York, 1938), p. 136.
10. See Keith Sward, *The Legend of Henry Ford* (New York, 1948), pp. 383-384.
11. "L'Homme Moyen Sensuel" and "National Song" (from "Poems of Alfred Venison, The Poet of Titchfield Street") in *Personae* (New York, 1949), pp. 244, 272.
12. Quoted by the syndicated columnist Victor Riesel in the *Los Angeles Daily News,* December 19, 1950.
13. The information on Watson I have taken chiefly from Vann Woodward's excellent biography, previously cited.
14. See the third letter in *Letters from an American Farmer* (London, 1782).
15. See "Song of the Universal" (Stanza 4) from *Birds of Passage.*
16. Treated by Richard Hofstadter, *Social Darwinism in American Thought 1860-1915* (Philadelphia, 1945).
17. See *The Iron Heel* (New York, 1907), Chapter 8.
18. See Sward, *op. cit.,* p. 146.
19. See Robert F. Byrnes, *Antisemitism in Modern France* (London, 1951), pp. 115-117.
20. See Paxton Hibben, *The Peerless Leader, William Jennings Bryan* (New York, 1929), p. 381.
21. For an exceedingly, if unselfconsciously, amusing picture of the Utopian idea, see Cabet's *Voyage en Icarie* (Paris, 1848).
22. See Alexis de Tocqueville, *Democracy in America* (New York, 1954), I, 33 ff.
23. See "Song of the Universal" (Stanza 4) from *Birds of Passage.*

13

The Ideology and Techniques
of Repression, 1903—1933

WILLIAM PRESTON

I

ON JUNE 25, 1952, President Truman vetoed a shameful immigration bill only to see a hysterical Congress override him on a wave of neo-Knownothingism, twentieth-century variety. The McCarran-Walter Act empowers the Attorney General to deport "any alien who has engaged or has had a purpose to engage in activities prejudicial to the public interest or subversive to the national security." Truman noted the lack of judicial guarantees and called attention to the departure from the "traditional American insistence on established standards of guilt. To punish an undefined 'purpose,'" the President said, "is thought control." [1]

The Immigration Act of 1952, as well as the Internal Security Act of 1950, represent, however, not a deviation from but an adherence to the twentieth-century treatment accorded aliens and radicals, an antidemocratic path along which the United States has been spectacularly progressing. This new nativism does not distrust the religion, color, or nationality of the immigrant so much as it dislikes his thought processes and intellectual associations. The contemporary fear that ideas can destroy the country symbolizes a real loss of nerve and of faith in the virtue of freedom. In perspective it can be seen that the current demands for ideological purity date back to the turn of the century, if not earlier. Ever since then the United States has been trying to reproduce a democratic society by sterilizing beliefs and opinions.

In 1903 the United States officially began the investigation of opinion among alien arrivals. From that moment its hostility to "subversive" ideas that might weaken the state or disturb the peacefulness of social and economic relations has steadily grown. The demands of an increasingly military administrative regime for conformity and reliability, while more intense, are certainly not new. Before the New Deal interlude a pattern of suppression was established, much of which became the root of present-day growth. The thirty years from 1903 until 1933 were the first phase of the red scare of today.

The nation's controversy with its political and economic heretics has been a long, bitter, and serious conflict. It has been waged on the local, state, and federal level by private citizens, volunteer groups, and public officials. There is no idea of telling all of that story in these pages. The concern here is with the federal government. Today its increasing authority and police power dominate the field of anti-radical surveillance and control, so tentatively embarked upon a half-century ago. A study of the earlier decades may throw into relief the development of the policies and practices from which the present spirit and structure emerged.

The struggle between the government and the radicals passed through several stages between 1903 and 1933. By the outbreak of World War I, bureaucratic procedures and attitudes towards aliens had become rigidly established. At the same time a growing consciousness of the "radical menace" enveloped the public mind. Before a large-scale deportation program could be instituted, however, wartime pressures diverted it into a series of emergency repressive measures. With the termination of hostilities, the government once more embarked upon a deportation crusade climaxed in the so-called Palmer raids of 1919-1920, in which thousands of alien radicals were jailed. The '20s witnessed a marked decline in deportations but a continuing fight with radicals over the release of political prisoners and the restoration of their civil rights. The first phase of the red scare ended with Franklin D. Roosevelt's Christmas pardon in 1933. It is only proper, then, to begin with the government's treatment of aliens. Had it dealt with them as human beings, it might have handled the radicals in the same way.

II

The Immigration Bureau brought to the deportation of radicals the same abusive tactics used in the apprehension and removal of all aliens. This has never been widely understood because it was obscured by the mythology created at the time of the Palmer raids. Contemporary observers were aware of the excessive and devious violations of fundamental rights—the roundup of many innocent people, the detentions incommunicado, the excessive bail, and the denial of counsel until confessions had been extorted. But these were pictured as the result of an unusual nationwide postwar hysteria. Reactionary-minded officials supposedly conspired to deny due process to "reds." The deportation process had been perverted by a great fear. The implication was that such things had never happened before and would never happen again. Later writers following the judgment of past witnesses perpetuated this interpretation and by repetition rewarded it with historical validity.[2]

Years of experience and policy making by immigration officers refute this facile analysis of the Palmer raids. They were conducted according to the highest traditions of the Immigration Service. This was simply the first time anyone had found out about these procedures and cared enough to fight back. The exposure was long overdue.

Due process in deportation was smashed on the rock of judicial decision in 1893 and has never been put together again. In *Fong Yue Ting v. United States* the Supreme Court determined the future pattern of expulsion in one simple interpretation: deportation was not a punishment for crime but merely an administrative process for the return of unwelcome and undesirable alien residents to their own countries. The United States deported aliens on the grounds of expediency, not crime, not as punishment but only because their "presence is deemed inconsistent with the public welfare." In subsequent action the Court has reaffirmed the absolute power of Congress to deport aliens summarily, by administrative fiat, and for any reason at any time, as "an inherent and inalienable right of every sovereign and independent nation."[3]

Once the definition of deportation as non-criminal has been made, all else follows. The guarantees of the Bill of Rights apply only where persons have been charged with crime. Expulsion often involved, therefore, a long detention, excessively high bail, unreasonable searches and seizures, the denial of counsel, self-incrimination, and trial without jury. There is no protection from the Fourth, Fifth, Sixth, and Eighth Amendments nor from Section 9 of Article I prohibiting ex post facto laws.

The hearings themselves, in which the examining inspector played the role of detective, prosecuting attorney, interpreter, stenographer, and judge, were summary and did not have to conform to the rules of courtroom procedure. Thus the file forwarded to Washington for action might contain unsworn statements, ex parte affidavits, hearsay or opinion evidence, and extraneous material not related to the charges. Usually the inspector attempted to obtain an admission of guilt during the so-called "preliminary hearing" before a warrant of arrest had even been issued. The Immigration Bureau's attitude in this respect was clearly outlined in a 1910 memorandum on the procedure:

> The reason for holding a preliminary hearing without the presence of counsel is to enable the immigration authorities to ascertain in their own way the true facts without the intervention of the dilatory tactics which some counsel are disposed to employ, including advice often given the alien not to answer questions put by the immigration authorities.[4]

The success of most deportation cases was closely related to the degree of the alien's self-incrimination, and the immigration inspectors came to rely heavily on this tactic. As one historian of deportation has written, it meant that the procedure in essence "afforded opportunity for deprivations of rights considered fundamental to Anglo Saxon law where personal liberty is involved."[5]

It must be difficult for an alien under arrest to realize that he is not undergoing a cruel banishment from a country where he may well have lived for many years. It must be even more incomprehensible to him that few of the rights he has come to associate with American judicial procedure are available to him.

If such reflections have disturbed the democratic sensibilities of departing aliens, they have never determined the decisions of more than a minority of the Supreme Court justices. After all, the Court might have decided that deportation *was* punishment. In the 1893 case Mr. Justice Brewer's famous dissent flatly asserted: "Deportation is punishment. It involves first an arrest, a deprival of liberty; and second, a removal from home, from family, from business, from property." Mr. Justice Field once said, "Brutality, inhumanity, and cruelty cannot be made elements in any procedure for the enforcement of the laws of the United States." But these and others like them have remained only vigorous dissents.[6]

III

The trend in deportation legislation after 1903 is an accurate symbol of the increasingly narrow and conformist ideology that has swept over the United States in contrast to its past experience and traditions. The American people had earlier survived some tremendously chaotic domestic disturbances and tolerated some extremely violent and critical expressions of dissent without feeling that their safety and self-preservation required the removal of foreigners with dangerous ideas. In fact, not since the end of the eighteenth century had legislation been passed against aliens on the theory that "those who corrupt our opinion . . . are the most dangerous of all enemies."[7]

The fear of "treasonable or secret machinations against the government" during the crisis with France in 1798 had led the Federalist government to pass the Alien Act of that year. Under it the President could deport any foreign agent whom he deemed a threat to the welfare and security of the country "without accusation, without public trial, without confrontation of witnesses, without . . . the right to have witnesses in his favor, without defense, and without counsel."[8] The Alien Act of 1798 became famous, not for the expulsion of foreigners (few were expelled), but for the displacement of the Federalist Party from its position of power in American politics. As the Kentucky and Virginia Resolutions so vehemently pointed out, the unconstitutional and despotic Alien Act "subverted the general principles of free government." The Federalist, not the foreigner, was the real alien. Within two years the discredited act had expired and with it went the idea of removing those aliens whose views or political commitments made them "dangerous to the public peace or safety."

Before the United States again singled out the alien as an enemy of opinion it successfully weathered an economic crisis of great magnitude after the Civil War. In addition, radical movements exhibited much vigor and influence without their immigrant component being attacked. The 1870s witnessed the desperate, spontaneous strikes and riots of the city unemployed and the revolts of armed miners. Nearly four hundred thousand workers joined in the movement for the eight-hour day culminating so tragically in the Haymarket riot of 1886. The Homestead and Pullman strikes of the 1890s further underscored the bitter seriousness of the struggle between capital and labor.

Socialist and anarchist groups also flourished in the '70s and '80s without frightening the government into repressive action against the incoming convert. Under the leadership of the German agitator Johann Most, the anarchist Pittsburgh Congress of 1883 demanded the "destruction of the existing class rule, by all means, i.e., by energetic, relentless, revolutionary and international action." [9] In 1885 the anarchists numbered some seven thousand organized in eighty localities. But after the Haymarket riot, for which the anarchists were blamed, "anarchism faded away completely as a political force in America." [10]

The United States, swept by economic crisis and labor revolt, tolerated anarchist immigration when anarchism was an alive and growing movement. A relatively calmer and prosperous United States raised ideological barriers when that movement was no more than the froth of an ebbing tide. Why did a country seek to overthrow an ideal by legislation years after its epitaph had been written by the American environment?

The public mind judged anarchism not by the underlying reality of its mass strength but by the superimposed illusion of its acts of violence. In addition, it accepted the incantation and ritual of a few traveling priests as the substance of a well-established church. The vividness of their prose invoking revolution has always stimulated horror more easily than have any reports of the numbers standing ready to carry out that revolution.

In 1901, history provided a reminder of anarchist violence that convinced Congress of the imperative need for some action. Leon F. Czolgosz, the mentally unbalanced murderer of President McKinley, had had a brief and shadowy association with anarchism, just enough to make his public identification as its instrument plausible. The ceremonial rites by which the nation sought to absolve its responsibility for the death of McKinley soon manifested themselves. Local police apprehended anarchists, mobs assaulted anarchists and other radicals, and several states passed criminal anarchy laws. If these were the immediate and excessive convulsions of popular disgust, they also had the transitory qualities of such seizures. By 1904, "the issue as a whole ceased to be of public interest." [11] On the other hand, federal legislation inspired by the assassination of McKinley permanently paralyzed a onetime vigorously libertarian immigration policy. The United States was on the road to 1798.

In the Immigration Act of 1903, the United States for the first time excluded certain immigrants because of their beliefs and associations. Section 2 made ineligible for entry "anarchists, or persons who believe in or advocate the overthrow by force and violence of the government of the United States, or of all government, or of all forms of law, or the assassination of public officials." Section 38 prohibited the admission of anyone who "disbelieves in or who is opposed to all organized government, or who is a member of or affiliated with any organization entertaining and teaching such disbelief in or opposition to all organized government." [12]

This law, however, and the subsequent act of 1907 limited the time within which deportation could be instituted for such views to three years from the date of entry. Congress still held that deportation of a man after he had been here three years or longer was an unfair hardship and it hesitated to banish individuals for views acquired during residence in the United States. The legislators assumed that conditions might well determine beliefs and were willing for the country to accept this responsibility. It was the departure from this position that constituted the major ideological retrogression of succeeding years. After 1912 the strength of the pattern was to be tested, not by the anarchists, but by the members of the Industrial Workers of the World. The Wobblies frightened a hostile government into laws and practices that extended the policy of 1903.

IV

The IWW, organized at Chicago in 1905 to create a labor union equivalent of the Socialist Party, recruited some of the outcasts of

Gompers's craft clubhouse into an organization that uniquely combined the practice of industrial unionism with the preaching of revolutionary ideals. During a brief but memorable solidarity, the Wobblies followed their class-conscious program with a militant and daring disregard for the conventional mores. As a result, they sent the reactionaries and the reformers of the time into an "hysterical recoil" [13] from which there emerged a further pattern of suppression.

Composed of the migratory miner, harvester, construction worker, and logger of the West and the unskilled factory worker of the East, the IWWs had framed their opposition to capitalism in a vivid, inflammatory, Marxist prose. Their language was as violent as their strikes were often peaceful; yet it suggested that force and violence would be met by force and violence. Wobbly orators familiarized the public with the concepts of "sabotage" and "direct action." In addition, the Wobblies rejected the church and the flag as the dishonest tools of the exploiting class. As if to make its alienation from the community complete, the organization never replaced the extremism of youth with the conservatism of middle age. There was always a proudly stubborn and defiant adherence to the original revolutionary zeal. And this eventually made them the easiest and most conspicuous scapegoat for the anti-labor and anti-radical passions of the country.

The IWW had at first a precarious, schismatic career, buried on the back pages of contemporary history. It had actually been lucky to survive. Then, beginning in 1909, a series of victorious free speech controversies gave the IWW the reputation of unbeatable militancy. In 1912 the Wobblies had again terrified conservative and respectable elements by dramatic strikes at the Lawrence textile mills in Massachusetts and in the West.

The resurgent vitality of the IWW between 1909 and 1912 was reflected in the appeals to Washington—all of which were characteristic of future anti-radical behavior. Local businessmen and political leaders demanded federal indictments, federal troops, and federal investigations. Lacking any evidence of criminal activity, the exponents of repression envisioned the federal government as a *deus ex machina* for their radical difficulties. Taft and, later, Wilson were eager to help, but until World War I they were equally embarrassed by the lack of laws suitable for the prosecution of dissident members of the community.

By all odds the IWW should have been suppressed in 1912 or close to it. In the years that followed, it did not become more dangerous, or extreme, or despised. Yet for some time the passions that came into being that year were not relieved by the official remedies of national action. At the height of IWW influence in 1912, there was no state law, no federal criminal law, and no deportation law with which to attack the organization. Eventually such deficiencies were more than made up. Congress led the way in 1912. Still adducing the alien nature of all radicalism, it determined to destroy the IWW by rewriting the deportation law.

Following the Lawrence strike and the free speech fights, Congress began the preparation of a new immigration law. The proposal to deport any alien "advocating or teaching the unlawful destruction of property" was aimed specifically at the IWW. Had this been all there was to the law, it might have passed in 1913 or 1914, but the literacy test was also a part of this very same bill. Presidential vetoes directed against the literacy test in 1913, 1915, and 1917 therefore afforded the IWW a triple stay of execution. On such fortuitous circumstances did the anti-Wobbly crusade depend.

The literacy test and the anti-radical clauses also shared a common intellectual paternity in the then generally accepted interpretation of the new immigration from southern and eastern Europe. Not only were the new immigrants supposedly more illiterate than the earlier arrivals from northern Europe, but also they presumably carried erroneous political ideas. President Wilson spoke of the later immigrants as lacking in "initiative" and "quick intelligence" and composed of "the more sordid elements," while the old "stock" was "sturdy," "vital," and "individualistic." [14] The chairman of the House Immigration Committee found that the new immigrants possessed "*inherited* misconceptions respecting the relationships of the governing power to the governed." [15] (Italics added.)

Shutting its eyes to the evidence of shocking industrial conditions uncovered by various investigating commissions, Congress keyed its solution of domestic unrest to a theory that described radicalism as a foreign import of the new immigration. Therefore, it sought not only to expel the alien agitator but also to exclude his ignorant, misguided follower. The literacy test was closely related to the anti-radical provisions of the immigration law. Theodore Roosevelt said as early as

1901 that the literacy test would "decrease the sum of ignorance, so potent in producing the envy, suspicion, malignant passion, and hatred of order out of which an anarchistic sentiment inevitably springs." [16]

The 1917 immigration law also abandoned the time limits during which deportation could be effected for violations of the act. No longer willing to recognize the principle of national responsibility for ideas and beliefs acquired during residence, the law in effect put the alien on indefinite probation. That an honest, hard-working foreigner could acquire radical views due to American conditions was simply too farfetched to be taken seriously. The alien worker to avoid banishment had to be, therefore, a conformist or, at least, a *silent* critic of the system. To the applause of his fellow Congressmen, a Texas representative indicated the direction in which official thought was moving:

> Now I would execute these anarchists if I could, and then I would deport them, so that the soil of our country might not be polluted by their presence even after the breath had gone out of their bodies. I do not care what the time limit is. I want to get rid of them by some route . . . or by execution by the hangman. It makes no difference to me so that we get rid of them. [17]

Despite the broad and indefinite nature of the clauses in the deportation law and the dropping of the time limit, not one Congressional voice had warned the nation against the potential injustices and obstacles in the untested legislation. Instead, officials favored deportation as the quickest and most effective method of suppressing the propagation of dangerous ideas because of its very antithesis to due process. They did not want to determine the rights of anarchists and other radicals by the long, slow procedure of courts. As one Congressman said, "a long delayed, snail-paced court trial" would only encourage radicals "to ply their trade" instead of making an example of them. [18] If repression was the aim, then a non-criminal, administrative method was far more efficient and gave the immigration official great latitude in defining guilt. How far was the Immigration Bureau prepared to go in deciding what constituted the advocacy and teaching of proscribed doctrines? In a memorandum on the new law, the Commissioner General suggested that the intention was not merely to destroy the active forms of the radical disease, but to attack the "passive and insidious germs." The government would, therefore, seek to eliminate the word as well as the deed, and in fact to "reach and suppress the underlying thought." [19] Since men have not as yet devised a scientific process for uncovering the convictions of the human mind, this policy sent officials off on the dangerous practice of judging intent, rather than evaluating acts. Should the immigration inspectors follow normal procedures, they would determine guilt by a self-incriminating confession of belief wrung from the radical alien during the preliminary hearing and before the actual warrant of arrest was issued. Before the government could adopt this program, however, the United States entered World War I. The anti-radical crusade then took on an entirely new character and tempo.

V

The war affected the course of repression in several ways. In the first place, a strike could now be described not only as a legitimate labor struggle, but also as a seditious interference with war production. In the second place, the IWW's most militant and dramatic surge in the lumber, mining, and agriculture centers of the West occurred during the summer of 1917. Finally, an atmosphere of war hysteria colored all decisions from the local to the national level. Thus, the apparent necessity and agitation for the repression of labor radicals coincided with their increasing demands for concessions. Local officials and businessmen in the Northwest at first assumed that the deportation of alien agitators would eliminate the threatened industrial strife. Based on their belief that the IWW was largely alien, the local proponents of suppression suggested a carefully selected purging of the agitators accompanied by a well-publicized but fictitious threat to deport all alien members.

Although the Immigration Bureau adopted the essence of this program by early 1918, it moved too slowly to satisfy the West. The drive to suppress labor radicals thereupon developed two additional phases: use of federal troops under the wartime emergency, and judicial prosecutions by the federal government, also under cover of the war. All three—troops, trials, and deportations—ran more or less simultaneously, but the deportation crusade always remained the favorite weapon. And to it the government returned when the war emergency had passed.

During July and August of 1917 business and public officials of the

West called in troops to eliminate the radical threat. At the very moment when the Wobblies seemed to be winning the lumber strike of 1917, the timber interests employed the federal army as their strike-breakers. The participation of federal troops in local strikes was unusual, unconstitutional, and linked to the war emergency. Constitutionally, the army may suppress disturbances only against federal laws and may put down insurrections against state authority only when the legislature or the governor certifies the state's inability to meet the emergency.

In reality the situation in the West hardly involved open insurrection or lawlessness. Prosecuting attorneys in Montana and Washington and special agents of the Bureau of Investigation testified to the peacefulness of the lumber strike and the lack of violence and intimidation by the IWW. Government action, however, was to be based not on realities of this sort, but on a deliberately created public hysteria against the IWW, an unreasoning anxiety that demanded the suppression of the Wobblies and the restoration of the community's sense of security. Behind this pressure were the bankers, businessmen, lumber operators, and farmers who desired to break the IWW strike with scabs and to force the IWW out of the harvest and fruit fields. They anticipated possible resistance and considered troops essential to the maintenance of order. New theories sanctified the new procedures that met this need.

War Department authorizations to local army officers to "sternly repress acts committed with seditious intent" and to protect "public utilities" essential to the war provided criteria vague and flexible enough to cover intervention in industrial disputes.[20] In addition, army officers could arrest IWWs who committed "acts in pursuance of pre-arranged plans contemplating violence" under the theory that such acts were disloyal.[21] The Administration told commanding generals to deal directly with local officials and businessmen in suppressing sedition and safeguarding "public utilities." This authority was in turn delegated to the platoon level, so that lieutenants and their men were available to county sheriffs and district attorneys. The army had become an illegal *posse comitatus,* not only for federal authorities, but for local and state officials as well. Neglecting the need for a Presidential proclamation or a declaration of martial law, the military assumed jurisdiction where the civil courts were functioning and where peaceable strikes were in progress. One way of preventing anticipated labor violence is to jail the laborer.

The pattern was similar throughout the Northwest. In Montana, troops raided IWW headquarters and put IWW leaders and members "in confinement in the city jail for a period of several weeks without filing any charges against them." [22] Elsewhere soldiers patrolled the towns, initiating a system of forced labor for Wobblies. In Washington, the army raided IWW halls, arrested delegates, broke up camp meetings, and searched freights for migrant workers. It held and questioned them on their membership and social and economic views, releasing only those the military felt confident would not be a "menace to the best interests of industry." [23] While a few Wobblies were legally detainable as draft dodgers or unregistered enemy aliens, over 90 percent were at least legally entitled to effect their release on habeas corpus. To meet this contingency, army officers, public officials, and local Councils of Defense agreed on the following plan:

> Persons arrested by the troops will be turned over to the sheriffs to hold, subject to release by the officer in command. The civil authorities, federal and state, will take charge of such as may be legally held by them; the others will be subject to the order of the military commander so that if petitions for habeas corpus are presented, return can be made that the prisoners are held by military power.[24]

The authorities justified the illegal detentions on the grounds that the IWW needed to be "protected against injury." According to the United States Attorney, "it is best for them [the IWW], too, because the people are of such a frame of mind that any slight disturbance on the part of the I.W.W.'s might cause most serious results." [25] Protective custody, of course, has often been the historical justification for the exercise of arbitrary power. The army preferred to preserve "law and order" by imprisoning an unpopular minority rather than by controlling the community violence directed against it.

By September 1920 the army had suppressed twenty-nine domestic disorders without resort to constitutional procedures. Apparently unconcerned by the widespread use of the armed forces as a local police, Secretary of War Newton D. Baker justified the relaxation of the rules as "necessary in the public interest." [26] It was realized, however, that no matter how successfully the troops suppressed radicalism, they were purely a temporary expedient. While the army could stabilize local emergencies, it was powerless to crush the leadership or to police the vast migratory areas of the Plains harvest fields. What it did and did well was to safeguard the threatened industries and communities until the Departments of Justice and Labor evolved their plans for the overthrow of the IWW.

VI

For a year and a half the Espionage and Draft Acts had now provided the heretofore missing statutes for the legal prosecution of radicals. The IWWs, anarchists, and many socialists were neutral or opposed to war. They had, moreover, for years denounced the government as capitalistic. The Administration now turned to this analysis and equated an attack on capitalism with hostility to a government at war. Through the judicial doctrines of constructive intent and indirect causation, the Department of Justice convicted radicals for their political and economic views. The United States attorneys reported almost unanimously that public sentiment was so inflamed against radicals that "if these cases are presented to the grand jury, indictments will necessarily follow, and, if indictments should be returned, convictions will be secured as a matter of course." [27] What the government was doing, in effect, was eliminating mob violence against IWWs and other nonconformists by removing the enraged citizen from the mob and placing him in the jury box. While this followed the form, it lacked the essence of judicial procedure. As Joughin and Morgan have suggested in their analysis of the Sacco-Vanzetti case, the jury system collapses in such cases because the community is "unfit to deal with any issue involving its hysterical passions." [28] With the outcome predetermined, therefore, the important thing is to know why the trials were initiated.

The IWW prosecutions depended on business pressure, community hysteria, and the relative eagerness or common-sense restraint of local federal attorneys. The Washington office of the Department of Justice indicted and tried only the first-string leaders at Chicago. The other cases reflected local needs and were not subject to national control or centralized direction. There was, thus, no real policy, but only local autonomy—responsive, as so often, to local crisis and unrest.

The local campaigns against second- and third-string Wobblies followed various patterns. When IWW organizers increased their activity in the mid-continent oil fields during the fall of 1917, the oil interests sought their suppression. They urged the federal officials at Tulsa "to arrest and intern every I.W.W. or person suspected of being such." [29] However, the United States Attorney considered the IWW agitation legitimate labor activity for increased wages and would not act unless the oilmen's committee could produce evidence of violation of federal law. He refused to arrest IWWs in anticipation of what they might do. In the eastern part of the oil field situated in southern Kansas, a different solution prevailed. There, the United States Attorney was responsive to the demands of the oil companies. While there had been no strike but only a concerted membership drive, the local Department of Justice office seized some hundred Wobblies. It justified the arrests and the indictments as "a preventative matter to prevent possible violence in the oil region in southern Kansas." [30] After two years of imprisonment, these Wobblies were tried and convicted of conspiracy to violate the war statutes. In California the IWW indictment climaxed a three-year battle between the Wobblies and the fruit and ranching interests of the San Joaquin and Sacramento valleys. The class war had been bitter and tense. In late 1917 a bomb explosion at the governor's mansion set off a widespread roundup of IWWs in and around Sacramento by an hysterical citizenry. For lack of evidence the local Department of Justice recommended the release of all but three of the fifty-four men seized. California officials were outraged, and their pressure on Washington was decisive.

These trials and indictments effectively suppressed the IWW. It became a defense organization, rather than a labor organization, and drained off its leadership, militancy, and finances in a fruitless resistance. Once the government realized the weapons the war statutes placed at its disposal, it used them decisively and without restraint "whenever the bare chance of successfully doing so presented itself." [31] The federal troops were the first and temporary solution to radical agitation; the medium of the courts the second and more permanent suppression. Yet deportation, always the first love of those who desired to rid the country of "isms," was not forgotten. It represented the third and final drive against radicals—a stage culminating in the Palmer raids of 1919 and 1920.

The Northwest witnessed the first mass deportation roundups of radicals in American history when Seattle, long a center of intense labor-capital bitterness, indulged in its anti-Wobbly hysteria in the winter of 1917-1918. Public officials and leading citizens pictured the annual fall migration of hundreds of workers from lumber camps and fields to the cities during the slack winter season as a seditious IWW conspiracy to seize Seattle. Moreover, the timber interests, which feared a revival of the still unsettled lumber strike in the spring, saw the winter layoffs as an ideal opportunity to crush the local Wobbly leadership and intimidate the members. Lacking specific evidence against individual Wobblies, Seattle's leaders called on the Immigration Service to detain for deportation an estimated five thousand alien IWWs. From January to March several hundred of them were arrested. Then, after filling its own detention station and every suitable county jail in western Washington, the Immigration Service called a halt for lack of space and appropriations. Secretary of Labor William B. Wilson also refused to approve the further roundup of *mere members* of the organization under an Immigration Act that called for some proof of *individual guilt*. With the settlement of the lumber strike and the spring departure of the workers, Seattle's hysteria subsided and with it the pressure for further arrests. While the Northwestern deportation crusade was important in the crippling of the IWW, more significant was the lesson it taught the Administration at Washington.

The Seattle experience convinced the Immigration Service that the test of individual guilt under the 1917 law was a requirement of proof that in most cases its inspectors could not produce. Fearing that most of the alien radicals under detention would win their freedom, the Bureau proposed to make them deportable by writing a new law and applying it ex post facto. Thus, the Immigration Act of October 1918, drafted and backed by the Departments of Justice and Labor, frankly proposed to remove any existing special immunities that favored radical aliens. Under the 1918 law the United States, for the first time in its history, made mere membership in an organization grounds for deportation. An alien was to be condemned not merely for his own personal acts and conduct but for the acts or conduct of an organization of which he might be a member. The country had now moved a long way from its policy at the turn of the century and had accepted the dangerous doctrine of guilt by association. It was this criterion alone that made possible the mass character of the "red" raids of 1919-1920. What made the raids probable, however, was the ending of World War I.

VII

Postwar America produced simultaneously an increasing reliance on and resistance to the deportation of radicals. A marked increase in unemployment, labor unrest, and radicalism accompanied the readjustment to a peacetime economy. Industry's open-shop drive symbolized its resolution not to remove the grievances responsible for much of the agitation. At the same time, the image and example of the Russian Revolution which invigorated the Left horrified the right-wing segments of society. These factors made the government and industry determined to expel the carriers of alien "isms." Yet with the postwar cessation of prosecutions under the Espionage and Draft Acts, the Department of Justice could no longer overthrow radical organizations in the courts. Freed from the restraining influence of a labor scarcity, the government's response was the initiation of wholesale expulsion.

A reawakened and reinforced defense was the response to this final drive against radicals. During hostilities, left-wing solidarity had disappeared, and liberals in their pro-war enthusiasm had abandoned radicals and civil liberties to the rape of the army and the Justice Department. By 1919 disillusion with the war and Wilson led many conscience-stricken liberals to fight further repressive measures. The IWW was also prepared to resist the deportation of its members. While earlier it had devoted its energy to the court battles, it could now supply legal and financial support to detained aliens. In February 1919, the first large group of IWWs arrived in New York for shipment overseas. Their cases provided the first real test of the relative strength of the government and the defense in the postwar environment.

A vigorous defense aided by the influence of outraged New York liberals forced the Department of Labor to reconsider most of the Wobbly cases. For the first time, the disregard of due process in deportation practices became clear to groups well organized and with adequate publicity channels. Discovering glaring inconsistencies and weaknesses in the cases, the IWW and its supporters were able to obtain the release of two thirds of the aliens whom the government had been ready to deport. In Washington, these radical victories forced a serious reappraisal of deportation policy and the evolution of a new plan.

During the summer of 1919, the Departments of Labor and Justice evolved an association culminating in the Palmer raids. They now realized that a few untrained immigration inspectors could not investigate or discover the existence of radical expressions or beliefs among aliens. The government also understood how difficult it would be to prove cases involving *individual* acts or thought. The Bureau of Investigation had the informers, the sleuths, the money, and the wartime experience in dragnet raids to recommend its participation. It planned quite illegally "a dragnet *inquiry* and a *search* for *suspected* anarchists and *radicals of all kinds*." [32] Using the membership provisions of the 1918 law, the government determined to strike at the mass bases of radicalism: specifically, the aliens in the ranks of the newly formed Union of Russian Workers, Communist Labor Party, and Communist Party. The federal agents hoped to prove membership through the seizing of membership cards and lists in the raids and through the secret testimony of planted informers. However, the Department of Justice insisted on the absolute necessity of "preserving the cover of our confidential informants," who had only recently been infiltrated into radical organizations. [33] Should the agents fail to obtain lists or cards, they expected that aliens might be induced to admit their memberships.

As defense lawyers became familiar with immigration procedures, however, aliens were becoming increasingly aware of their rights. This determined the final peculiar characteristics of the Palmer roundups. During late 1919, George F. Vanderveer, chief counsel of the IWW, in a widely publicized article advised all aliens to refuse to answer questions until provided with legal aid. Since Bureau of Investigation agents had already discovered that it was often "next to impossible to prove actual membership," the government had only two choices. Either the Department of Justice could uncover its informers to prove membership, or it could resort to the historical deportation technique of self-incrimination. J. Edgar Hoover and his subordinates chose the latter, and the Bureau of Immigration agreed that it was "extremely desirable" that the alien should give his testimony "without being hampered by the advice of counsel"! [34]

The dragnet raids, the unlawful searches and seizures by Bureau detectives, the levying of excessive bail, the intimidating preliminary interrogations of aliens held incommunicado, and the denial of counsel followed from that policy decision in the January 1920 raids on the Communist organizations. The Department of Justice concerned itself with the preservation of its informers rather than with the protection of the rights of alien defendants. An extorted sworn confession became the substitute for due process.

These arbitrary extremes proved to be their own undoing. The protest from all segments of society forced the Department of Labor to introduce greater conformity to due process into deportations and induced the Justice Department to abandon its plans for further dragnet inquiries into alien radicalism. It was, moreover, impossible for the two authorities to resume the peculiar relations that had made possible the raids. Unfortunately, critics of the government interpreted the events of 1920 as a merely momentary persecution of radicals by federal agents. They failed to realize that deportation procedure had historically mistreated all aliens and that the anti-radical crusade itself had developed over many years.

VIII

Although the 1920s witnessed no repetition of the concerted wartime attack on radicals, the fear and hatred of left-wing "isms" constantly influenced official policy. If there was little federal activity, this was not due to a conviction that the class war had been won. Rather, it signified the reassertion of authority by the states over the discontented elements within their borders. The national guards and the state criminal-syndicalism laws provided effective methods of combating radicals. Wherever it could, the federal government clearly indicated its distaste for rebellious ideologies. At the beginning of the decade it delayed the release of alien enemies whom it had interned solely because of their radical beliefs and associations. Yet it freed the active pro-German, the near-treasonable businessman who had traded with the enemy, and the ordinary enemy criminal or saboteur. The Justice Department would release, however, radical alien enemies who renounced their former affiliations and "adopted a more reasonable attitude towards American institutions." [35] The war was over, but the class war went on.

The War Department recommended the formulation of a program for, and the training of officers in, the handling of "radical rebel groups" attempting the overthrow of the government. Conscious of the successful Soviet revolutions in Russia and Europe, the army argued that local "reds" might try to disrupt the food distribution, capture local arms depots, and starve the populace into submission. The Military Intelligence and the War Plans Division estimated that the danger was "not a transitory affair," but was likely "to be present as a permanent feature to be reckoned with." The army prepared, therefore, a lengthy plan known as "War Plans White" to deal with both minor and major emergencies arising out of labor and radical unrest.[36]

The Department of Justice and its Pardon Office also acknowledged the persistence of the class war in opposing the amnesty of wartime political prisoners. Amnesty supporters recalled that the war with its passions and hysteria was over, urged a reconciliation by forgiveness, and pointed to the historical precedent of Lincoln's Civil War amnesty proclamation. To these people Pardon Attorney James A. Finch replied that "at the time that proclamation was issued, slavery was dead, the South was defeated, and there was no possibility for further revolution." In contrast, Finch indicated that in postwar America, "bolshevism, anarchy, and lawless discontent are rampant and growing . . . not dead, but just beginning to spread . . . and to think of liberating these prisoners at this time, when it needs a firm hand to show such malcontents that this government is strong enough to hold and keep its prisoners, is, to my mind, a matter which should be well considered." [37] The government also hoped that further confinement would have a corrective effect on the radical views of the prisoners by teaching them "the needed lesson in citizenship" and by making them "amenable to constituted authority." [38] While admitting in confidential memorandums that "there is very little evidence that many of these defendants ever did anything to constitute a violation of the Espionage Act," [39] the government delayed liberating radicals until their recantation or a relaxation of the class war made their freedom innocuous. The amnesty of political prisoners depended on strikes, unrest, and domestic radicalism rather than on the justice of the convictions or the adequacy of the punishment. Favoring those who renounced their radical beliefs with earlier commutations of sentence, the Coolidge administration finally released the last unregenerated radicals in December 1923.

From 1923 on, the American Civil Liberties Union fought for the restoration of the radicals' civil rights by a general pardon. At the very peak of prosperity in 1929, the Pardon Office cautiously approved such a proposal, but before President Hoover could act, the crash had initiated the great depression. In 1933 the Pardon Attorney was once more fearful of the encouragement such a pardon would provide to the radical movement. But Franklin D. Roosevelt in his first year in office disregarded this alleged danger and offered a Christmas pardon to all those convicted under the Draft and Espionage Acts of the first World War. Fifteen years after the prosecutions and during a much greater crisis, a New Deal administration was ready to close the wounds opened by the anti-radical hysteria of its Democratic forebears.

IX

On May 24, 1954, a 7 to 2 Supreme Court decision upholding the deportation of an ex-Communist indicated that the United States had continued down the narrow, intolerant road marked out in 1903. The nation's highest court had validated the constitutionality of the 1950 Internal Security Act when applied ex post facto to aliens who had been Communists at any time before its passage. An alien who had been a member of a legal political party from 1944 until 1946 found himself deportable under an act passed four years after his rejection of the Communist faith. While even the majority opinion recognized that the action in question "shock[s] the sense of fair play which is the essence of due process," the justices respected the power of Congress to handle alien affairs.[40] Similar decisions in recent years have also acknowledged the "absolute" and "unqualified" right of Congress to determine the deportation of an alien for any reason or for no reason and at any time. Nor is the alien as yet protected by constitutional guarantees in deportation procedures.[41] The Immigration Service lapsed back into its historical practices soon after the Palmer raids; the reforms intended to quiet public criticism had largely been abandoned by 1924. As the President's Commission on Immigration reported in 1953, "The present hearing procedure . . . fails to conform to the now generally accepted standards for fair hearings." [42] Until the Supreme Court reverses the decision of 1893 in *Fong Yue Ting v. United States,* it will continue to uphold deportation legislation and practice regardless of "how deeply such policies may offend American traditions."[43] The Court has referred critics of these undemocratic and unjust processes to the body that is responsible for them.

The Congress has given no sign that it will reverse the trend toward sweeping anti-radical and anti-ex-radical legislation. The New Deal interlude of the 1930s was just that, a short and temporary respite that did nothing but create a false optimism in the radical mind. The Smith Act and the Alien Registration Act of 1940, the Internal Security Act of 1950, and the Immigration and Nationality Act of 1952 have made the radical-catching bills of this century's first two decades seem in comparison simple and harmless. Then the country punished individual advocacy or, at most, contemporary membership in illegal organizations. Present legislation penalizes conspiracy to advocate, *past* membership (no matter how far back), and membership, association, or affiliation with any organization required to register under the Subversive Activities Control Act of 1950. Vile and degrading as the practice was, a radical could once recant and save himself from deportation. Now he must face deportation unless his recantation involves five years' *active* opposition to a formerly held ideology. In the early 1900s the nation accepted its responsibility for domestically induced radicalism. Today it has made the radical or ex-radical everlastingly liable for what he once was or thought. It has reserved the right to create new classes of radicalism and enlarge the index of dangerous ideas and associations for which an individual may find himself deportable in the future. In addition, Congress has chopped away at the protection formerly afforded by naturalization. Citizenship is much more difficult to obtain and much easier to lose for any radical or ex-radical. The country seems to have accepted the 1922 suggestion of the Bureau of Naturalization that, "as long as the advocates of these malignant and un-American doctrines remain aliens, they may be deported and their gospels may be overthrown at their inception."[44]

In the security-conscious twentieth century, the rights of a large portion of the population—aliens, naturalized citizens, and native-born radicals—have been sacrificed to the alleged safety of the state. These groups are becoming the real displaced persons of the cold war, less free and less protected than the rest of the population. There has been a steady progression toward a federal policy based on fear rather than faith in people. Not only are we afraid of our own shadow, but we also would like to deport it. Politicians, journalists, and others have raised the crisis issue involved in the cold war and the threat of sub-version as a justification for present policies. Senator Thomas J. Walsh of Montana replied to such proponents of expediency during the anti-radical hysteria after World War I. "It is only in such times [as the present] that the guarantees of the Constitution as to personal rights are of any practical value," he said. "In seasons of calm, no one thinks of denying them . . ."[45]

In 1912, an anti-Wobbly editor predicted the future course of events. The IWW, he wrote, "are the waste material of creation and should be drained off into the sewer of oblivion, there to rot in cold obstruction like any other excrement."[46] The United States has followed the sugges-tion of that editor for too long. For a future that is democratic and vital, it must evolve a more generous, humane, and decent policy for the aliens and radicals of succeeding generations.

NOTES

1. The President's Veto Message, *Whom We Shall Welcome,* Report of the President's Commission on Immigration and Naturalization (Wash-ington, 1953), p. 281.
2. Accounts of the raids and the interpretations of them may be found in Louis F. Post, *The Deportations Delirium of Nineteen Twenty* (Chicago, 1923); Constantine M. Ponunzio, *The Deportation Cases of 1919-1920* (New York, 1921); Max Lowenthal, *The Federal Bureau of Investigation* (New York, 1950); and Robert K. Murray, *Red Scare* (Minneapolis, 1955).
3. Fong Yue Ting v. U.S., 149 U.S. 698; Japanese Immigrant Case, 189 U.S. 86; and see Milton R. Konvitz, *Civil Rights in Immigration* (Ithaca, 1953), pp. 40-44, 97-98, 102-103.
4. William Williams to Commissioner-General, May 21, 1910, Immigration and Naturalization File 53244/1 (hereafter referred to as I & N).
5. Jane Perry Clark, *Deportation of Aliens from the United States to Europe* (New York, 1931), p. 487.
6. Fong Yue Ting v. U.S., 149 U.S. 698, 737, 740-741 (1893). Justice Field's remark is quoted in Clark, *op. cit.,* p. 48. Other justices have objected to the idea that deportation is not punishment. Chief Justice Fuller dissented in the Fong Yue Ting case. More recently Justices Black, Douglas, Murphy, and Rutledge have criticized or challenged the historic position of the Court. See Konvitz, *op. cit.,* pp. 103-106.
7. Quoted in John C. Miller, *Crisis in Freedom: The Alien and Sedition Acts* (Boston, 1951), p. 164.

8. Konvitz, *op. cit.,* p. 96.
9. Quoted in Sidney Fine, "Anarchism and the Assassination of Mc-Kinley," *American Historical Review* (July 1955), LX, 792.
10. Daniel Bell, "Marxian Socialism in the United States," in Donald Drew Egbert and Stow Persons, editors, *Socialism and American Life* (Princeton, 1952), I, 239.
11. Fine, *op. cit.,* p. 798.
12. 32 *United States Statutes at Large* Secs. 1214, 1221.
13. Charles A. Madison, *American Labor Leaders* (New York, 1950), p. 264.
14. Quoted in *Congressional Record,* 63d Congress, 3d Session, p. 3031.
15. Congressman Albert Johnson's foreword in Roy L. Garis, *Immigration Restriction: A Study of the Opposition to and Regulation of Immigration Into the United States* (New York, 1927), p. vii.
16. Quoted in Garis, *op. cit.,* pp. 102-103.
17. *Congressional Record,* 63d Congress, 2d Session, p. 2892.
18. *Ibid.,* 64th Congress, 1st Session, pp. 5166-5167.
19. Commissioner-General Anthony Caminetti to the Secretary of Labor, I & N 54235/36.
20. H. P. McCain, Adjutant General to the Commanding Generals of all Departments, March 21, 1917, Adj. Gen. File 2560557.
21. General Bell to the Adjutant General, April 21, 1917, Adj. Gen. File 2581689.
22. County Attorney T. H. MacDonald to Attorney General T. W. Gregory, August 21, 1917, Department of Justice File 186701-27-14.
23. Jones to Dentler, July 14, 1917, Exhibit C in Report of Lt. Col. C. W. Thomas, Jr., to the Inspector General, Adj. Gen. File .085 I.W.W.
24. U. S. Attorney F. A. Garrecht to the Attorney General, July 14, 1917, D. J. File 186701-49-10.
25. *Ibid.*
26. Secretary of War Newton D. Baker to the Chief of Staff, December 2, 1920, Adj. Gen. File 370.6.
27. U. S. Attorney Clarence Reames to the Attorney General, D. J. File 186701-49-119.
28. G. L. Joughin and E. M. Morgan, *The Legacy of Sacco and Vanzetti* (New York, 1948), p. 204.
29. U. S. Attorney W. P. McGinnis to the Attorney General, December 5, 1917, D. J. File 186701-37-14.
30. U. S. Attorney Fred Robertson to the Attorney General, December 11, 1917, D. J. File 189152-1.
31. The Assistant Attorney General to Frank C. Dailey, August 24, 1917, D. J. File 186701-14-26.

32. Anthony Caminetti, Memorandum of Conference with James W. Good, Chairman, Committee Appropriations, House of Representatives, August 19, 1919, I & N 54568/General.
33. Bureau of Investigation Instructions, July 28, 1919, I & N 54670/A.
34. Anthony Caminetti to the Acting Secretary of Labor, December 30, 1919, I & N 54645/378.
35. Special Assistant R. W. Sprague to the Attorney General, March 30, 1919; John Lord O'Brien to R. W. Sprague, April 5, 1919, D. J. File 9-16-12-7519-87½.
36. W.P.D. Files 1835, 5215, 5763; Adj. Gen. File 381.
37. Pardon Attorney James A. Finch to the Attorney General, December 10, 1921, P. A. Records, Box 52.
38. Finch to Attorney General, December 10, 1921, P. A. Records, Box 52.
39. Finch to J. T. Williams, September 7, 1922, P. A. File 39-241.
40. United States v. Galvan, reported in *Washington Post and Times Herald,* May 25, 1954.
41. Konvitz, *op. cit.,* pp. 97-103.
42. *Whom We Shall Welcome, op. cit.,* p. 162.
43. Konvitz, *op. cit.,* p. 103.
44. *Bureau of Naturalization Radio Release No. II,* October 16, 1922.
45. Quoted in Post, *op. cit.,* p. 304.
46. *San Diego Tribune,* March 4, 1912.

BIBLIOGRAPHICAL NOTE

Bell, Daniel, "Marxian Socialism in the United States," in Egbert, Donald Drew, and Persons, Stow, editors, *Socialism and American Life,* 2 vols. (Princeton, 1952).

Clark, Jane Perry, *Deportation of Aliens from the United States to Europe* (New York, 1931).

Fine, Sidney, "Anarchism and the Assassination of McKinley," *American Historical Review,* LX (July 1955).

Garis, Roy L., *Immigration Restriction: A Study of the Opposition to and Regulation of Immigration Into the United States* (New York, 1927).

Joughin, G. L., and Morgan, E. M., *The Legacy of Sacco and Vanzetti* (New York, 1948).

Konvitz, Milton R., *Civil Rights in Immigration* (Ithaca, 1953).

Lowenthal, Max, *The Federal Bureau of Investigation* (New York, 1950).

Madison, Charles A., *American Labor Leaders* (New York, 1950).

Miller, John C., *Crisis in Freedom: The Alien and Sedition Acts* (Boston, 1951).

Murray, Robert K., *Red Scare* (Minneapolis, 1955).

Ponunzio, Constantine M., *The Deportation Cases of 1919-1920* (New York, 1921).

Post, Louis F., *The Deportations Delirium of Nineteen Twenty* (Chicago, 1923).

NOTE. The writer has also used in the preparation of this chapter the files of the Department of Justice, the Immigration and Naturalization Service, the Pardon Attorney, the Department of Labor, and the War Department, all in the National Archives, Washington.

14

Walter Weyl and the Class War

CHARLES B. FORCEY

I

"Bertha has been suggesting to me that I go to Lawrence to see the strike there," wrote Walter Weyl in his diary early one morning in January 1912.[1] By midnight of the same day he had traveled from New York to Massachusetts and was ready to begin reporting the strike for the *Outlook* the next day. It was his first chance to see the radical International Workers of the World in action.

For the moment Weyl had reached an impasse in his work. Three months earlier he had finished *The New Democracy,* his first major work in political philosophy, and now awaited its publication and the "enormous influence" it might have.[2] During the wait, Weyl had done some research for Senator LaFollette; he had written several pot-boilers for the *Saturday Evening Post* and a weightier article for the *North American Review;* for a few days he had even tried to write a play. The chief source of his restlessness, however, had been the roughing out of a new book, one he planned to call "The Class War." Where his forthcoming book advocated middle-class progressivism, the new one would attack proletarian socialism.

When Weyl plunged into reporting the strike, he was on familiar ground. For fifteen years, since finishing his Ph.D. in economics at the University of Pennsylvania, he had been a student and partisan of the labor cause. He had worked closely with the United Mine Workers' leader, John Mitchell, in the great anthracite strike of 1902; he had traveled with Mitchell in Europe in 1904 and later had ghost-written a book on labor for him. Weyl had also written labor articles for such muckraking magazines as *Charities,* the *Survey,* and the *Outlook,* and had made extensive surveys for the United States Bureau of Labor of working conditions in Mexico, Puerto Rico, France, and England.

He spent three days at Lawrence. The strike was already gripped by the mounting tension that made it one of the most famous industrial disputes of the day. The Industrial Workers of the World had moved into the East for its first great strike. To many, it seemed that Lawrence might measure the appeal of the union's "Western radicalism." The town was already under siege; the mills were barricaded, with private guards roaming their empty aisles. State militia patrolled the streets, while the strikers girded themselves for the long struggle ahead.

Tall, dark, affable, with handsome features, Weyl wandered through the streets and meeting halls of the town, talking to politicians, militiamen, and strikers. Going from meeting to meeting he was struck most of all by the drama of a collision between Haywood and Ettor of the IWW and an investigating committee of the Massachusetts legislature. Feeling the fire of Haywood's syndicalist faith, Weyl felt almost sorry for the legislators, "smitten by a logic they could not understand." [3]

When Weyl returned home to write about the strike, he recognized that the days at Lawrence had been "one of the most fruitful experiences of . . . [his] life." The success of the IWW in arousing and uniting the workers had excited his "enthusiasm." But, for the moment at least, he was convinced that there was "nothing to it." "The Lawrence strike would be won by a man like Mitchell," he wrote, "but will be lost by Haywood and Ettor." [4]

Resolving to write about the strike "from the point of view of . . . [his] book on the Class War," Weyl produced a piece for the *Outlook* that emphasized his faith in conservative trade unionism. His attitude toward the Wobbly leadership of the strike was one of sympathetic skepticism. He dismissed the IWW's syndicalist aim of worker-controlled industries as an impossible ideal. "I do not believe that society can be changed as Haywood wishes to change it, or could remain 'put' if once organized on such a basis," wrote Weyl. "His is a Utopia of too generous a faith." [5]

Despite the distraction of laudatory reviews of *The New Democracy,* he turned back to work on "The Class War." "For the sake of . . . [the] book," he resolved "to go . . . to one manifestation after another of the class struggle." [6] He read more deeply in the works of American and European socialists, and concluded that the American writers were "second raters, . . . merely weak repeaters of other people's thoughts." [7] He experimented, too, with Socialist club meetings in New York, and generally came away unimpressed. "The evening left me with a sense of utter contempt for the methods of this little group," he declared after one of the meetings. "They are Parlor Socialists—& that is all there is to it." [8]

In March Weyl went again to Lawrence, where the workers had held out longer than he expected. There had been all the violence, misery, and suppression he had foreseen, yet the workers had not deserted the IWW's red banner. This time Weyl could not so easily dismiss what he saw. "My experience at Lawrence shook me up mightily," he noted upon his return. "I feel that it compels me to test all my theories." [9]

II

Weyl, in 1912, was a man heavily committed to a theory that seemed to be contradicted by the evidence before his eyes. Just when the IWW at Lawrence was shaking his own faith in middle-class reform, *The New Democracy* was giving him a national reputation as a philosopher of progressivism. The book was reviewed widely and favorably in most of the leading magazines and newspapers. In December, Theodore Roosevelt himself assured his Bull Moose followers that it was "one of the true books of the movement." [10]

One of the things that gave *The New Democracy* so broad an appeal was its strong faith in democracy. Unlike some other political theorists, Weyl saw no need for inspired leadership or a guiding elite to coerce the people toward reform. Nor, for all that Roosevelt endorsed his book, was Weyl entranced by the nationalism that became the Colonel's creed in 1912. Democracy itself, economic as well as political democracy, was the burden of his appeal.

In working out a moderate position, Weyl sought a middle ground between revolutionary socialism and laissez-faire liberalism. He wanted first of all to refute the Marxist dogmas that attracted so many of his friends in the socialist movement. Equally, however, he intended to disprove the liberal assumptions of the English classical economists, whose works had been the basis of his own economic training. "The old *laissez-faire* philosophy is done for," wrote Weyl, "and the old absolute socialism is dying in the embrace of its dead adversary." [11]

He rejected Marxism largely because he had long been convinced that capitalism had not developed and would not develop as the Marxian dialectic predicted. He came upon the first contradictory evidence as early as 1898, when he analyzed a six-volume French report on wages and hours to show that the real wages, the actual standard of living of French labor, had risen considerably in the latter half of the nineteenth century. Collecting vast quantities of such data, Weyl marshaled them in *The New Democracy* to prove that, contrary to Marxist prediction, "no progressive impoverishment of the working classes . . . [had, in fact] taken place." [12]

He conceded, however, that Marxism was at least an honest effort to meet crushing social evils. For laissez-faire liberalism he had less patience. The philosophy's individualism, he declared, had been the source and justification of the "monopolist" and "railroad wrecker." Manchester liberalism merely masked the inhumanities of the sweatshop, the chicanery of graft and rebates that blighted American progress. It deluded Americans into seeing equality and democracy where exploitation and oppression actually ruled. All efforts at reform, Weyl argued, were blocked "by ancient political ideals which still encumber . . . modern brains, by political heirlooms of revered—but dead—ancestors." [13]

In searching for a substitute for the old philosophies, Weyl found the key in America's great wealth. His basic concept was the "social surplus." By the social surplus, he meant the great increment of wealth the United States had produced over basic human needs. The surplus was social because it was the product of all society and not of particular individuals. Furthermore, being "surplus," it could easily be directed toward social ends. America's enormous prosperity, Weyl believed, had annulled the grim predictions both of classical economists like Ricardo and Malthus and of revolutionary theorists like Marx. What remained to be done, however, was to discover how the social surplus could be distributed so as to be shared by all.

The social surplus itself, Weyl thought in 1912, had destroyed the revolutionary socialist solution to the problem. The trend of American capitalism had not been toward decay but toward continuing material progress. Karl Marx had taught that progress would come through poverty—the crippling contradictions of capitalism, the revolt of the proletariat, then the socialist millennium. But Marx had made the crucial error of thinking the impoverished proletariat the source of social revolution. The truth was that Marx's utterly degraded proletariat would lose all capacity for revolt in the depths of its own misery. "A man or class crushed to earth," said Weyl, "is crushed to earth." [14]

With the proletariat hopeless as a regenerative force, with the ideals of liberalism merely justifying the marauding tycoons, some new force had to be found to foster economic and political democracy. A class to be effective either for revolt or reform, Weyl argued, had to be economically above the poverty line, intellectually above the literacy line, and politically above the suffrage line. In the United States, almost alone, had the great mass of the people been lifted by the social surplus above such levels. Calculating roughly, Weyl asserted that perhaps twenty of America's ninety millions were either too rich or too poor to concern themselves with democratic reform. Seventy millions, however, remained for the purposes of the "new democracy."

Weyl still questioned, nevertheless, whether the great amorphous mass of the middle class could be organized in an effective movement. Noting the progressive movement that already burgeoned around him, Weyl thought much had already been done. The very malignancy of the tycoons had bred a reaction. Furthermore, the magnitude of American wealth had created an ideal to spur the movement, the ideal of a "full life for all the members of society." Still, an impulse toward reform could not wax strong on protest and idealism alone. Some positive conditioning circumstance had to be found to bind the seventy millions to reform. "For," said Weyl, making his compromise between determinism and freedom of the human will, "it is ideas born of conditions that rule the world." [15]

Looking about for the motivating circumstance that the seventy millions might share, Weyl found it in their common lot as consumers. Why, he asked, had Americans protested against the tariff, why against the trusts, why against the grab of the nation's resources by the few? The progressive movement obviously represented the protest of consumers against the prices of monopoly. "A new insistence," Weyl declared, "is laid upon the rights of the consumer, and political unity is based upon him." [16]

Recognizing that, historically, man's common lot as consumer had been a rather tenuous political bond, Weyl argued that as a result the program of his "new democracy" must be moderate and gradual. Rapid or revolutionary reforms would only divide the seventy millions. Even so, the very size of the social surplus promised success for peaceful, gradualist methods. "Where wealth is growing at a rapid rate," said Weyl, "the multitude may be fed without breaking into the rich man's granary." [17]

III

The New Democracy inevitably committed Weyl more deeply to the cause it espoused, a cause the Lawrence strike had already led him to question. Gone now was the independence of all parties and persuasions that had been his pride before 1912. Wooed by the contending progressive factions that partisan year, Weyl could hardly avoid lending himself and the influence of his book to one of the battling candidates. After several months of hesitation, Weyl made Theodore Roosevelt and the "New Nationalism" his choice.

Support of Roosevelt unquestionably forced Weyl to sacrifice ideals to political expediency. The Colonel's militarism, his homilies on "race suicide," his desire for a disciplined labor movement, his emphasis on leadership, all violated the spirit of Weyl's "new democracy." But on the major issues of the campaign—the need for strong social reform and the control rather than busting of the trusts—Roosevelt and he could agree. Thus in August, Weyl pledged Roosevelt his help in the "struggle for national reorganization and regeneration." [18]

For three months Weyl labored in the Progressive Party headquarters in New York. He organized an "educational campaign" among the foreign-born, joined Roosevelt on a campaign tour, and became a member of the party's national committee. Even after Roosevelt's defeat, Weyl remained enthusiastic both about the politician and his new party. By the end of the year his own fortunes seemed much melded with the Progressive cause.

All during this exciting year of affirmation, however, Weyl had still continued to question the whole basis of the progressive movement. When he turned to "The Class War" again after his second visit to Lawrence, he blocked out several more chapters and decided that just as in *The New Democracy* he had personified American History "in the figure of the Pioneer so . . . [he would] figure him this time as the Proletarian." [19] Participation in a discussion where William J. Ghent and Morris Hillquit argued against syndicalism led Weyl to conclude that, like them, he was "tremendously against it." [20] But still he made little progress on his book. He resolved to read several other books on socialism, among them William English Walling's *Socialism As It Is*. Two weeks later he recorded that he was "working steadily through Walling's book and getting lots of good through . . . opposition to it." [21] In May, he went as an observer to the Socialist Party convention in Indianapolis, where he watched the parliamentarian Berger faction drive out the Haywood syndicalists. But neither reading nor the naked clash of issues brought him to any new resolution before he joined the Bull Moose campaign.

After the election, still engrossed in trying to forestall class war, he sought ways to arouse the middle class, "to appeal to other people than the workingman to face the problems." "We shall have class war unless we prevent it," he wrote. "It is up to us." Somehow, "united interests" had to be developed between the working class and the middle class. The welfare tactics of *The New Democracy* now seemed not enough. "We cannot be little brothers to the workman," Weyl declared, seeking some way for the workers to share control over the social surplus. What was needed, he thought, was "industrial democracy," a system where worker and employer would share control of industry, where the workman would become "an equal citizen . . . [in spite of] a worse environment." [22]

During much of 1913, despite the distractions of writing magazine articles, or helping Roosevelt revise the labor chapter of his *Autobiography,* or serving with Louis Brandeis on the New York garment workers' Protocol, Weyl kept turning the possible arguments against class warfare over in his mind. Reconsidering the themes of Roosevelt's "New Nationalism," he wondered whether the threat of class war itself could bring national unity, whether a "unitary conception of the nation [was] possible." [23] Perhaps a fundamental reform of the wage system was necessary. The purpose of his book became finding "a policy for the reformation & improvement of conditions & even of the very nature of paid labor." In this respect he thought the work of John Dewey in education suggestive. "Education became pleasant," said Weyl; "why not labor?" [24]

His main theme, however, remained "industrial democracy." He now definitely discounted the chances of class warfare, and significantly he changed the title of his book to "The Social Concert." It would "stand or fall," he thought, "on its *Constructive Labor Program*." [25]

IV

In 1914, Weyl joined Herbert Croly, Walter Lippmann, and others in organizing the *New Republic,* a magazine intended as a rallying force for the progressive movement. When war broke out in Europe, he turned his mind to foreign policy and produced two strongly internationalist books on world affairs.[26] Not until January 1918, less than two years before he died at the age of forty-six, did Weyl again list among things to be done "especially *The Class War Book*." "The Old Class War Conception. . . ," he reflected, "To what extent has this been invalidated by the war." [27]

The war had revived his faith in middle-class reform, which had wavered after 1914, when he saw the progressive movement seemingly dissolving around him. The war seemed to have promoted "an evolution towards a centralized, highly organized State Socialism." Moreover, it was doing so without violence, or at least violence between classes. "The conflict is not between the wage-earners & the capitalists," wrote Weyl, "but more like that presaged in *The New Democracy* between the Plutocracy and the People." War expansion of the government had trimmed the power of the plutocracy; for had not the railroads been taken over? The idealism and unity of the people had been reaffirmed in a war to end war. But Weyl's serenity was short-lived. The blood-letting in Europe dragged on. The Wilson Administration, once a fruit of the progressive movement, seemed bent on the suppression of all dissent. War hysteria in the United States mounted. Weyl found his own war books attacked as "Teutonic internationalism," "Bolshevik," or, with a sneer, "*New Republic*-type thinking."

As the peace conference approached, Weyl saw the real issues of war and peace more and more in terms of an underlying class conflict. Revolutions that had broken out all over Europe would "determine the plans and . . . shape the deliberations [at Versailles]." [28] Though he went to Paris early in 1919 to watch the conference, he was convinced that it would "accomplish next to nothing." [29] He had long believed that Wilson's peace program was foredoomed to failure: "It was a capitalistic, legalistic, middle-class conception; it was an appeal to an international class interest, . . . but it failed to exert any moderating influence upon rival nationalistic greeds." The old world of the middle class was done for, Weyl concluded. "There now comes to the surface a new group, and the war for democracy begins with the end of the war." [30]

The war, Weyl decided, had been "a terrible & perhaps permanent calamity." [31] The conferees at Versailles he saw merely as "solemn gentlemen, meeting daily, talking, . . . while Europe . . . [was] on fire." Noting the poverty, unemployment, and bankruptcy that followed the fighting, Weyl felt that the war had made "a clean sweep of the Bourgeoisie." [32] "Marx," he wrote, ". . . stated the wage-earning class must await the slow evolution, but he could not have foreseen that the bourgeois themselves would create conditions so abnormal." What was happening was "the suicide of capitalism." [33]

Though convinced that some of Marx's predictions were coming true, class war still had for Weyl no iron inevitability. The recovery of Europe might be accomplished "by a new and more capable bourgeois class." [34] Nor, if socialism did triumph, would it solve all world problems. He did not expect the workers of the wealthy nations to surrender "their privileged position in the world." "We must not believe that wage-earners are noble merely because the attainment of many of the ends they strive for runs parallel to the line of social development." [35]

The final event that convinced Weyl that socialism in some form would come in the future was the survival of the Bolshevik republic in Russia. Weyl analyzed the new Soviet constitution when it was published in July 1919, and concluded that despite the efforts of the Allies, the Communist experiment would not "be easily crushed." [36]

He was unwilling to dismiss the Soviet experiment merely on the charge that it was undemocratic. "Mr. Charles M. Schwab denies that Lenin is democratic," he declared, "[but] . . . curiously enough Lenin [also] denies that Mr. Schwab is democratic." The issue, he thought, was "not one of political forms but of class supremacy within a nation." [37]

Turning to the United States, however, Weyl declared himself "not in favor of Bolshevism." The great steel strike of 1919 convinced him that America was "approaching ignorantly and blindly the most disastrous (or the reverse) labor crisis in . . . history." But, he added, "we do not need or want—as I see it at present—a dictatorship of the proletariat." True, the United States had "sweatshops, industrial exploitation, spies, strike-breakers, corrupt industrial intriguers," but without a "czar, [or a] . . . large standing army, [it was] in a different situation from Russia." The United States, Weyl concluded, would progress much as it had before, "but more rapidly in the future, [and] by the unfolding power of the wage-earning class." [38]

The rise of Communism in Russia, in fact, was the final dissolving acid for Weyl's middle-class progressive faith. The apparent success of the Soviets completed the disintegration that the Lawrence strike, the decline of the progressive movement, the war, and the lost peace had already begun. In August 1919, in the last political entry of his diary before the throat cancer that killed him three months later stopped his work, Weyl raised again the central question of his still unfinished "The Class War." "What," he asked, "is the issue presented by this Bolshevik denial of democracy? . . . Are our own skirts clean? . . . Is our democratic government adaptable & can it be made adaptable . . . to a real Industrial Democratization such as the people want?" "The ultimate test," said Weyl, answering a lifelong question for the last time, "is survival." [39]

NOTES

1. Weyl, MS. Diary, January 24, 1912 (hereafter cited as Diary).
2. *Ibid.*, October 15, 1911, January 20, 1912; Weyl, *The New Democracy* (New York, 1912).
3. Weyl, "The Strikers at Lawrence," *Outlook*, C (February 10, 1912), pp. 309-312.
4. Diary, January 29, March 6, 1912.

5. Weyl, "The Strikers at Lawrence," *op. cit.*, pp. 309-312.
6. Diary, January 29, 1912.
7. *Ibid.*, March 2, 1912.
8. *Ibid.*, March 1, 2, April 18, 1912.
9. *Ibid.*, March 11, 1912.
10. Theodore Roosevelt, *An Autobiography* (New York, 1913), p. 25.
11. Weyl, *The New Democracy, op. cit.,* p. 188.
12. *Ibid.*, pp. 174-176.
13. *Ibid.*, p. 108.
14. *Ibid.*, pp. 169-190.
15. *Ibid.*, p. 199.
16. *Ibid.*, p. 251.
17. *Ibid.*, p. 260.
18. Weyl to Roosevelt, August 8, 1912, Roosevelt Papers.
19. Diary, February 25, 1913.
20. *Ibid.*, April 18, 1912.
21. *Ibid.*, April 13, 29, 1912.
22. *Ibid.*, December 3, 1912.
23. *Ibid.*, December 24, 1913.
24. *Ibid.*, March 16, 1913.
25. *Ibid.*, August 13, 1913.
26. Weyl, *American World Policies* (New York, 1917); *The End of the War* (New York, 1918).
27. Diary, January 12, 1918.
28. *Ibid.*, December 25, 1918.
29. *Ibid.*, March 22, 1919.
30. *Ibid.*, November 28, 1918.
31. *Ibid.*, March 18, 1919.
32. *Ibid.*, March 22, 1919.
33. *Ibid.*, April 16, 1919.
34. *Ibid.*, March 22, 1919.
35. *Ibid.*, June 13, 1919.
36. *Ibid.*, July 20, 1919.
37. *Ibid.*, August 14, 1919.
38. Undated workbook entry [1919].
39. Diary, August 15, 1919.

BIBLIOGRAPHICAL NOTE

Works by Weyl

The New Democracy: An Essay Concerning Certain Political and Economic Tendencies in the United States (New York, 1912).

American World Policies (New York, 1917).
The End of the War (New York, 1918).
Tired Radicals (New York, 1921).

Works on Weyl

Brubaker, Howard, and others, *Walter Weyl: An Appreciation* (Philadelphia, privately printed, 1922).

Forcey, Charles B., "Intellectuals in Crisis: Croly, Weyl, Lippmann and the New Republic, 1900-1919" (Unpublished Ph.D. thesis, University of Wisconsin, 1954).

VI

To the Roots of
American Civilization

"We have frequently printed the word Democracy. I cannot too often repeat that it is a
word the real gist of which still sleeps, quite
unawakened, notwithstanding the resonance
and the many angry tempests out of which its
syllables have come, from pen and tongue.
It is a great word whose history, I suppose, remains unwritten, because that history has yet to
be enacted."

Walt Whitman, *Democratic Vistas*

15

Thorstein Veblen and the Culture of Capitalism

ARTHUR K. DAVIS

I

PROBABLY NO AMERICAN ACADEMIC FIGURE has been the focus of so much controversy as Thorstein Veblen (1857-1929). Born of Norwegian immigrant parents, he spent his youth on poverty-stricken homestead farms in Wisconsin and Minnesota. Parental thrift and his own intellectual curiosity managed to secure him an education at nearby Carleton College (A.B. 1880) and at Yale (Ph.D. 1884). Not until 1892, however, at the age of thirty-five, did he find an opportunity to begin his teaching career in economics at Chicago. For a quarter-century he maintained an uncertain footing, sometimes interrupted by involuntary withdrawals, in various universities. In 1918, he left the academic profession for writing and occasional lecturing in New York City, dying finally in obscure poverty in California.

Veblen's great achievement is the sequence of the eleven books he wrote, beginning with *The Theory of the Leisure Class* (1899), his only really famous work. But his ideas proved to be too iconoclastic for the conservative spirit prevailing in American academic life. Hence he never attained the professional status he so clearly merited. Was he an agitator? In no sense. Veblen shunned all contacts with organized social movements. His lifelong role, relaxed but never wholly abandoned after he left the academic life, was that of the Olympian analyst, dispassionately dissecting the social customs of the past and the present. His indirect style partly veiled the critical implications his work had for the existing social order. That he was *persona non grata* to college authorities, despite these large concessions to the bourgeois academic code, is telling evidence for two important points: Veblen's nonconformity was far deeper than the skepticism he outwardly assumed; and the academic freedom professed by the universities was much more shallow than they wished to admit.

Doubtless his case is best summed up by the man himself, writing ironically about the lot of the social scientist in American universities: "No faithful inquiries into these matters [of social institutions] can avoid an air of scepticism as to the stability of the received articles of institutional furniture. . . . Scepticism is the beginning of science . . . [but] vulgar sentiment will tolerate a sceptical attitude toward vulgar convictions only as regards the decorative furnishings, not as regards the substance. . . . Some slight play of hazardous phrases about the fringe of the institutional fabric may be tolerated, but in such cases the conclusive test of scientific competency, in the popular apprehension, is a serene and magniloquent return to the orthodox commonplaces after all such playful excursions. Substantially nothing but homiletics and woolgathering will pass popular muster as science." [1]

Veblen's social science was anything but a woolgathering affirmation of the virtues and permanence of existing capitalist society. Not merely skepticism, but change, was the heart of his thought—change either toward some sort of socialism or (somewhat less likely) toward a revival of semi-feudal military reaction. His analyses of contemporary society pointed up its wastefulness, its coercion, and the basic maladjustment of its major institutions.

II

The core of Veblen's social theory is largely Marxian. A second but much less important pair of not unrelated elements in his work is utopian anarchism and agrarian populism. A third aspect is Darwinian evolution, which serves mainly as a façade and as a source of terms, the content of which usually turns out to be quite non-Darwinian. Finally there is a stiff dose—a saving dose, some may say—of skepticism, ranging in its manifestations from Veblen's tongue-in-cheek literary style to his ostensibly above-the-battle scientific objectivity.

Veblen's Marxian foundation consists of his insistence on change as the prime reality of social life, and on the leading role of economic, property, and class institutions in history, with ideological phenomena remaining secondary. It underlies his emphases on the inherent and chronic nature of capitalist economic crisis due to overproduction, on the existence of two antagonistic classes of occupations (business and industrial), on the role of the state as an "executive committee for the businessmen," and on the built-in propensity of modern capitalist powers to militarism and colonial wars.

Of the main Marxian propositions concerning capitalism, Veblen slighted only two: the dynamic role of capital accumulation (which yielded his inadequate analysis of imperialism) and the inevitability of socialism. His acceptance of the latter was guarded, usually implicit, and somewhat qualified by his conception of an alternative—a reversion to the predatory dark ages of a feudal-like barbarism.

To classify the majority of Veblen's leading ideas as principally Marxian in character implies a relatively broad conception of Marxism as a developing tradition of thought, not a set of rigid dogmas. The general framework of this tradition may be defined as follows: (1) Change is inherent in nature, the social aspects of which—societies— must be viewed as evolving wholes and as products of their historical past and of their natural and social environments. Whatever abstractions may be used as analytical aids in understanding change and societies must be reassembled into concrete wholes. This first premise is sometimes called—or obscured—by the term "dialectics." (2) The productive (including reproductive) and distributive institutions, and social classes, are the primary molders of social life. This second premise is "historical materialism." (3) Applications of these two premises to particular historical epochs produce explanatory theories of specific social systems, thus far mainly modern Western capitalism, though theories for feudalism and socialism are integral to the same approach. The Marxian tradition includes not only the original works of Marx and Engels, but also the later contributions and criticisms of numerous others, such as Kautsky, Hilferding, and Lenin.

Given this broad conception of Marxism, many if not most of Veblen's apparent departures from Marxism (such as his criticism of Marx's overemphasis on rational class consciousness in history) become either corrections of particular Marxian propositions or original contributions to that tradition. An example of the latter is Veblen's analysis of conspicuous consumption as a symbol of class status—a point Marx mentions but nowhere develops. Although only minor portions of his work belong in non-Marxian categories, Veblen never acknowledged (at least in his published work) any indebtedness or allegiance to Marxian ideas. His terminology is entirely un-Marxian. But the biographical evidence is overwhelming that Veblen became permanently and intensely interested in Marxism early in his career.

The second distinctive tendency in Veblen's thought is two-pronged: anarchism, in the sense that social life without organized institutions is tacitly assumed to be not only possible but ideal; and populism, or the idealization of simple agrarian communities. Neither is prominent. The anarchist tendency is manifested in his theory of social evolution, especially in his conjectural picture of the prehistoric "Savage State" as a primeval golden age. It also underlies Veblen's consistent polarization of social life between "bad" institutions and "good" human instincts. He listed only three of the latter: the parental bent, workmanship, and idle curiosity. By themselves, these could hardly serve as adequate bases for organizing any conceivable earthly community. Though it doubtless weakens his empirical analysis at certain points, Veblen's anarchism does not greatly alter the Marxian character of his main thought. The Marxian tradition is not without a generous sprinkling of similarly utopian elements, quite apart from Veblen.

The populist aspect of Veblen's minor "flight from reality" shows up in his largely implicit idealization of agrarian simplicity, in the almost Tolstoyan austerity that is the opposite of "conspicuous consumption," in his preoccupation with the exploitation of the countryside by the towns, in his comparison of the Russian soviet to the New England town meeting,[2] and in his recurring notion that modern machine culture may be incompatible with original human nature.[3]

Veblen divided the span of social evolution into two major phases:

an indefinitely long savage state, wherein social life was guided by man's benevolent instincts; and predatory society, roughly signifying historic times. The slow advance of technology in savagery finally gave rise to an economic surplus, whence followed the appearance of private ownership, a ruling class, the state, priesthood, and war. These institutions, in Veblen's eyes, have two dominant characteristics: they are predatory, dedicated to "getting something for nothing"; and they are wasteful.

Predatory society has two subdivisions: barbarism, wherein coercion was by direct military and priestly devices, as in the ancient empires and medieval feudalism; and pecuniary society (modern times), with exploitation carried on by indirect, semi-peaceable means, chiefly business enterprise. Veblen treats this epoch in terms of its early and late phases, the handicraft economy and the machine economy.

That we write off the third strand in Veblen's thought—the Darwinian—as chiefly (except for one point) a façade and a source of terminology may seem questionable to some. Yet no other conclusion seems possible. Despite his repeated praise of Darwinism as the model science, Veblen avoided its central concepts of natural selection, struggle for existence, and survival of the fittest. This seems strange at first, especially since these concepts, in the form of Spencer's and Sumner's social Darwinism, dominated the orthodox academic social science of Veblen's time. But the matter becomes clear when we observe that social Darwinism reinforced capitalist institutions and expressed capitalist values, and that Veblen rejected capitalism unreservedly.

What Veblen mainly took from Darwinism was its premise of change—blind, impersonal change. The Marxian concept of change tended to overemphasize rational change stemming from class-conscious interest. Veblen's correction of Marx on this point is one of his more important contributions to the Marxian tradition. He developed his argument in two notable essays on "The Socialist Economics of Karl Marx and His Followers." [4]

Veblen discussed human behavior largely in terms of three analytical categories: habits (the more persistent of which he called institutions), culture lag (the maladjustment of institutions to each other), and instincts. In his most ambitious theoretical book, *The Instinct of Workmanship* (1914), he defined instincts in biological terms. But he used these Darwinian concepts as social norms. The parental bent means a vague altruistic feeling for one's kin and fellows. Workmanship comprises two basic norms: maximum productivity of goods and services (this was also Veblen's definition of social welfare), and doing a job well for its own sake. Idle curiosity likewise has two meanings, the lesser being the disinterested pursuit of scientific knowledge—than which, in Veblen's personal philosophy, no other value rated more highly. In its more important meaning, idle curiosity is Veblen's awkward way of referring to the molding of a society's ideologies by its basic socioeconomic institutions. The parallel to Marx is obvious. For example, the autocracy of the ancient empires made for religious monotheism, and the late-modern dynamic machine economy brought forth a world view of material causation and impersonal evolution, which in turn have furthered the rise of science. It follows that the first meaning of idle curiosity is actually a special case of the second. It is erroneous to link idle curiosity directly with science, though Veblen himself tends to do so in *The Higher Learning*—doubtless because of his own occupational bias and personal predilection for science. Yet almost every commentator on Veblen, from Homan to Riesman, has misinterpreted idle curiosity as a mere static value—scientific inquiry. In his chief writings on the matter, however, Veblen unmistakably conceived it as a dynamic institutional relationship. Could there be a clearer case of the static and taxonomic character of our academic social science than this drastic distortion—otherwise inexplicable—of Veblen's dynamic concept?

Though most of his thought is social rather than Darwinian, there are in Veblen (as also in Marx) some minor manifestations of racial and biological determinism not warranted, or only partly warranted, by our present scientific knowledge. Among these are Veblen's occasional statements concerning the hereditary nature of "instincts" like workmanship, his belief in the inheritance of individual, specific mental traits, and his affirmation of the innately limited capacity of races to adapt to new cultural environments. What is remarkable, however, is not that these errors are present, but that they are of such relatively minor importance in Veblen's work. For the currents of opinion prevailing in his day were heavily weighted in favor of a thoroughgoing biological determinism. Here as elsewhere Veblen was far ahead of his contemporaries.

III

The amazing insight with which Veblen unlocked and laid bare some of the controlling historical trends of the present was due, in my opinion, to his mastery of the "Marxian key." Like Marx, he saw a basic tension between the community's industrial arts and its institutional framework. Institutional principles, perhaps well suited to the earlier epoch in which they were developed, persist beyond their useful span to hamstring the progressive potentialities of the present. Progress, we must remember, Veblen equated with the advance of the peaceful industrial arts toward maximum productivity.

Recognition of the importance of culture lag, of the sheer dead weight of unplanned social drift, is one of Veblen's great contributions to social science. Although this idea is implicit in Marx's concept of the contradiction between the productivity and the relationships of capitalism, many Marxists (and occasionally Marx himself) have tended to give more attention to the rational aspects thereof—self-interest and class consciousness. Perhaps this overemphasis helps to explain why, to Marx and Engels, revolution was sometimes just around the next corner. Veblen gives us the other side of the coin. True, his well-nigh exclusive emphasis on institutions as "survivals" goes too far in the other direction. For social customs survive not only because of inertia and culture lag but also because certain groups profit from their survival. The Marxian and Veblenian viewpoints are complementary, and they both belong in the same general tradition. With respect to formulating and executing social policy, the Veblenian emphasis is doubtless the weaker of the two, in that it conduces to do-nothing inactivity. The Marxian emphasis incites to concerted efforts to change society, but it also may invite premature disillusionment by underestimating some of the most important factors in the situation.

In capitalist society, Veblen saw the decisive tension as that between "business" and "industry." By the former term, he meant the profit-oriented and managerial occupations; by the latter, the technically productive ones. Industry now is an endless chain of specialized and mutually adjusted segments—the machine process, Veblen called it. But by virtue of the persistence of the institution of private ownership, business controls industry, although the industrial arts are the inherited, collective, and cumulative product of the whole community. Business systematically upsets the adjustment of the segments of the machine process, appropriates its product, and restricts total productivity—these policies being undertaken in the interest of maximizing business profits, and all of them being detrimental to the general welfare. Against this background, we can understand why Veblen referred to private enterprise as "getting something for nothing" and as "waste."

Veblen was one of the first business-cycle theorists. The advance of technology, he held, combined with its antiquated pecuniary controls, precipitates depressions, which he judged to be inherent and chronic features of business enterprise. In a competitive regime, newer and more efficient firms undercut older ones and force their liquidation when creditors recognize overinvestment in the field. Depressions are thus a phenomenon of business, not of industry. Veblen correctly anticipated as counterweights to depression a marked trend toward monopoly (in order to restrict output), the rise of salesmanship and associated functions, and the growing reliance upon wasteful (unproductive) consumption by government and the "kept classes."[5] That he considered all three responses to the threat of overproduction as "waste" goes without saying. He expected the chief reliance to be placed upon the first two, obviously underestimating the capacity of governments to spend for wars.

How closely Veblen was in touch with the significant developments of his day—in sharp contrast to most of his academic colleagues—is hard to appreciate at this distance in time. If he failed to realize adequately the role of the state in modern capitalism, he sensed at once the significance of the rise of monopoly, of the growing separation of corporate ownership and corporate management, of the expansion of the "new middle classes" dependent upon salesmanship occupations, and of the crucial importance of duress in modern economic life— "getting something for nothing." Only in the next generation did certain of these pioneering ideas become common currency in academic social science—for example, white-collar classes, separation of ownership and control. Others were too devastating to enter into general circulation.

Veblen believed that the real threat to business enterprise—he rarely used the term capitalism—came, not from the business cycle as such, but from the basic incompatibility of business and industry. The machine process, he argued, fosters impersonal, matter-of-fact habits of thought and hence undermines the older conventions of nationalism, devout observances, the patriarchal family, and similar traditions surviving from earlier epochs. The corrosive effects of city life in the machine age make for socialistic ideas of property, the equalitarian family, religious agnosticism, and so on.

In 1904 in *The Theory of Business Enterprise* Veblen stated his famous theorem concerning the transitory character of business enterprise. Either it would give way to some form of socialism, or to a reversion toward a semi-feudal barbaric militarism. As to whether progress or reaction would prevail Veblen ventured no opinion. But in *Imperial Germany* (1915) he applied the same formula with more definite results. He pictured Germany as a semi-feudal militaristic regime, to which had lately (since 1865) been joined a highly efficient machine process. Temporarily Germany had become a berserk nation, Veblen wrote, but eventually the machine economy would undermine the old dynastic institutions and disciplines. He viewed Japan as a parallel case, only more so—one of his most notable perceptions, for Japan was then fighting on the Allied side.

Although not well known, *Imperial Germany* is one of Veblen's best works, and certainly one of the few substantial English-language books about Germany. Its chief failing is an overemphasis on culture lag. The German imperial regime was not merely a dynastic survival; it was also an uneasy alliance of industrial and agrarian aristocratic interests caught up in war-generating imperialist rivalries. Discussing England's industrial revolution in the same book, Veblen makes telling use of one of his most important original concepts, "the penalty of being first." [6] His concept is clearly of prime value for understanding not only capitalist England, but also Communist Russia.

The net impression of Veblen's analyses points toward socialism as the successor of capitalism. But not without serious qualifications. In his last major work, *Absentee Ownership* (1923), he sketched three sets of factors as the decisive determinants of the future of America—business enterprise, the machine process, and nationalism. Veblen was keenly aware of the hold of nationalism upon the masses, and of the way the vested interests exploited national sentiment "by night and cloud" for their own economic and political gain. Whether the "underlying population" could shake off the combined hold of business principles and nationalism and come through "alive and fit to live" was a question he could never answer without resorting to *if's*. The long-run fall of capitalism he did not doubt, nor did he ever feel uncertain about the desirability of a new social order based on rationally planned maximum production for use. Yet he knew that rational logic does not always fashion historical change—the opposite relationship was the more likely one, to his way of thinking. The chief obstacle to progress was not the coercive repression of one class by another, although that was assuredly part of it, and a growing part, too. The real enemies were the massive drift of large uncontrolled social forces and the grip of traditional and obsolete institutions, such as nationalism, upon the minds of average people. "And the common man pays the cost and swells with pride." [7]

Perhaps this darkening view in Veblen reflects the cultural malaise—or bourgeois pessimism—which has been manifest in Western literature for many decades. Perhaps it reflects simple tragedy. For all his uncertainties, however, Veblen never abandoned his basically Marxian outlook. Joseph Dorfman's indispensable biography of Veblen reports:

> Six months before his death in 1929, Veblen said in substance to his neighbor, Mrs. R. H. Fisher: "Naturally, there will be other developments right along, but just now communism offers the best course that I can see." The youth movement in China was the last revolutionary flash which deeply interested him, and he was greatly distressed over its failure.[8]

One of Veblen's greatest contributions to social science is his *Theory of the Leisure Class* (1899). While this work is cast partly in terms of leisure-class customs considered as survivals of an earlier barbarism, its main theme is the analysis of "conspicuous consumption" and "conspicuous leisure" as symbols of class status. Veblen was the first major academic thinker in America to develop the great realm of covert motivation and latent or unintended effects of social phenomena. Dress, sports, idle wives, servants, ornate houses, animal pets, Latin studies, devout observances, gambling—all these Veblen looked on as devices for public exhibition of one's ability to waste time or money or both. His examples may be dated, but his argument has become part of our culture, familiar to many who have never heard of its author.

In his little-known *Higher Learning in America* (1918), Veblen dealt caustically with the effects of business culture upon universities.

To the extent that business principles come to dominate university policy, they make for "decorative real-estate, spectacular pageantry, bureaucratic magnificence, elusive statistics, vocational training, genteel solemnities and sweatshop instruction." [9] But he emphasized that the dominance of higher education by businessmen trustees and business values does not ordinarily require overt duress on the faculty. The situation is far more subtle. True, he said, academic social scientists rarely dissent from the status quo. But this is because "their intellectual horizon is bounded by the same limits of . . . commonplace insight and preconceptions as are the prevailing opinions of the conservative middle class. That is to say, a large and aggressive mediocrity is the prime qualification for a leader of science. . . ." [10]

IV

There is no better evidence of Veblen's "Marxian key" than his observations on the conditions of permanent peace in the war-weary world of the early 1920s. So enduring are his brilliant reflections that today they almost appear to have been written about the era after the second World War rather than the first.

In his *Nature of Peace* (1917), he concluded that nationalism, especially the intensified version then rampant in Germany and Japan, is the prime source of modern war. That he considered England and France as relatively peaceful regimes (an opinion he soon changed) is an indication partly of his short-lived wartime enthusiasm for the Allied cause and partly of his inability to shake off enough of his preoccupation with culture lag to get a full-length view of the imperialist state. But he went on to say that permanent peace would require not only the elimination of nationalism but also the end of colonies, tariffs, the existing ruling classes everywhere, and—as a sort of afterthought—the price system, meaning capitalism.

Other necessary conditions of peace, he said, would be an international Peace League including the defeated nations as equal members, and a peace treaty avoiding a vindictive settlement which would only leave the real enemy of peace—German nationalism—untouched and nursing a patriotic grievance. Veblen clearly saw that a league of sovereign powers, dominated by their present "kept classes," would tend to become the tool of the owning classes against the have-not classes wherever class conflict might break out. That such a clash was brewing Veblen had no doubt, well before 1917. He made no bones about his belief that the Versailles Treaty merely restored the old system of vested interests that generated the war.

The Russian Revolution seems greatly to have sharpened his vision. He recognized that the socialism of the Second International was a dead horse, and that the future, whatever it might be, belonged to the Bolshevik "out-and-outers." Bolshevism he saw as the disallowance of absentee ownership, the final answer of the common man to the vested interests. And he also felt that the crushing of Bolshevism in and out of Russia had become the controlling consideration of the "elder statesmen's" policy.

In "Dementia Praecox," in many ways his most brilliant postwar essay, Veblen held that complete defeat of Germany would have meant Bolshevism in Berlin and probably also in Paris. "When Germany, with Austria, had fallen out of line as a Power, the rest of the line of Powers would be in a precarious case for want of something formidable to lean against. A practicable Power has to rest its case on a nerve-shattering popular fear of aggression from without." [11]

American intervention, he continued, saved the war system and saddled America with a severe case of dementia praecox, manifested in illusions of persecution and treason, attacks on civil rights, official inquisitions, and vigilante groups like the American Legion and the Klan, with the "Secret Service kept faithfully on the job of making two suspicions grow where one grew before." [12]

We may appropriately conclude this section with a composite quotation from a 1921 essay:

> . . . the only practical line of policy still open to the safe and sane statesmen whose duty it is to avert the Bolshevist menace is further warlike enterprise . . . and the sedulous fomenting of a warlike temper in the underlying population. . . . Visibly, but with decently voluble disclaimers, the constituted authorities in all the civilised nations have chosen this way out of the dilemma [between Bolshevism and war]. . . . So long as the underlying populations . . . are taken up with patriotic blare and national jealousy the division of interest within these nations, between those who own more than they can use and those who have urgent use for more than they own, will be held in abeyance; a symphony of national hatred and suspicion will be heard in the land,

and absentee ownership will be secure. . . . America is taking war by the forelock—with very decently voluble disclaimers of course. . . . The established order, economic and political, rests on material circumstances which ceased to exist some little time ago; and it can be maintained only by artificially preserving the spiritual counterfoil of that materially obsolete past. . . . It is plain that absentee ownership and business as usual are at cross purposes with the country's industrial needs. All of which argues that it is wise for the statesmen to take repressive measures and keep the popular temper irritated about something else.[13]

V

It has lately become fashionable to look upon Veblen as a psychological curiosity, or as an outdated satirist whom we can still read pleasurably for "the period flavor of his hatreds and affections"—to borrow Riesman's patronizing phrase.[14] That this view has gained a certain ready following in various intellectual circles is perhaps a better measure of those circles—and of how isolated from the workaday world they have become, "sitting on a dry shoal upstream"—than it is of Veblen. Veblen paid his respects to such intellectuals in *The Higher Learning,* as we have seen, and there we can let the matter rest, decently interred.

For the rest of us, burdened with the critical pressures of the historical present—however differently we may conceive them—it is surely time to remind ourselves of the permanent value of Veblen's powerful insights. Among the professional academic economists of the twentieth century, perhaps only Keynes and Schumpeter belong with Veblen in the first rank. Certainly, there has been no American sociologist, before or since, who could carry Veblen's bat for him. His stature looms ever larger with the passing of the years, and he will someday be recognized for what he clearly was—the most original American social thinker of his time.

Finally, is it not time also to recognize the Marxian character and source of Veblen's brilliance? And to acknowledge Veblen as a notable and original contributor to the Marxian tradition? We believe that the future will record an affirmative answer to these questions. On this subject, Sweezy wrote "that Marxism was one of the decisive factors shaping Veblen's thought and that for the last forty years of his life he was a good deal more sympathetic to socialism than he was to the order of society under which he lived." [15] We believe that time will prove that this is, if anything, an understatement. Like Veblen himself, the tradition of which he was a part is greater than most of us have yet recognized.

NOTES

1. *The Higher Learning in America* (New York, 1918), pp. 180-182.
2. *Essays in Our Changing Order* (New York, 1934), p. 441.
3. *The Instinct of Workmanship* (New York, 1914), pp. 318-321.
4. See *The Place of Science in Modern Civilization, and Other Essays* (New York, 1919).
5. See especially *The Theory of Business Enterprise* (New York, 1904).
6. *Imperial Germany and the Industrial Revolution* (New York, 1915), p. 132 and *passim*.
7. *The Vested Interests and the Common Man* (New York, 1919), p. 137.
8. Joseph Dorfman, *Thorstein Veblen and His America* (New York, 1934), p. 500.
9. *The Higher Learning in America*, pp. 175-176.
10. *Ibid.*, p. 186.
11. *Essays in Our Changing Order*, p. 424.
12. *Ibid.*, p. 432.
13. *Ibid.*, pp. 444-449.
14. David Riesman, *Thorstein Veblen: A Critical Interpretation* (New York, 1953), p. xiii.
15. In Donald Egbert and Stow Persons, editors, *Socialism and American Life* (Princeton, 1952), I, 473.

BIBLIOGRAPHICAL NOTE

Works by Veblen

The Theory of the Leisure Class (New York, 1899).
The Theory of Business Enterprise (New York, 1904).
The Instinct of Workmanship (New York, 1914).
Imperial Germany and the Industrial Revolution (New York, 1915).
The Nature of Peace (New York, 1917).
The Higher Learning in America (New York, 1918).
The Vested Interests and the Common Man (New York, 1919).
The Place of Science in Modern Civilization, and Other Essays (New York, 1919).

The Engineers and the Price System (New York, 1921).
Absentee Ownership (New York, 1923).
The Laxdaela Saga (trans.) (New York, 1925).
Essays in Our Changing Order (New York, 1934).

Works on Veblen

Daugert, Stanley, *The Philosophy of Thorstein Veblen* (New York, 1950).
Dorfman, Joseph, *Thorstein Veblen and His America* (New York, 1934).
Hobson, John A., *Veblen* (London, 1936).
Riesman, David, *Thorstein Veblen: A Critical Interpretation* (New York, 1953).
Schneider, Louis, *The Freudian Psychology and Veblen's Social Theory* (New York, 1948).
Sweezy, Paul M., "Thorstein Veblen: Strengths and Weaknesses," in *The Present As History* (New York, 1953).

16

Charles Austin Beard: The Intellectual as Tory-Radical

WILLIAM APPLEMAN WILLIAMS

Editor's Note

THE FOLLOWING ESSAY BY PROFESSOR WILLIAMS on the great historian Charles A. Beard differs considerably from most of the other chapters. It is essentially interpretative, stressing the central purpose of Beard's work, rather than expository, setting out the details of his life and career. For clarification, therefore, it has seemed useful to preface the essay with a biographical note.

Charles Austin Beard (1874-1948) was born in Spiceland, Indiana, of a family which enjoyed property in both farmland and business. Though his home tradition was Republican and conservative in politics, young Beard became conscious in the 1890s of some of the worst abuses of American industrialization and urbanization. While a student at De Pauw University, where he received his bachelor's degree in 1898, he had taken many trips to Chicago and had witnessed the exploitation of labor by employers and the degradation of politics by city machines.

Having decided upon a scholar's career, Beard did half a year of graduate study at Cornell before leaving for Europe, where he passed more than three years in study and travel. In Germany, he was impressed with the program of social security; but it was in England, where he spent most of his time, that he first made close contact with a growing labor movement. Strongly influenced as an undergraduate by the elder Toynbee's piercing criticism of the industrial revolution, and greatly moved later by Ruskin's moral injunctions against capitalism, Beard plunged enthusiastically into various aspects of British labor politics. He addressed audiences of workers, wrote in 1901 a short work on *The Industrial Revolution* (which went through ten printings), and met many of labor's political leaders.

Beard returned to the United States in 1901, however, to complete his work for the Ph.D. in history at Columbia University, receiving the degree in 1904 after writing his dissertation, "The Office of Justice of the Peace in England in Its Origin and Development." He joined the Columbia faculty at once, but his interest in social and economic questions took him from the traditional pattern of teaching and research to a fresh evaluation of basic American history. "Beard was one of those who found his vocation in the effort to arrest the emergence of a plutocratic America, self-confident, determined, even arrogant, that was seeking to subdue the promise of American life to the service of a narrow oligarchy." [1] The first important products of this vocation were those two epoch-making books, *An Economic Interpretation of the Constitution of the United States* (1913) and *Economic Origins of Jeffersonian Democracy* (1915), which blazed a new trail in American historical study.

Beard never confined his activities to the classroom or the study. He demonstrated this most dramatically when he resigned from the Columbia faculty during World War I (on October 8, 1917) because President Nicholas Murray Butler had dismissed Professors Harry Dana, J. McKeen Cattell, and Leon Fraser for their association with allegedly disloyal persons. Consistent in his fight for academic freedom, Beard always urged courage upon teachers. In answer to attacks on teachers by the Hearst press, he replied thus in a famous speech in Atlantic City (February 24, 1935): "There is not a cesspool of vice and crime which Hearst has not raked and exploited for money-making purposes.—Only cowards can be intimidated by Hearst." [2]

Beard's public activities were varied and notable. He worked especially hard for improvement of state and local government. As director of the Training School for Public Service from 1917 to 1922, he was called upon to direct many studies of governmental machinery, which ultimately led to reform. Such surveys as those of Delaware (1918) and Newark, New Jersey (1919), were so noteworthy that he was called abroad to make studies in Japan (1922-1923) and Yugoslavia (1927). As a political scientist and the author of the brilliant textbook *American Government and Politics* (1910), Beard could not stand aside from practical political problems.

He continued to pour forth a stream of distinguished historical writing, the high point of which was probably the monumental, two-volume *Rise of American Civilization* (1927) "in which Charles Beard with his wife wrote what is certainly one of the half dozen most effective general narratives of a people's history that any nation possesses." [3] Profundity was no bar to popularity, and his works reached and influenced a wide audience.

Beard's last years were given over to a searching criticism of American foreign policy, the nature of which is discussed in the essay below.

H. G.

I

Late one night in 1929, aboard a train clickety-clacketing northward along the Atlantic coast from the Carolinas, Charles Beard gave away a vital insight into his intellectual and public career. He was cornered in the smoker, defending himself against, and explaining himself to, some professional historians who challenged his emphasis on economics in history. One can imagine him: his patience gone, his blue eyes sparking like high-voltage electricity, and a scalpel's edge on his voice.

"I never said that economic motives explain everything!" he roared. "Of course, ideas are important. And so are ethical concepts. What I have always said and all I have said is that, among the various motives impelling men to action, the struggle for food, clothing, and shelter has been more important throughout history than any other. And that is true, isn't it?—*Isn't it?*" [4]

Here, in one piercing paragraph, is the essence of Beard's intellectual personality. He was a radical in rooting to the heart of the matter and insisting that man's economic struggle was the "most important" part of history. But his conservative's caution was equally apparent. He refused to stereotype the relationship between the economic struggle and other phases of man's activity, or the future nature of the struggle itself. He declined, in short, to grant the inevitability of any pattern of development. Spengler's *Decline of the West* left him as unconvinced and as unsatisfied as Darwin's middle-class utopia or Marx's prophecy of a communal Eden. Beard accepted only the certainty of change and conflict.

This suggests that Beard may most aptly be described as the intellectual as Tory-Radical. He had little, if any, confidence in revolutionary efforts to wrench mankind out of its historical continuity. For this reason some radicals have said that he was short-sighted and worse, that he lacked the nerve of failure. But he did believe that people could improve their lives by controlling more rationally and more equitably the economic system under which they lived. And for this the conservatives have called him subversive.[5]

The right-wingers are far closer to the truth. Beard contributed much to the currently neglected intellectual foundations of an American radicalism. He insisted that economic conflict and development is unending, and that it must constantly be analyzed, whatever the institutional organization of society. The American Left may be aware of this truth. It has failed, by and large, to act upon it since the days of its ideological romance with the New Deal's *noblesse oblige*. Beard also maintained that rulers who say one thing and do another, whatever the legal framework within which they act, undermine democracy. This morality is as important to those of the Left who close their ethical eyes while defending Franklin Delano Roosevelt's *conduct* of foreign affairs from 1938 to 1941 as it is to those who do likewise when discussing Soviet purges.

Thus Charles Beard's great legacy to American radicalism was not programmatic. Rather was it his persistent assertion, with great personal courage, that economics and morality are, respectively, the cornerstone and the keystone of the good life. Economic maladjustment will undermine morality; but the lack of ethical integrity will corrupt the best economic system. Beard never wholly neglected either of these propositions at any time during his career. Nor did he separate his intellectual and political activity. But he did tend to stress economic factors from his early maturity through the first years of the Great Depression. Thereafter he emphasized the ethics of power. Thus it may be helpful to review Beard's career within this framework: first his development and employment of a theory of social change; then his efforts to warn of the disastrous consequences of amoral politics.

II

Throughout both periods, of course, Beard's actions were in keeping with his analyses and morality. He considered the ivory tower as a refuge for the intellectual and moral coward—or scoundrel. The unity of theory and practice was to Beard a bit of Indiana common sense, not an alien philosophy to be disparaged or damned. In the earlier years, for example, he committed himself to educational and pragmatic efforts designed to increase his fellow citizens' understanding of causal forces, and to instruct them in the use and control of such forces to build a better society. Thus his vigorous work within the British working-class movement, his efforts to improve and extend American education, and his extremely practical proposals for rationalizing existing political institutions. During these years he worked primarily with other men, whether informally or in organized groups. But when he saw what seemed to him the rise of an essential immorality in American politics, Beard withdrew from group agitation to stand alone, unencumbered by conflicting loyalties, and to unmask in his writing the self-deceptions and public fabrications which he saw.

In a sense, of course, Beard stood so straight and so tall that he always stood alone. But he was not the lone wolf that some have pictured him. Only once before his attack on Roosevelt's foreign policy did he stand so much apart. That was in a similar situation, when, on October 8, 1917, he resigned from Columbia in defense of the principle of academic freedom. From the perspective of 1956 that act looms even larger than it did at the time.

"I am sure," he declared, "that when the people understand the true state of affairs in our universities they will speedily enact legislation which will strip boards of trustees of their absolute power over the intellectual life of the institutions under their management." [6] For it will not do to blame the people. The trouble was, and is, that Beard overestimated the extent to which his colleagues were concerned with discovering "the true state of affairs"—let alone communicating that knowledge to the people and acting on it themselves.

But Beard was a different kind of academic man. His troubles were always caused by his efforts to establish and publicize "the true state of affairs." His resignation from Columbia, for example, was the first major consequence of his dedication to the task of developing and using a theory of social change. He left Columbia as the final act in a series of events which began with the publication, in 1913, of *An Economic Interpretation of the Constitution*. Thus the *New York Times* (October 10, 1917) discussed Beard's resignation in a representative fashion—burying the issue of academic freedom in a diatribe against that book. And in this instance the *Times* is a source of accurate information, for the top levels of Columbia's administration had been fighting Beard ever since the publication of the volume. Their attacks on academic freedom were but a specific demonstration of their general antagonism to Beard's ideals and objectives.

A later generation of conservatives, realizing that the search for a general theory of social change is not in itself proof of radicalism, have acted less hysterically, though not necessarily less effectively. A theory of social change can be used to oppose radical innovations and reforms as well as to encourage them. Most recent research along this line has been motivated and financed, in fact, by those who have such a negative purpose. But Beard's early opponents thought that his case study of the origins of the Constitution established his desire for radical change, and so struck back vigorously and viciously. Beard never wholly committed himself, however, to using a theory of change in any one manner. He wanted to save what was best, yet improve it along with all the rest. Hence the ambiguity of his career.

III

Basically, though, Beard was more of a radical than he sometimes found it easy to admit to himself. For the commitment to search for a theory of social change undercuts the assumption of uniqueness upon which the theory and practice of the majority of American liberals and conservatives have been based. Such a denial that the United States is unique confronts those who understand it with a private and a general problem. It lays bare the uncomfortable truth, so personally pleasant to camouflage, that the evasion of basic issues ultimately becomes a terribly expensive flight from reality. And it thereby forces one either to continue such escape knowingly or else to grapple directly with the question of how to limit individual liberty without also destroying freedom.

Beard understood this. Prior to 1929 he was able to deny American uniqueness in theory while enjoying it in practice. But the Great Depression put an end to this idyll. And from that time forward Beard can only be understood in terms of a man wrestling with this central dilemma. These considerations also explain the changing nature of the criticism of Beard. His early opponents fought him because of his specific intellectual and political acts. His later critics, aware that he confronts them with the basic issue, assault the entire body of his work.

Save perhaps for a brief period early in the depression, Beard never came to grips directly with the theoretical and practical problems arising from the curtailment of individual liberty which was implicit in the idea of America living with and within itself. But Beard's own thesis that politics follows economics forced him, after the depression, to project two alternate paths for America's immediate future: rapid involvement in another general war, or self-containment within existing continental boundaries or, at most, the Western Hemisphere. This is not a happy choice for a man (or a society) who matured in the tradition of "anything is possible," and the shock of its harshness may do much to account for Beard's seeming shift to relativism during the early '30s. Yet Beard always returned to the central question of whether it necessarily follows that freedom is lost when liberty is curtailed. He never worked out a simple, programmatic solution for this problem. But he never denied, and only briefly evaded, the issue, and his basic answer was negative.

Beard's concentration on these key issues of causation and freedom does much to account for his interest in, and debt to, Karl Marx and James Madison. Those men labored all their lives over the same questions. But those who hope for a precise bookkeeping-style analysis of Beard's debt to these men will wait in vain. Beard was an on-going intellectual, concerned primarily with understanding and improving the world. He had little interest in, and even less time for, analyzing and defending himself.

Combined with his early experience in Chicago during the 1890s, Beard got from Marx a deep consciousness of change and an abiding sense of the importance to that change of the latent, long-run consequences of decisions made on the basis of short-term analyses. This emphasis on long-term generalized patterns helps to explain, for example, Beard's tendency to overlook immediate functional conflicts between economic groups. Beard's over-all interpretations, like those of Marx, are extremely difficult to destroy, whereas specific aspects of their analyses can be seriously modified or disproved.

Such weaknesses can not be inflated into proof of intellectual failure. It is possible, as several scholars have recently done, to demonstrate that some details of Beard's analysis of the origins of the Constitution are wrong.[7] Thus, as a case in point, his stress on the role and importance of the men who held obligations of the Continental Congresses can be interpreted to deny Beard's entire interpretation. But such concentration on functional analysis can lead the critics even further from the mark. For there is a very considerable difference between saying that Beard was mistaken about bondholders, and going on to argue that economic alignments were not the central dynamic of the movement for the Constitution. Critics who attempt the second assertion would seem to be forgetting that a historical generalization is not an answer to every specific question.

Beard's intellectual relationship to Madison is also easy to confuse or misconstrue. Some scholars have taken Beard's sometime assertion that he was a Madisonian at face value. More of them have claimed that he merely used Madison as camouflage for Marx. Both judgments seem a bit wide of the mark. It is more probable that Beard viewed Marx and Madison as complementary thinkers. An analysis of his famous essay on *The Economic Basis of Politics* (1922) supports this view. The over-all prognosis of Marx and Madison is very similar, as attested by Madison's famous forecast, in 1829, that the United States would suffer a serious economic and social crisis a century later. Beard also realized that Madison's system of factions was nothing less than an unsystematized anticipation of the functional school of sociological analysis. And, in some instances, Beard followed Madison's model in his own work.

At times Beard failed to use these ideas of Marx and Madison as well as he might have. He was always in a hurry, for one thing, and seldom took the time to dig out the facts on every faction. Sometimes his insights as to which groups were the most important were correct, and the finished essay was brilliant. In other cases, however, his research hypothesis was awry, and the error was compounded in the completed work. It was not that Beard ignored or monkeyed with the evidence, for he was fanatically honest. But he tended, in his concern and haste to find clues for the present, to work *with* his hypothesis instead of *from* it. But for Beard specific mistakes were of far less concern than the validity of his general analysis of American history. For he considered himself not so much an ivory-tower historian as a functioning student of history.

IV

What did Beard mean when he called himself a student of history, not a historian? The crucial difference between them lies in the former's emphasis on his study as a means, whereas the latter considers his work as an end in itself. True, the historian's work may be the means to a personally satisfying life, but such an argument either misses or begs the issue. So, too, does the claim that all historians are also students of history. A difference of degree does lead to a difference of kind. Beard studied history to equip himself to comprehend and change his own society: to understand the direction and tempo of its movement, and to pinpoint the places at which to apply his energy and influence in an effort to modify both aspects of its development.

Analyzed from this perspective, it becomes very difficult to demolish his two central interpretations, *The Rise of American Civilization* (1927) and *The Idea of National Interest* (1934). For what Beard did in these books was to confront his readers with the hard fact that it was specific Americans who made American history, and that for the most part they had acted on the basis of a materialistic calculus. He ripped aside the appearances and the rationalizations to reveal the realities. No wonder he was attacked, for his lesson was quite outside any connection with existing politics. It was radical in the deepest sense of the term. And so it remains.

Though obviously pointing the moral of responsibility, and spelling it out in case after case, Beard's writing prior to the Great Depression was not characterized by any overriding sense of urgency. Neither were his actions. A man anticipating and dreading imminent and catastrophic crisis does not center his efforts on educational and political reform. Save for the academic freedom episode, the tenor of Beard's writings and actions was that of a concerned and responsible man who assumed that there was plenty of time to go slowly. It seems probable that this outlook was a product of Beard's American experience reinforcing his awareness that Marx's sense of time was quite foreshortened.

But the depression brought Beard up short. Here was deep and general crisis. And there is little doubt that his intellectual and personal outlook responded immediately. The tone of his " 'Five Year Plan' for America," written in 1931, was markedly different from that of his volume on *Public Service in America* (1919), or the concluding pages of *The American Party Battle* (1928). The earlier work is characterized by the assumption that there is plenty of time. His essay on a five year plan is urgent, and probes far deeper in an effort to suggest new and significant changes.

Beard did not, however, launch any frontal attack on private property. His proposal was no more, in essence, than an intelligent and rather extensive development of the idea of a corporate society, previously advanced in America by such men as Herbert Croly and Herbert Hoover. This concept of a corporate society is based on the proposition that every individual holds membership in two of the three basic units of all industrialized societies. All people are citizens, hence are part of the government. And, in addition, they belong either to capital or labor. Thus the state, in theory at least, is at once the common ground where both parties adjust their differences, and an independent power capable of enforcing judgments on both groups.

But corporatism is not a radical concept, for it is tied intimately to the principle of private property. And this weakens both its theoretical and its practical value. For unless the power to control investments, so vital to balanced economic growth, is exercised on the basis of a public choice between alternate programs and policies, one half of the economic life of society remains in the hands of a tiny minority.

Thus Beard's radical insights into the malfunctioning of the existing system were never matched by an equally fundamental program for its renovation. His predilection for such a corporate solution does explain, however, his support for much of the New Deal's domestic legislation. Beard and Roosevelt did see eye to eye on one point: they saw through the myth of rugged individualism. But when it came to the question of what to put in its place they turned first to a vague sort of corporatism, and then back to the dream of restoring competition. Neither of them looked forward to socialism.

V

The same disparity between radical analysis and conservative preference and program bedeviled Beard on foreign policy. There are few short analyses, for example, which match the quality of Beard's treatment of foreign affairs in *The Rise of American Civilization*. It is even more difficult to name a volume that is more rewarding in insights and suggestions than *The Idea of National Interest*. Beard stressed three points in these analyses of foreign policy: (1) it is intimately connected with domestic affairs, (2) empires are not built in fits of absent-mindedness, and (3) expansion does not in and of itself solve problems, and often complicates and deepens them.

These conclusions forced Beard to deal with several related problems. Both as a student of history and as an acting citizen it was vital for him to comprehend the system of ideas which first rationalize, and in turn further motivate, imperial expansion. In conjunction with his intrinsic intellectual ferment, and the shock of the depression, this need makes sense out of his sudden concentration on the work of German historians who were working on the general problem of *Weltanschauungen,* or conceptions of the world. This study was of key importance to Beard, for if he could come to grips with the general view of the world that was held by the expansionists, then he could attack it more directly and effectively.

He never carried through on this phase of his intellectual pursuits. It is, indeed, the weakest of all his performances. The reason that Beard never gave full attention to these studies, and rather shortly dropped them, lies in his growing concern over the drift of Roosevelt's foreign policy. Thus, after 1937, Beard gave less and less attention to the narrowly academic aspects of his work. It was not that his mind slowed down, but rather that his heart speeded up. Beard cared too deeply about America to bother with the formal rigmarole of the professional intellectual. And his love for his homeland brought him, deep in emotional turmoil, face to face with the multiple contradictions between his radical analyses, his strong concern for his fellow man, and his personal and philosophic commitment to private property. It would appear, on a close reading of his last books, that he sought a way out of this difficulty by emphasizing the primacy of moral integrity in public life.

One can only sympathize with Beard as he confronted his cruel dilemma. He realized, to start with, that the depression threatened the entire fabric of American society. This led him to cut through the cant of the claims of recovery and propose some serious modifications in the American economic system. He was quite aware, of course, that it was too late to "save capitalism" in the sense that the phrase was used by the New Dealers. Beard's fear was that the old order, though dying, would dominate the future. And he grew ever more disturbed as he realized that the New Deal was not economically successful. Nor could the failure be blamed only on the businessmen, for the New Dealers had few ideas about—let alone for—the future.

Then worse yet: he came to feel that the people in power were submerging the basic domestic problem in a foreign crisis, and defending this shift of emphasis by defining the new issue as the central danger. Here Beard confronted himself, for he too had to give an answer to this question of which was the crucial issue. It has been said, and often, that Beard failed this test. But the judgment is not that simple. Several things need to be kept in mind when appraising Beard's reaction. There was no radical program backed by organizational strength. Beard's position has often been misunderstood or misrepresented. And finally, the implicit import of Beard's criticism of Roosevelt is usually evaded.

It is possible to argue that an American socialism, structured around political and civil liberties and centralizing none but the economic power necessary to plan and administer balanced economic growth, leaving other property untouched, would have won Beard's support. Beard can hardly be blamed for the lack of such a choice. Indeed, a psychological analysis might well point to the conclusion that the New Deal intellectuals' attack on Beard is really indicative of their own sense of failure.

It will not do, furthermore, to argue that Beard would have opposed such a program because it carried the strong probability of entering the war. For Beard did not oppose the war that was fought. He did oppose the way that Roosevelt led this country into war, and the New Deal's strong inclination to think it was America's job to reform the world.

This vital difference demands considerable emphasis because it is central to an understanding of Beard's thought and his importance. Beard made three central points in his attack on Roosevelt: the domestic crisis was being "solved" in a manner that only postponed and deepened it; this "solution" was being carried out in a manner—deceptively —that undercut democratic morality and practice; and the assumption by the United States of the right, or obligation, to police the world would compound both crises.

It is extremely difficult to deny the force of these arguments. Recovery and prosperity at the price of an extremely poor strategic position in World War II, a police action in Korea, and an atomic diplomacy based on cultivating the cold war *have* deepened the basic crises of the '30s. Nor were any of these developments inevitable. The consequences of Roosevelt's deceptive methods are perhaps less obvious, but perhaps even more dangerous. The practice of protecting the people from the truth in order to save them from themselves damages the fiber of a society. And, as Beard knew, no society can survive its own hypocrisy.

Thus Beard lived by the creed of grappling directly, honestly, and democratically with any problem, be it economic, social, or moral. And he fought hypocrisy and political chicanery with all the militance he could muster, a worthy example for American radicals.

NOTES

1. Harold Laski, "Charles Beard—An English View," in H. K. Beale, editor, *Charles A. Beard: An Appraisal* (Lexington, Kentucky, 1954), p. 13.
2. George Counts, "Charles Beard, The Public Man," in Beale, *op. cit.,* p. 246.
3. Laski, *op. cit.,* p. 13.
4. The story is reported in H. K. Beale, "Charles Beard: Historian," in Beale, *op. cit.,* p. 123.
5. Beard carried on a running battle with many prominent American historians, who accused him of lack of objectivity for his economic interpretations and his interest in contemporary problems. See, for example, the criticisms of him by Theodore Smith, "The Writing of American History in America, from 1884 to 1934," *American Historical Review* (April 1935), XL, 439-449; see also Beard's response to "objective" historians in his review of Arthur M. Schlesinger's *Rise of the City,* in

the *American Historical Review* (July 1933), XXXVIII, 779-780. The most strenuous attack on Beard immediately after publication of *An Economic Interpretation of the Constitution* was by Professor Edward Corwin who attributed to Beard the aim of establishing "the truth of socialistic theory of economic determinism and class struggle." *History Teacher's Magazine* (February 1914), V, 65-66.

6. From Beard's letter of resignation of October 8, 1917, cited by Counts, *op. cit.*, p. 245.

7. See the article by Robert E. Thomas, "A Reappraisal of Charles A. Beard's Economic Interpretation of the Constitution of the United States," *American Historical Review* (January 1952), LVII, 370-375.

BIBLIOGRAPHICAL NOTE

Works by Beard

The Supreme Court and the Constitution (New York, 1912).
An Economic Interpretation of the Constitution (New York, 1913).
Economic Origins of Jeffersonian Democracy (New York, 1915).
The Economic Basis of Politics (New York, 1922).
American Foreign Policy in the Making, 1932-1940 (New Haven, 1946).
President Roosevelt and the Coming of the War, 1941 (New Haven, 1948).

   With Mary Beard:
The Rise of American Civilization, 2 vols. (New York, 1927).
America in Midpassage, 2 vols. (New York, 1939).
The American Spirit (New York, 1942).
A Basic History of the United States (New York, 1944).

   With George Smith:
The Idea of National Interest (New York, 1934).
The Open Door at Home (New York, 1934).

Works on Beard

Beale, H. K., editor, *Charles A. Beard: An Appraisal* (Lexington, Kentucky, 1954).
Williams, William A., "A Note on Charles Austin Beard's Search for a General Theory of Social Change," *American Historical Review* (October 1956).

WITHDRAWN

Kelly Library

3   7